in the water they can't see you cry

a memoir

AMANDA BEARD

with Rebecca Paley

A TOUCHSTONE BOOK
PUBLISHED BY SIMON & SCHUSTER
NEW YORK   LONDON   TORONTO   SYDNEY   NEW DELHI

Touchstone
A Division of Simon & Schuster, Inc.
1230 Avenue of the Americas
New York, NY 10020

First Touchstone paperback edition April 2013

TOUCHSTONE and colophon are registered trademarks of Simon & Schuster, Inc.

For information about special discounts for bulk purchases, please contact Simon & Schuster Special Sales at 1-866-506-1949 or business@simonandschuster.com.

The Simon & Schuster Speakers Bureau can bring authors to your live event. For more information or to book an event contact the Simon & Schuster Speakers Bureau at 1-866-248-3049 or visit our website at www.simonspeakers.com.

Designed by Akasha Archer

Manufactured in the United States of America

10   9   8   7   6   5   4   3   2   1

Library of Congress Cataloging-in-Publication Data is available.

ISBN 978-1-4516-4437-1
ISBN 978-1-4516-4438-8 (pbk)
ISBN 978-1-4516-4439-5 (ebook)

For Sacha and Blaise, who make me smile every day

in the water
they can't
see you cry

I could feel it coming. An angry, pulsing energy started to grow inside me. Sitting on the edge of the bathtub, I tried to zone out to the symmetry of the white subway tiles lining the wall in front of my face. But it always came too fast. I knew that. The only light in the bathroom arrived through the wall of opaque glass bricks behind the tub where outside the sun beat hot on Venice Beach. I blocked the daylight with my back, trying to keep the room dimmed out, as if that would help anything.

My toes curled up. That's how it always started. Then the nervous energy drove up my body. My knees bounced hard. My fingers refused to stop wiggling. One ran against the inside of my palm as if foreshadowing the inevitable. I made a fist but the energy was now up around my face, clenching my jaw and grinding my teeth back and forth.

Rushing around my bloodstream, it started to overwhelm me. When it got to my brain, which would be soon, I wouldn't be able to think at all. Then, at least, it would almost be over.

My heart pumped like crazy, and my breathing was heavy. Suddenly it was hot, too hot.

Let it out.

I felt like a cartoon character with steam coming out of my ears.

Let it out.

Something had to happen. Something had to be done to release the pressure, or it would be released by my exploding. I was going to scream my head off, smash the bathroom mirror, or grab one of those tiny little eyebrow razors and cut my arm.

I grabbed the razor, a two-inch handle in a cheery shade of pink with an extremely thin and sharp blade at its tip. I surrendered to the object so tiny in my palm. With the razor in my right hand, I revealed the underside of my other arm, cradling it close to my body. The energy ran too fast to contemplate the moment before the half-inch silver blade hit my arm. It flashed briefly in the sunlight before slicing into the meaty part between the wrist and the elbow. One. Two. Three. I made the small lines as I had done so many times before. I didn't have to press hard, only run the razor across my skin as lightly as a blade of grass moving across the leg of a child running through a field.

I knew immediately. Something was wrong. The calm that usually washed over me as soon as I made my light little cuts with their delicate beads of blood was replaced by a new fear. In the moment when thinking was not possible and the energy took over, I must have applied too much pressure, because one of the cuts gushed blood. This was not in control.

Within a second or two, blood spread across my arm, dripping down from my elbow to the white tile floor below. It was getting all over the place, on my tank top, my jeans, my feet. I yelled at my boyfriend, Sacha, all the time for the messes he made around the house we shared. I was never the cause before.

The sight of too much of my blood, a creepy red-brown color, sent a wave of panic over me. This wasn't the satisfaction of the cuts that put things back in control. Scared, I grabbed a towel and threw it on my arm to try to stop the bleeding. Soon enough the towel was soaked in blood. I tried to grab another towel that was hanging on the door, but in my panicked state I knocked over a roll of toilet paper. I stood up and continued to drip blood on the floor, now covered with red drips and toilet paper.

I threw the tissue in the toilet and tried to clean up the disaster on the floor with the fresh towel, but everything was chaos and I couldn't stop the bleeding. I was like a kid who, trying to hide the evidence of her mistake before getting caught by Mommy or Daddy, just winds up making everything worse.

How did it get to this point? I was a three-time Olympic swimmer and world record holder who had appeared on the cover of national magazines in skimpy bathing suits that made everyone think I had all the confidence in the world. I made money in a sport where no one makes any. I owned my own home and paid my own bills. Lots of Americans who didn't know anything about swimming knew my name and the face under the goggles. I also had a wonderful boyfriend, who made me feel like the sexiest, smartest, most important woman in the world. And yet I was miserable to the point of this. Bleeding and broken on a bathroom floor. I felt embarrassed and ashamed. Why was I such a loser?

I might have been an idiot, but I didn't want to die. So I stood and looked at myself in the mirror to clean myself up. With my face and eyes red from crying, mascara running down my cheeks, and blood all over me, there was no masking this disaster.

I opened the door to see Sacha standing right outside. When he looked at me, I could see in his face just how terrible I was.

"What happened?" he asked.

"I'm so sorry," I said. "I went too deep this time."

chapter I

I wanted to get to the pool so badly, I was practically running. The
July sun had already dried all the dew on our neighbors' matching
green lawns, and I was hot. Why were they taking *so* long?

I turned around to watch my family, almost half a block behind
me. Mom and Dad, laughing as usual about some story, carried all
the junk. They had packed a cooler filled with drinks, sandwiches,
and chips that'd last us the whole day of hanging out in the pool
and on the surrounding soft, grassy hills. Though we lived only two
blocks away, my mom had enough towels, books, and blankets that
we looked as if we were moving to the pool.

Okay, I could understand my parents' slow speed, but what were
my sisters' problems? Lagging even farther behind, Leah and Taryn
had their heads close together the way they always did when they
were gossiping, which was a lot of the time. The three of us were
like variations on the same theme. Despite the age differences
(Leah was two years older than Taryn, who was five years older than
me), we were all beanpoles with olive skin, dark brown hair, bright
blue almond-shaped eyes, and huge California-girl smiles. But we
couldn't have looked more different.

Leah's hair was feathered as it always was, and even though we
were headed for the pool, she had put on the blue eyeliner that was
her current style obsession. I had to admit, she looked really good.
Taryn was just as pretty. Her short hairstyle made her neck look

graceful like a dancer's. It was so different from the long, mostly blonde hair that practically every girl in our town had. But she hated doing her hair so much that Mom had threatened to cut it all off if she didn't brush it. Taryn didn't brush it, and my mom didn't make idle threats. So Taryn had hair like a boy's, which was fine with her.

However, I was the real tomboy. I never heard of a sport I didn't want to play, and I never wavered from my uniform of shorts, T-shirt, and sneakers. Today I had jazzed it up with my acid-washed shorts and New Kids on the Block tank top. But the heat was beginning to make my bathing suit underneath stick to my torso.

"Come on!" I shouted at my family. They just ignored me.

I could have run ahead without them. I knew the site—the pool (nine feet at one end, four feet at the other), the grassy hills, the showers, the covered area with picnic tables—like I knew the back of my hand. And I loved everything about the place: the buttery smell of sunscreen, the feel of hot concrete under my feet, the shock of the first jump into the pool. It didn't matter that I spent all day, every day of the week, around the same pool during swim team practice. On the weekends, it was different; I had to be with my family.

Instead of bolting ahead, I waited for my sisters, who agreed to play Marco Polo with me as soon as we arrived. After they grew bored, my dad chucked me across the pool a few times before he had to get out and help my mom set up the chairs and cooler near the encampment of parents. Luckily a group of neighborhood kids started a fierce game of sharks and minnows that went on until we were starved and our skin was puckered and white. I hopped out of the pool and bolted toward my mom, who greeted me with a clean towel, a turkey sandwich, and a cold Dr Pepper. After gobbling down lunch, I went straight back into the water. And that's where I stayed, where we all stayed, until the sun started to go down on that perfect summer day.

Perfect. That's the word that describes where I grew up. Irvine, California, had cul-de-sacs and identically manicured lawns, kids on bikes and parents who let us do pretty much as we wanted in what seemed like the safest town in the world. It was straight out of a John Hughes movie where the biggest problem is a fight with your best friend. You never saw a single piece of litter on the streets. Even the bright blue sky was straight out of a Hollywood set. Located in Orange County (not exactly known as a land of hardship), my home-town was sunny, on average, 325 days a year. And because it's on the coast, the average temperature is a comfortable seventy degrees. We never had to worry about the town's Easter Egg Hunt or Fourth of July Bike Parade getting rained out. As I said—perfect.

My parents fit right in. High school sweethearts from the Puget Sound region in Washington State, they got married when my mother, Gayle, was twenty and my dad, Dan, was twenty-one. He had been the captain of the football team, and she had been captain of the cheerleading squad. I made fun of them for their cheesy per-fection (my mom was homecoming queen), but secretly I was proud to have them as parents.

With his dark skin, black hair, and blue eyes, I thought my dad was the most handsome guy in the world. A basketball player at Washington State, he kept his six-one frame in great shape by con-tinuing to play lots of sports. My petite mom, a lighter beauty with sandy-blonde hair and pale-blue eyes, fit right into my dad's side.

You couldn't have asked for better parents. They were like best friends who never fought. Because they were both teachers—my dad taught hotel and restaurant management at Orange Coast College, and my mom taught art at various local schools—they always seemed to be around. Over boring, balanced breakfasts and dinners prepared by my mother, which we ate together every day, my siblings and I competed to see who could be the goofiest and get the most atten-tion. Whether it was acting out *Annie* during a family camping trip or telling the best fart joke over chicken and broccoli, Mom and Dad encouraged us to have fun. Everything was about having a good time.

There was always something crazy going on in our house. That's why all the neighborhood kids gravitated to our four-bedroom tract home in a development called the Colony. My parents, in their very laid-back way, welcomed every single one of our friends. They kept the fridge and cabinets stocked with all the best junk food and allowed us to act young and silly. That meant not freaking out if someone spilled soda on the carpet, hit a lawn ornament with a hockey puck, or lay around watching MTV all afternoon.

Some kids liked it so much, they hardly ever left. One summer, Bobby Lanza, a boy I was really close to from the age of two on, spent every minute that he wasn't sleeping at our house. That wasn't such a big deal; lots of kids did that. But Bobby, who was eight at the time, wore his Speedo for every single one of those minutes. "Jeez, Bobby, give that thing a rest," my sister Taryn said by early July.

"Maybe you *should* give it a wash and wear something else," Leah said.

"Do you sleep in your Speedo too?" Taryn laughed.

Bobby was unfazed, and so was I. Teasing was the price we happily paid to hang out with (or at least around) my older sisters and their friends. Although we were on the fringes—listening to the new Huey Lewis and the News album through an open door to the living room or using the terms *face!* or *bitchin'* even if we had no idea what they meant—it was still an exciting place to be. Growing up, I thought Leah and Taryn were the coolest people on earth. Anything they did, I wanted to do too. When they started wearing huge socks scrunched down by their ankles, I begged my mom for a pair and wore them piled around my toothpick ankles. They used mousse to get their bangs to stand straight up, then so would I—well, at least once before I decided hair was a waste of time. I even posed the same way they did in photos, with their head tilted way over to one side.

Taryn wasn't tolerant of my copycat ways. To her, I was nothing more than the annoying little sister. If my parents ever left her to babysit me, we'd both cry to try to get out of the arrangement. Leah, on the other hand, treated me like her special little baby. She would do anything for me, including play endless sessions of Barbie. If Leah had jumped off a bridge, I would have followed in a heartbeat. While I didn't leap off Golden Gate, I did take tap, jazz, and ballet because Leah was a big dancer. I stuck with it for several years until it was obvious to me and everyone else that I wasn't very good at it.

While I adored Leah, the best times were when the entire family was together. And there was no better time in our family than Christmas. In our house, Christmas was not a subtle affair. We were those guys who got our tree the minute after the Thanksgiving dishes had been cleared. We played Christmas music and Christmas movies nonstop, decorated the house like crazy, and drank hot cocoa even though it was Southern California. I lived for our traditions, which included my mother and grandma baking trays of *fattigman*, an exotic savory cookie popular in Sweden and Norway, and my dad reading the children's book *The Polar Express* to all the kids at our annual holiday party. We also used the holiday as an excuse to sneak in a few practical jokes, like the time we gave our grandfather—my dad's dad, who had been a strict high school principal—a black lace thong for Christmas just to see his reaction when he opened his present. My mom, dad, sisters, and I all wound up laughing too hard to see the expression of shock on his face.

While I recognized that my parents, my town, our home, the pool, and my sisters (even Taryn) were perfect because of their natural, easygoing, and carefree ways, for me perfection could be achieved only through a kind of vigilance I had known ever since I could remember.

Hyperorganized, a neat freak, kind of compulsive: call it what you like, I needed order. All my stuff was perfect. In my sixth-grade classroom, my little desktop stood out like an empty island in a sea of chaos. My pencils were lined up in descending height order next to my pens at the top of the desk, schoolwork and notes to the left, books to the right. When kids knocked my display askew with their backpacks, the disorder sent a cold feeling directly to the pit of my stomach. Until I righted it again.

No one ever had to tell me to clean my room; it was always clean. That was no small feat considering I had two parakeets (Goldie and Zeba), two lovebirds (Peaches and Big Mouth), and our family cats (Angel and Dodger), who used my room as their hangout. Those birds were a mess, constantly throwing their food out of their cages and all over my floor. The vacuum was practically attached to my hand, I used it so much. They were worth it though. I spent hours with my animals, dressing up the cats in outfits and teaching the birds to sit on my finger, which I thought was so cool. They were like best friends.

It wasn't just my room that I cleaned. I would have sooner died than have my human friends come over to a dirty house. Before a playdate, I cleaned the house—and I don't mean tidy but what my mom called a "deep clean." I busted out the wood cleaner for the coffee table, dusted the bookshelves, put all the dishes away, Windexed the sliding glass doors, and made sure my Chipmunks record collection was nicely organized. My sisters—whose rooms appeared to have been hit by bombs that sent their Huey Lewis and Andre Agassi posters askew and their clothes across the floor—looked at me like I was crazy.

My mom, on the other hand, thought her youngest daughter giving her house a good scrub-down was hilarious.

"When I grow up, Mom, I want to be your maid," I said. It was my fantasy job because I could live with my mom *and* clean.

"Fantastic," she said.

I didn't know my Windexing was weird—my parents certainly never made me feel that way. In fact, they made me feel as if anything I did was okay. Limitations never crossed my mind, especially when it came to the physical. Rambunctious to the extreme, I loved a goal, a competition, a challenge of any kind. There's an old family video from one of our hiking trips to Yosemite where my sisters stop at a soggy, moss-covered log to discuss whether they can use it to cross a rushing creek. Suddenly the camera pans to me; with tall alpine trees as my backdrop, I flip my hair brazenly and then start to run across the log. No contemplation, no strategy, no taking it slow—just going for it. In the next scene, I fall off the log like a cartoon character and land smack in the gooey mud. I was completely humiliated, but no fall could erode my fearlessness. Nothing bad was ever going to happen to me. I was sure of that.

My combined fearlessness and high energy made for a lot of showing off. To expend a little bit of the energy that drove my parents nuts, they enrolled me in every activity under the sun. By the time I was four years old, I was taking swimming, soccer, gymnastics, and dance. And still, I had enough steam left over to play endless roller hockey with the neighbors.

When it came to sports, I wanted to do it all. And in Irvine that was a completely realistic goal. Everything was at our fingertips, with pristine basketball and tennis courts, fields, and pools that anybody in the community could use for free. I didn't care if they were "boys' sports" or not, I played softball, football, and basketball—you name it. Dad couldn't have been happier; I was the son he never had.

Even when my dad and I rode our bikes to the basketball court to play horse, I felt the rush of competition and pedaled hard to keep up with him. On the court, he towered over me, his broad shoulders, lean torso, and powerful legs completely eclipsing my spaghetti-thin frame. But I thought I still had a shot. *I'm faster, smarter. I can beat this giant.* We both had the squinted look of people taking a game really, really seriously.

For hours we played horse (there was no way I could out-dribble my six-foot dad), forgetting about the time of day, trying crazier and crazier shots. My dad didn't let me win. I had to really win. That hardly happened, but when it did, I bragged to my family how I had schooled Dad on the court.

In the whirlwind of activities that I did on any of the trim fields or bright, shining facilities in our town, swimming held a special place. Swimming was major in Orange County. Every kid did it, and every rich kid tried to do it well. For me, the love was real. From my earliest memories, the pool was the place of long, happy summer days having fun surrounded by everyone I knew. It was also the only sport shared by my oldest, girlie-girl sister; my middle, rebellious one; and me.

Before I had even turned two years old, my parents toted me to the community pool to watch my sisters' practices and swim meets with their team, the Colony Red Hots. Hanging from my father's arm or toddling with the help of my mother's hand, I thrust my hands out, trying to reach the moving shapes in a spray of blue. By three, I was a full-on water baby who longed to be a part of the team, even though I wasn't eligible to join the summer league until the following year. I was such a pest that the coaches got me a tiny black swimsuit with red piping, the uniform of a Red Hot.

It was official (at least to me!): I was part of the team. My parents and the coaches let me spend all summer pretending. I followed swimmers alongside the pool during races as if I and not they were swimming. During free swim, I dove like a dolphin between the legs of the older kids horsing around and challenged my sisters to see who could hold our breath underwater the longest. I stayed in the pool until my lips were blue and someone finally yanked me out.

In the summer of 1986, it was truly official. Old enough to really be in the league, I curled my toes around the edge of the starting block, as I had been taught, and stared at the long stretch of shining blue in front of me. In the periphery of my goggles I could detect the movements of my competitors, but I didn't look at them. Just straight ahead.

Bang! A shot announced the start of the race.

I pushed off the block, trying to fly as far as I could through the air, and plunged into the water. In a flurry of reaching and kicking, my brain repeating every instruction again and again, I moved like a fish through the water. No, that's too slow. More like a speeding bullet. Definitely. My heart pounded with the effort and my four-year-old muscles began to strain. How much longer could I go? Then, *bam*, my hands hit the hard wall, and I shot up out of the water. An entire lap! And I had done it. I won!

I scanned the crowd through the watery view of my goggles and found my family cheering wildly. My sisters, in their Red Hot suits, were making whooping sounds while my mom clapped happily. But my dad was the most excited, pumping his fist into the air. I felt as if I had won the Olympics. I was hooked.

That summer I practiced for a half hour in the morning every day of the week with the other kids my age and then spent the rest of the day hanging around the pool, watching the older team members work out, or playing games until the sun had finally ducked behind the hills, which meant it was time to go home for dinner. The pool was the place to be. Mom and Dad, who had the summers off from teaching, were always waiting alongside the other parents at picnic tables covered in sandwiches and drinks for their ravenous kids. When my sisters weren't in the pool, they joked around and gossiped with their friends in the shade of the trees or moved to the grassy hills for more serious discussions.

Out of the whole week, Saturdays were my favorite. That's when we had swim meets. My three or four races were each only a lap long, which I knew wasn't as hard as what the older kids did, but it didn't matter. They were races and I was going to win. I put everything I knew how to put into those fifty-second bursts of crazy energy, and it usually paid off.

If anyone singled me out as a swimmer, it wasn't for talent. It was for love and belonging. With the sun shining, my sisters as teammates, and my parents as cheerleaders, I would have been happy to stay in the water forever. Life would always be like this, because why change what's perfect?

chapter 2

I raced up the front walkway of our house, leaving my dad to deal with our bags. I couldn't wait to tell Mom all about the trip.

It had been even more awesome than I imagined it would be. When Dad had told me I could come along on his business trip to Orlando, I couldn't believe it. We were always on a budget, so vacation usually meant driving and camping, which was great but nothing like this. Everything was amazing, even going on the airplane, where Dad and I opened our mini snacks and sipped from drinks brought to us by friendly and pretty stewardesses.

I grabbed the doorknob and pulled, yanking my arm against the unexpected resistance. *Locked?* The house was never locked. Maybe Mom, nervous with us away, had locked the door at night and had just forgotten to open it. *Whatever.* I rang the doorbell and waited for my dad, impatient for one of them to get here.

Mom was going to love hearing about the hotel we'd stayed in. It was so huge it had a fake lagoon with a water slide. Then there was Spaghetti House, a delicious restaurant where they gave you a free glass at the end of your meal! "We have to come back here," I begged Dad, who finally said okay, although he looked a little sad about it. The next night, I ordered the same thing, spaghetti and meatballs, and got another glass, which I decided I'd give to Taryn.

Dad hardly had to work at all. He had to go into an office for about an hour one day, while I sat in the waiting room. It seemed like a racket to me, but I wasn't about to complain. Not when he was taking me to MGM Studios, where I got to see all these cool sets from famous TV shows. The high point of the trip, however, was Disney World. In my book, a world dedicated to rides was nirvana. Pirates, the Wild West, underwater adventures: Who came up with this stuff? Epcot was the only bust (I had no idea it was a *learning place*). I almost died of boredom as we slowly inched through the big globe that I thought was going to be a roller coaster. Luckily, one ride on Space Mountain was all it took to carry me back to my happy place.

When Dad finally got to the front door, he took out his keys as if he knew it was locked. He looked at me kind of weird, smiling a little too hard. Maybe he was sorry the trip was over.

As soon as I heard the lock click open, I pushed past my dad and ran inside. Instead of bolting through the house until I found my mother, I stopped dead after only a few feet. *Where am I?* Most of the stuff in the living room was gone—the couch, the lamps, the coffee table, the side tables—missing. *We've been robbed.* The justification quickly disappeared when I saw the stereo. Thieves don't take an old couch and leave the electronics.

If my dad was near me, I didn't know it. He didn't call to me, and I didn't reach out to him. I was in my own world as I started to walk through the house. In a daze, I took a mental inventory of what was left. I roamed from room to room, looking for proof of something I couldn't grasp. My mom was gone.

The family room was the same. I guess she hadn't wanted the TV. And there wasn't any stuff missing in the kitchen or dining room, even though those had been primarily her realm. I wandered upstairs, going first into my parents' bathroom, where I knew the old cup holding my mom's eyeliner, mascara, and other stuff would be gone. Then I opened the door to their bedroom—I guess my dad's bedroom now. The bed was gone; the room looked huge. *Where is Dad going to sleep now?*

A cold feeling moved from my throat down to my chest and then on to my stomach as I settled into my room, where my dad had left my bag. *Feeling* isn't exactly the right word. The coldness was the absence of feeling as confusion and anger pushed any trace of emotion to someplace so deep, I didn't even know it existed. I started to unpack, putting the dirty clothes in the hamper and finding places for my new treasures, as if it were any ordinary day. Even though I was only twelve years old and my mom had left, I wasn't the kind of person to start bawling. That's not the Beard way.

I don't remember the moment I learned my parents were splitting up. One day I just seemed to know. Like most emotional stuff in our family, it was a nonevent. There were no big talks, no TV-style family sit-downs where they told me it wasn't my fault and that they still loved me. My parents weren't into confrontation. In fact, they weren't really into communication. I had no idea why they were breaking up. I had never ever seen them fight.

There had been that one unsettling moment about a year earlier. Coming into the house after playing roller hockey, I found my mom and dad snuggled up on the couch in front of the fireplace. I almost jumped, the scene was so out of place. Just as they didn't fight, they were never ever lovey-dovey. It was too emotional, too intimate. Taken aback, I mumbled a few awkward words and ran up to my room. *Something's not right.* I shoved aside the premonition with the rest of the emotions that didn't fit with our goofy, easygoing family.

We were lighthearted and fun. Anything else wasn't real, or didn't matter. I didn't want my parents to sit on the side of my bed and give me the Mommy-and-Daddy-are-splitting-up speech. I didn't want to talk about it with them, or with my sisters. I didn't want to talk about it at all—not even with my best friend, Yvette.

If I was going to open up to anyone, it would have been to Yvette, the most nurturing person I know. We had met in seventh-grade keyboarding (a class to learn how to type on computers) because our desks were next to each other—and next to one of the school phones with a directory of the internal codes for every single teacher's phone in the school. This was a gift from the middle school gods.

Our glassed-in keyboarding class looked directly into Mr. Kelley's science room. With his big buzzed head that made him look like a member of the military ready to shoot on sight, the chemistry teacher was the biggest jerk ever. Even if I didn't understand something he was talking about in class, I would never have asked a question. He was just too mean.

Mr. Kelley was, however, the perfect prank target. Yvette and I didn't have to discuss the plan; it arrived intuitively like kicking a ball you find in the street. She picked up the phone and dialed his extension, her long tight curls bouncing in excitement. We watched as he stopped his lesson and walked over to his desk. But when he picked up the phone, she hung up. After a second of confusion, he hung up the phone and returned to teaching. We kept at it all class long, interrupting Mr. Kelley, sending him to pick up the ringing phone, and then leaving him hanging.

"Hello!" he bellowed, before slamming the receiver down. "Whoever this is, this is *not* funny."

We begged to differ.

After that we were inseparable. Yvette's fiery personality complemented my sillier self. She talked a mile a minute, much of it funny, so that I was always laughing my ass off when around her. Despite a seriously sarcastic side, Yvette was also one of the most kindhearted people I had ever known. Soon her house became like a second home (it was the only place I was allowed to sleep over during the week). Her parents, who had thick foreign accents from their native British Guiana, were just as hilarious as Yvette, and I pretended her two little sisters were my own, since I had always wanted younger siblings.

There was nowhere I felt more comfortable than by Yvette's side or in her house. Still, I didn't let her know that my parents were having problems. My whole universe was threatening to come apart, but I went about life as a normal twelve-year-old. I confided in no one, maybe because I wanted to pretend as if it wasn't really happening.

Now the half-empty house proved undeniably that this *was* happening. Nothing felt more real than seeing things my mom had picked out specifically for our family gone. I didn't need to ask my dad; my mom was gone. What was the point of asking a whole bunch of questions when I was sure they'd just make me feel worse? And what I wanted to do in that moment was not feel anything at all.

My dad eventually came into my room and sat down. With his long legs stretching from my single bed, he looked really uncomfortable. I concentrated on making sure my records all stuck out the same distance from the shelf.

"Hey, I know your big dream is to be an interior designer when you grow up. Right?" he said. "Well, since the living room is empty, how about you design the room and pick out new furniture? This could be your first official project."

There was only one moment, much later, when I cried about my parents' divorce. I had come home from a long day at school and swimming to overhear my dad talking on the phone in the kitchen.

"No, that's fine," he said. "I'll have them Christmas Eve and morning, and you get them the rest of the day."

Suddenly my arms felt too weak to hold my backpack and my legs too weak to keep me upright. As soon as I heard him put the phone down, I ran noiselessly up to my room and threw myself into bed, where I sobbed into my pillow. We were never again going to have a family Christmas or Thanksgiving again. We were never again going to enjoy a family trip together. What I couldn't grasp in the beginning broke my heart with stunning force. All my best memories—putting on plays for my parents, making s'mores by campfires, walking to the pool—would never ever happen again.

But in my bedroom with my dad, I let him whisk me past tragedy, accepting his positive spin on Mom moving out. I turned to him and gave him a big smile, a signal of excitement over a new project.

"Cool," I said. "When can we go to Ikea?"

I became a master at distracting myself from pain. It was almost like a party trick; the more I added to my schedule, cleaning regimen, or athletic training, the less I felt. My coping mechanism won most people's approval. Adults were unusually impressed. Who doesn't like a kid with a serious work ethic? One of my biggest flaws turned into my best asset. *A hard worker. Determined. Unstoppable. Tireless.*

Not long before my parents split, I had switched from my summer league to much harder, faster, and intense club swimming. During my last couple of years with the Red Hots, I had been undefeated. And while I loved winning more than most anything else in the world, my mom and dad could see the tiniest edge of boredom creeping into my races. I wasn't being challenged, so they asked me if I wanted to try swimming with the Irvine Novaquatics. The coaches had agreed to let me join the team for a couple of weeks to see if it worked.

The Novas were a universe away from the Red Hots. In the summer league, just six weeks long, no one really had to be in shape. It was just for fun. The Novas were a full-throttle year-round program filled with focused and competitive kids who wanted to be recruited into top colleges or even make the Olympics. To compete on a national level, the Novas demanded nine training sessions a week. That meant four to five hours of swimming a day with practices before, during, and after school (before was 5:30 a.m.). The coaches were tough and unforgiving, unlike the Red Hots' coaches, who were mostly high school kids like my sisters. The Novas traveled all around the nation to face kids who had trained just as hard and wanted to win just as badly.

I was totally game.

I arrived early to the Irvine Nova pool for my first practice. Located in the high school, it was part of a huge complex of three big pools. (The Olympic trials were held there in the early eighties.) Even though I had swam in the pool during big meets with the Red Hots, it still scared me. It was a lot bigger and deeper than our community pool, but that wasn't the problem. It was the gutter system.

In most normal pools, the gutter runs around the perimeter as a totally unnoticeable feature where all the stuff you don't want in the water—hair, bugs, dirt—floats away. In the Novas' pool, the gutter was a beast. A yawning eight-inch gap between the ledge and the wall of the pool dropped down into a rushing sewer-like system of water. During Red Hot meets, I involuntarily slowed down only the tiniest bit when I neared that murky gash. When I joined the Novas, I was still small enough that I could have easily fallen in and been washed away like a hairball.

The gutter threatened me like a dark, evil force when I jumped from the edge, joining the other ten-, eleven-, and twelve-year-olds in the pool. The coach, Brian Pajer, a very tan former swimmer, paced along the edge with a mild-mannered, almost goofy-looking smile on his face. I dove under the water and started to relax a little in these new surroundings. Below the surface I checked out the competition stretching their quads and hamstrings. With their skinny legs and small torsos, they didn't look so tough. There was nothing to worry about.

I popped back up for air just as Brian was laying into a swimmer for being late.

"What are you thinking?" he screamed. Suddenly the mild-mannered guy had turned red-faced and really, really angry. The object of his wrath, a boy with a sunken chest and a blond bowl haircut, kept his mouth shut.

"We're here to work," Brian continued. "And if you're not willing to do that, you need to leave."

The boy didn't speak or budge.

"Leave!" shouted Brian, who demanded perfection and complete accountability from his swimmers, even the youngest on the team.

What time was it anyway? As the boy scuttled out the door, I looked up at the clock. It read 3:02 p.m., two minutes past the start of practice. Then I looked around and realized all the other swimmers were already at the wall waiting for our first drill. I swam as fast as I could for the wall, no longer worrying about the gutter. Getting chewed out by Brian, especially on my first day, was way worse than getting sucked into the sewer.

I felt confident lined up next to the other kids. Swimming was swimming, and I was good at it. Nobody could touch me on the Red Hots. Sure, I probably wouldn't be the best Nova, not yet anyway.

Then Brian gave us our first drill: twenty-five laps at thirty seconds a lap. *Thirty seconds?* I could do a lap in thirty seconds, maybe, if I tried really hard. But I sure couldn't do twenty-five of them. There was no time to think. Brian blew his whistle and we were off.

I used everything I had to speed through the water. Still, the rest of the swimmers were much faster. I was trying as hard as I could, but all I saw were the frothy bubbles left in their wake. I made the first interval but just barely. Everyone else had arrived with at least several seconds extra in which they could rest and catch their breath. I had to turn and push off immediately with my heart pounding in my chest.

People continued to pass me in the pool while lactic acid burned through my muscles. But I kept going and going. Overwhelmed, intimidated, and on the verge of throwing up, I kept my head down and kept swimming.

By the end of practice, it was clear that I wasn't that good. In fact I was the worst one in the group. By far. I couldn't believe it. I had been awesome in the summer league, and all these kids on the Novas could just kill me.

Even though I was left shaking and depleted, I wasn't discouraged. During those first couple of months on my new team, I discovered something new about myself. While I hated to be slower than the others around me, I understood this was an adjustment period. My speed didn't dictate my dedication. There was no way I was going to give it up just because I wasn't the best. I loved being in the pool; I loved swimming.

Water had become my getaway. The silent sanctuary was my biggest distraction from the troubles with my family now that my dad and I lived alone. My parents had decided it was best for me to stay with my dad, since he had remained in our house in the Colony. My mom, the one who needed to get away from everything, had moved to a little apartment near the beach like a bachelor. It didn't make sense for me to move to a small apartment away from sports, school, the pool, and friends. Leah and Taryn were both already out of the house by this time, so that left just me and my dad. Our home, which before had been cozy and chaotic, was now lonely and empty. My mom and dad had hoped to disrupt my life as little as possible by maintaining my routine. I should have told them not to bother; my life was already destroyed.

In the water, I didn't have to think about any of that. The moment I jumped in (always feetfirst), there was a rush of cold while the water swept up my legs, swimsuit, goggles, face, and swim cap. I was glad to become completely consumed in a cleansing weightlessness. Everything was washed away. The top of my head down to my toes was so light as to not exist. I didn't worry for my dad or myself. I wasn't angry at my mom or resentful of my sisters. I just wasn't.

All my focus and energy went into completing the interval. The harder the training, the better. Challenges with the Novas offered the purest mental break. I wanted the work to take everything I had in order to achieve it. And being the slowest swimmer, getting beat all the time, was definitely a challenge. Watching my teammates pass me ignited my competitive sparks. If the urge to win hadn't consumed me, I never could have withstood the pain. After less than a half hour into most practices, I found myself completely exhausted. My muscles started to go limp and give up on me; keeping a consistent rhythm became impossible. What was worse than the lack of oxygen and my Jell-O body was the thought that I'd have to fight through it for the next hour and a half.

Again I turned to my powers of distraction. I went deep inside my head and started doing math, a lot of math. It was ironic, since I hated math in school. Numbers on a sheet of paper were about as real to me as the tooth fairy. The problems I did in the water were real. I'd play with the intervals Brian had given us. (If we are going to do twenty-five laps at thirty seconds a lap, how many minutes will the entire set take?) I parsed time in as many ways as I could come up with, and when I ran out of ideas, I used the eight black lines at the bottom of the pool for my computations. (How many strokes per line? Multiply that by eight for strokes per lap, then by the number of laps for the interval.) Unlike the fractions or the equations where you had to solve for x that brought me to my knees in school, the random numbers that found me in the pool soothed my brain. I escaped from the pain—of home, of intervals—but remained sharp. All that number crunching turned me into a precision instrument in the pool. Knowing exactly how many strokes it took me to do a lap, I could swim with my eyes closed.

No one would have noticed if I had. On most levels, swimming is very individual in nature. It's the most antisocial sport in the world. You say a sentence before practice and then another to announce when you're leaving. It's impossible to gossip when your face is in the water. In swimming, that fact weeds out a lot of people, but I was grateful for the isolation.

I was happy to be in charge of myself and no one else. It meant more pressure. There was no one else to blame if I didn't swim well. I was accountable for showing up, getting in the pool, and working my ass off. But I was also in complete control of my success. I wanted to earn every single win and suffer every loss myself.

Mostly though, I was happy just to be alone. In the water, I didn't have to deal with all the questions. *How are you? What's happening with your parents? Are you sure you're okay?* People meant well, especially Yvette's parents, who voiced their concern over homemade mac and cheese with their still-perfect family. I know they were trying to help me through my parents' split, but probing the emotional realm felt like an attack on me and how my family did things. We didn't talk, and I didn't want to talk.

The pool drowned words with its primordial silence. With my ears tucked under my hair and swimming cap, only the faintest sound of water, like a dulled-out river running, could be detected. Hardly anything broke through the ambient noise that became as quiet and resonant as my heartbeat, not even the coaches who screamed out my time at the top of their lungs when I hit the wall. This was my own world, quiet, contained, and tough. Here, in the water, no one could see me cry.

chapter 3

"One salad coming up!"

My dad worked furiously over the kitchen counter, cutting carrots, cucumbers, and a tomato, dumping the colorful heap onto the crunchy iceberg lettuce. From the kitchen table I could smell the spices as soon as he opened the bottle of Italian dressing. I was still rubbing my eyes awake—no matter how early I went to sleep, waking up at 4:30 a.m. for morning swim practice was never easy—when he put my current favorite breakfast in front of me.

"Here you go," he said cheerfully, sitting down to his own breakfast even though it was still pitch-black outside.

I dug into the huge, delicious salad and was thankful there was no one to say a word during each tangy bite. Back from college and visiting home a week earlier, my sisters had made fun of us for my unusual morning menu.

"You're serving your child a salad for breakfast?" Leah had asked, raising her eyebrows in serious disapproval.

"That is *so* like a dude," Taryn piled on. "Cold pizza in the morning. Cereal at night. It's just sad."

Dad and I shrugged off their judgments. My sisters could make fun all they wanted. There was nothing weird about how we ate. Food was food. As long as I was getting the necessary calories and nutrients into my system, Dad didn't care what time it was served. He was glad to indulge my cravings. For the last three months, it had been a salad with Italian dressing for breakfast. Before that I wouldn't eat anything but waffles with powdered sugar. And before that it had been Top Ramen noodles (my sisters might have called child services if they had seen that).

I didn't care what anyone thought, my dad had stepped into the role of Mr. Mom like a natural. As we settled into our new routine, he happily prepared and served me my unusual meals, drove me to 5:30 a.m. practice, and picked me up without fail after my last practice at 6:30 p.m. He was a rock, strong and together, even though he was also hurting. Like me, he hadn't wanted the divorce; his family had fallen apart. But if he was heartbroken, he never showed it to me, not once. It takes a lot to get my dad upset. There was only one time in my entire life I remember seeing my dad cry, and that was when his father died. Otherwise, he was always smiling. Always.

Instead of moping around like two depressed roommates, we rested on sunnier common interests, such as sports. I hadn't veered from my tomboy ways even as I entered my teen years, so we had a lot to occupy us. There were moments, however, when I needed my mom and really missed her immediate presence in the house.

The worst was when I got my first period. With stuff like that, I was the shiest person in the world. I was like a stereotypical guy; emotional, personal things made me really nervous. I would have given anything to ignore them completely. And that's exactly what I tried to do when I got my period while returning from a trip with my mother to visit her family in Washington State. Too embarrassed and scared to say anything, even to my mom, I decided to handle the situation by shoving toilet paper down my underwear at every rest area we stopped at during the long drive back to Irvine.

That wound up not being a great long-term plan. Back at home, I wasn't any better equipped to deal with this very unexpected and uncool turn of events. Unsure of what to do, I began privately freaking out. My stupid period wouldn't stop, and I had swim practice coming up on Monday, where my toilet paper solution would be a disaster. There was no way in hell that I was going to talk about this with my dad. He was such a dork. Plus you just didn't talk to your dad about periods. I think we would have both died on the spot.

Despite the obvious mess I was in, it took me two days to work up the courage to call my mom. I was so uncomfortable that the minute my mom picked up the phone, I began crying.

"Baby, what's wrong?" she asked.

My sobs choked my words so that it took me a dramatically long time to get it out. "I got my period."

"Oh, honey . . ."

"I don't know what to do. I can't go to the grocery store myself. I'll die if I have to do that. And I can't tell Dad. I mean that's too weird. This is the worst thing that's ever happened to me. . . ."

My mom immediately drove over to the house with half the feminine hygiene section of the pharmacy and helped me figure everything out while my dad lurked around downstairs, thankfully staying very much out of the way.

My mom wanted me to know that even though she wasn't in the same house with me, she was still available. We talked on a daily basis, and my parents were always friendly with each other. There were never any fights, drama, or saying bad things about each other. They made it as easy as they could on me. Still, it was hard.

No matter how many swim meets my parents cheered me on at side by side, life had become strained and strange. I knew Mom understood and felt guilty about that even though, like everything else in our lives, it remained unspoken.

One day when we were having our daily telephone chat, she said out of the blue, "I'm going to pick you up tomorrow morning and take you to swim practice."

"Why would you do that?" I said. "You're going to drive twenty-five minutes from Balboa to drive me three minutes to the pool? You'll have to wake up at four thirty a.m. for us to make it on time. That's crazy. Dad'll just do it."

"No, I want to come. I wake up early anyway, and there's a masters swimming class for my age group at the pool during your practice time, which would be a good workout for me. I'm looking forward to it. I already discussed it with your father."

There was no point in arguing. Because I was too young to drive to see her in Balboa, she used any excuse to come to Irvine. If my mom was willing to sacrifice sleep to be able to spend three minutes in the car with me, there was no way I could talk her out of it.

Despite my parents' major attempts at creating normalcy, the most helpful thing in adjusting to life post-split was the fact that I was way too busy to think about it. Being gone from 5:00 a.m. to 7:00 p.m. five days a week and traveling many weekends didn't leave much time for brooding in the house.

My dad kept me on a tight schedule that I gratefully adhered to. He'd pick me up from swim practice at 6:30 p.m., which meant we'd get home by 6:45. Knowing I returned from practice as starved as a stray animal, he would have a nice, hearty dinner ready to serve by 7:00. Broccoli was his go-to vegetable, so we had it practically every night. Then he would make some sort of meat; barbecued chicken or pork chops were a staple. I always started my meal with a salad and washed it down with a glass of milk.

The two of us would eat our dinner in front of the TV, usually watching a sitcom since half an hour was all the time we had. Our favorite show was *Home Improvement*. My dad and I both thought it was hilarious, so much so that we had *Home Improvement* T-shirts that we wore once a week while it aired. (For Halloween, I went as the character Al in a fake beard, flannel shirt, and a hat that read "Tool Time.") After dinner and a show, I had about an hour and a half to get my homework done, and then it was straight to bed. I never gave my dad any trouble about going to sleep. I had to be unconscious by 9:30 p.m. if I didn't want to be completely wrecked the next day, which was absolutely no problem. I was so exhausted from my day that the minute my head hit the pillow, I was asleep.

Swimming with the Novas was like a full-time job—especially in the beginning when Brian discovered that what I called my breaststroke had little in common with the stroke that typically goes by that name.

"What the heck is that?" Brian said, disgusted after a breaststroke set. "What you just did was totally illegal. I can't have a swimmer on my team who doesn't know how to swim legally. You'll be disqualified if you swim like that."

It turned out that while one of my legs was doing a correct breaststroke kick, the other was doing a scissors kick. Instead of booting me from the team, Brian overhauled my stroke. He spent an extra fifteen minutes with me every day after practice trying to retrain my unruly legs.

The breaststroke is the slowest stroke, but it's also the most technically challenging. Not only does most of the stroke take place underwater—unlike the freestyle or butterfly, where a swimmer's arms and legs move above the surface—the right and left sides of the body have to be perfect mirror images of each other. When done correctly, the breaststroke looks like a little frog moving uniformly and swiftly through the water.

Mine was nothing like that. One leg was doing a poor imitation of a frog while the other was slicing the water. When you have done something one way for eight years and all of a sudden someone says, "No, you need to do it completely differently," it's not easy or fun. I swam one lap and Brian stopped me.

"Turn your toes out."

Half a lap.

"Get your heels up to your butt."

Picking apart my stroke, Brian had so many comments and changes that by my second lap, I felt as if I had forgotten how to swim and was on the verge of drowning. He was asking me to change what seemed as natural to me as walking. On my third lap, I might as well have drowned, I was so bad.

"Slow yourself down, Amanda," Brian shouted. "Think about what you are doing."

The last thing I wanted to do was slow down. I pushed off the wall angrily, reverting back to a more pronounced version of my original kick. Brian must have realized my frustration, because his only comment when I completed the lap was, "Let's come back to this tomorrow."

I was irritated with my body and brain that couldn't put this new information together immediately—but not with Brian. I was grateful to him for taking time out of his schedule to help me. He didn't have to stay after practice; he didn't even have to keep me on the team. I felt special having him pay that much attention to me.

In the coming weeks, we made countless minor adjustments to turn my breaststroke from an illegal one into an efficient underwater machine. Any really great athlete knows where his or her body is in every moment. Ever since I was very little, I had that ability to detect every part of me in the pool. I sensed pain at its first fiery itches and a cramp at the very beginning of a tightening muscle. Eventually, I also understood Brian's directions—all ten million of them.

I figured out how to cut through the water, making myself hydrodynamic. Almost every swimmer can do freestyle, but the technicality of the breaststroke weeds out a lot of folks. People either can do it or they can't. There's no middle ground. I might have originally been a butterflyer while swimming with the Red Hots, but after three weeks' working with Brian, I was a breaststroker. Each swim, I coordinated the kick with the pull a little bit more and pulled my chin up while taking a breath a little less.

Then I started to go fast. Really fast.

While warming up before my race at the Santa Clara Grand Prix in July of 1995, I was full-on staring—just as I had been doing the whole weekend. I snuck little glances and then quickly looked away when she tried to make eye contact. I didn't want her to know I was looking. I wanted to be cool, but it was hard; I was only three strokes away from my swimming idol Summer Sanders.

I first fell in love with Summer while watching the 1992 Olympics. Although I was only ten, I knew I wanted to be just like her. For sure she was pretty: strong and lean with perfect light-brown hair that looked good wet or dry. Her beauty was so effortless, I'm pretty sure she woke up looking gorgeous. But it wasn't her looks that I admired. Summer was the whole package. A world-class butterflyer, she won more medals than any other U.S. swimmer that summer in Barcelona, including two golds, a silver, and a bronze. That was just the start. Her reach went far beyond the small world of swimming. She attended Stanford University, acted as UNICEF's special ambassador for sports, and had an amazing presence on television. Summer had already done commentary for CBS Sports and cohosted a sports show on MTV.

More impressive than her cool TV gigs or her amazing legs was her graciousness as a competitor. You can tell a lot about athletes by the way they handle success. Something as small as the way a swimmer touches the wall after she's won a race offers insight into her character. It always made me uncomfortable when people flailed their arms and started screaming after getting first place. Maybe they were just caught up in the moment. But that didn't keep me from wanting to swim over and tell them to cool it. No matter how wildly happy you feel, you're surrounded by others who've lost, so it's important to win with a little humility. You need to celebrate yourself but also be courteous to your fellow racers. When Summer won her two gold medals during the 1992 Olympics, she didn't go crazy and rub it in everyone's face. In my living room at home, I watched in awe as she simply touched the wall and bowed her head.

Now my idol wasn't on television but in the same pool as me while we warmed up for our race at the Santa Clara Grand Prix. I really wanted her autograph but I couldn't whip up the courage to ask her—not at sign-in, not when I saw her in the hotel lobby, not in the locker room. I had blown all those chances worrying that I'd come off like a complete idiot. Right before the race, I tried to talk myself into it again, but my mouth wouldn't open. Okay, after the race. I'd definitely do it then. I had no other choice.

On the block, everything faded—even Summer's allure. It was me and swimming, something at which I had known I was good but, as it turned out, I might actually be awesome. The last year had been a whirlwind of improvement. Every time I swam my new and not illegal 100-meter breaststroke, I dropped huge chunks of time. While most swimmers are lucky if they can budge one-hundredth of a second off their last best time, I'd shave a handful of seconds off each time I dove into the water. In January 1994, I swam the 100-meter breaststroke in 1:33; by August of that year, I was down to a 1:15. My times were dropping so fast that I qualified for the Junior Nationals. But before I even had the chance to swim in that meet, I qualified for the Senior Nationals.

It was really fun to go from having a disqualifying stroke to being one of the top-ranked breaststrokers in the nation in an absurdly short time. I was cool about the whole thing because I didn't know any better. My nonchalant attitude wasn't a put-on for the press but rather sheer ignorance. I had no idea that my meteoric rise was unheard-of.

Just as I did with every other race, I took for granted that I'd rock it in Santa Clara. Free of worry and any notion of failure, that's exactly what I did. I won the 100-meter breaststroke, beating Summer Sanders. To the media it was a huge deal that I swam faster than her, but the truth is I should have. This wasn't her event; it was mine.

Whatever the press would say later, the only thing I was thinking about when I got out of the pool was that autograph. How many more moments would I have to be near her? By my calculation: none. I propelled myself forward by imagining how upset I'd be in my room that night if I didn't have her signature on something.

Dripping wet and still breathing hard from the race, I tentatively approached Summer, also wet on the pool deck. She looked up, staring directly at me. This was stupid! What was I thinking going up to her two minutes after the race? What a jerk. My hand was shaking, I was so nervous, but it was too late to turn around now.

"Uh, Summer, can I have your autograph?" I said, so quietly I could barely hear it.

Giggling and taking the pen and T-shirt from my death grip, she said, "I should be asking you for *yours*."

Summer's compliment was lost on me. It wasn't until a month later—when I qualified for my first international meet—that I was truly impressed with my own success. Here I was, a thirteen-year-old at the Pan Pacific Championships in Atlanta, Georgia, a dry run for the Olympics the following year, representing the United States against the best twenty-five-year-olds from all over the world, who were twice my size. And it was a blast.

The meet was the biggest I had ever done and the first time I was away from my parents for two whole weeks. I couldn't have felt more grown-up. Homesickness was no longer a problem for me, since I had started traveling as far away as Hawaii and Colorado for swim meets when I joined the Novas. Instead of worrying about being alone, I concentrated on what I'd do with my freedom. I mapped out my day as carefully as if I were planning a rocket launch: Where would I walk in the mall that joined our hotel; what would I choose for dinner at the T.G.I. Friday's I'd already found; what was I going to watch on TV back in the room? These all felt like vital questions to be answered as I thrived on my independence.

I couldn't understand my other U.S. teammates' stress. The older kids were edgy during practice, the pressure growing with the mounting hype. Just as in Santa Clara and all year long, I was totally clueless. The press and the internal politics of swimming were not part of my universe. To me, the Pan Pacs hardly felt any different from local meets. There were the same rhythms and routines. The same pool length and depth. Basically, just step on the block, dive in, and go.

There were perks that I had not found swimming in Southern California. Not only did I take my first taxi ride at the Pan Pacs but we got tons and tons of free clothes from swimming companies— and two hundred dollars in cash to spend on food! For me, a girl who got seven dollars a week for chores, the wad of bills felt like a million bucks. I dined at T.G.I. Friday's to my heart's content and still had enough left over to buy a bracelet and the delicious sugar-covered, peach-flavored hard candies I discovered at the mall.

The swimming was the icing on the cake, a fun activity in between Parmesan-crusted chicken combo platters and window shopping. At the Georgia Tech pool, which was fully souped-up for the upcoming Olympics, I won bronze medals in both the 100-meter and 200-meter breaststroke events and a silver in the women's medley relay. While I stood on the podium as a crowd of a couple of thousand cheered, my only thoughts were that this is what happens when you love swimming and are good at it. You get money, cool outfits, taxi rides. It was as natural and easy as training, improving my time, and winning medals. It was all good.

So I was kind of confused with the reporters' line of questions in the mix zone. For about twenty minutes, dozens of press people asked me many variations on the same basic theme: Was I nervous?

Was I nervous for the race?

Am I nervous about what's ahead?

Am I nervous that my friends back home will treat me differently now?

Am I nervous that I won't have what it takes to go all the way to the Olympics?

What's wrong with these people? Don't they know swimming is a game?

Standing behind the microphone, this thirteen-year-old, who looked more like a ten-year-old, weighing in at just under a hundred pounds, couldn't give the reporters the drama they were looking for. They dug for that little nugget of emotion—some nail biting before stepping on the block or tears in my eyes after I had won. But it just wasn't there. Swimming wasn't a crazy out-of-this-world thing. It was jumping in a pool. It was *fun*.

If the reporters wanted drama and nerves, they wouldn't find it in the pool. I was fine in this grown-up world of pain and triumph, winning and losing. There *was* a place that was killing me, but the journalists would have been surprised to hear its name. It was a place for kids, normal kids. School: I hated it.

Because I suffered from a mild form of dyslexia that gave me trouble when I read on white paper, I had never been a terrific student. The harsh white made it hard for me to focus on the words or problems. Instead I'd see weird shapes, like little squiggles, moving around the corners of my eyes, distracting me from the content of the page. I didn't know what was going on in my brain, but I'd flip the order of words, easily reading a question in reverse. It took so much concentration and time to focus on reading things right that I had barely any energy left to answer questions on quizzes.

Don't ask me why, but purple paper made reading easier. The color dulled down the distractions. All my teachers were supposed to know about my disability and print my tests on purple paper, but somehow whenever that first quiz or test landed on my desk, there it'd be, a blaring white page burning my eyes. Of course, I could have told my teachers directly: "Hey, I'm messed up. Can you give me my tests on purple paper, though I'm not sure where you can get purple paper unless of course you don't mind stopping off at an art store on your way home? Thanks a bunch." But I never did. I didn't want anyone to know, and I certainly didn't want to be the pain-in-the-ass kid who needs her tests on special paper. No, white paper would do just fine.

But it wasn't fine. And it only got worse after I joined the Novas and homework time was crunched into the short hour or so after dinner and before sleep. When I got bad test grades, which was all the time, I tore into the house in tears, which in turn tore my father apart. He'd never gotten mad about my doing poorly—he knew how much effort I put into my schoolwork. He shoved aside any helpless feelings of watching me fail and instead did his best, as an educator and a dad, to support me. "It's okay," he said. "We'll work harder for the next test."

We tried. I spent an entire Saturday struggling over a chapter of *The Old Man and the Sea*. The words were simple and the sentences short. But all put together, it was as if I were in the sea, and I was drowning. I followed word after word after word. But when I finally emerged from my room for dinner, I was in tears. For the life of me, I had no idea what I had spent all day reading.

After a long hug and the healing properties of an episode of *Home Improvement*, Dad came up with a plan; he'd read to me. So when it came time to read *Lord of the Flies*, each of us flopped on one of the two big couches in the family room and he read me everything—the book, the CliffsNotes on the book, and my homework. He also helped me with my papers, giving me notes for second and third drafts.

Nothing worked. No matter how much time and effort I put into school, I was lucky to pass, let alone succeed. In English class, I poured my heart into a personal essay for which I chose to write about my experience swimming. My dad and I had revised it (or as he said, "polished it") a couple of times, adding to my excitement as I proudly handed it in to my teacher.

So when she returned it to me with an ugly, giant C minus and so many red marks that each page looked as if it had just returned from war, I hit bottom. I ripped up the paper and threw it into the trash. "Nothing I do pleases these people."

I had put everything I had into that paper, done multiple drafts, and it still wasn't good enough. Even worse, I knew that my teacher, a nice-enough lady who worried about me, had been charitable giving me a C minus. I'm sure she thought my work was worth only a D or F. What was the point of trying? When I tried my hardest, I got a D or a C, and when I didn't, I got the same result. It wasn't worth the heartache.

Despite my repeated, demoralizing failures, I couldn't give up. Not trying wasn't in my nature. I didn't want anyone to look at me as a charity case or a dummy—even as I improved in swimming, and my teachers were more willing to give me passes for my lack of aptitude. Once I missed a whole week of class for a big swim meet, which meant I missed a whole chapter and test in history. You might as well have told me the chapter I needed to read was on the top of Mount Everest. The idea of making up work when I couldn't even keep up with the regular load was suffocating.

My teacher must have seen the terror in my eyes because he said, "Don't worry about it. Just move on." And like that, the Hundred Years' War and the end of feudalism were forgotten. What a relief. I knew catching up would be so overwhelming it might break me permanently. But another feeling quickly gnawed away at the relief. I wanted to be smart like Yvette and my sisters (Taryn graduated from high school in three years as if it were some part-time hobby), not that dumb jock for whom teachers look the other way. I hated that I was living up to an awful stereotype.

I didn't give up, but I didn't stop suffering either. School made me cry out of frustration or humiliation on a daily basis. I felt like a complete idiot struggling with tasks or concepts that came like a snap to my classmates. Reading out loud in class was the worst. Reading to myself was difficult enough, but out loud was pure and utter torture. While reading excruciatingly slowly so as not to jumble my words, I broke out in sweats, and my heart rate spiked. Needless to say, I didn't get called on a lot.

Math and science weren't any better. That stuff made absolutely no sense to me. I was in awe of Yvette, who understood everything in an algebra class we had together. She suggested we study together for tests, but it was just a ruse to give me an anxiety-free tutoring session.

"See, you're solving for x," Yvette explained patiently. "You have these three formulas to choose from. Do you know which one you need here?"

I must have looked at her with that familiar terror, which really seemed to work on people.

"Okay, it's this one," she said.

I still did the steps all wrong and she had to walk me through the whole problem like a math teacher. Despite Yvette's best efforts, I failed algebra and had to repeat the nightmare the following year.

School was murder. Homework and tests were a daily mental and physical beat-down. My frustration was so bad it hurt. I didn't see how I could work through this kind of pain—the pain of being really bad at something without hope of improvement.

It made the physical pain of swim training seem like a vacation. In fact, it was a vacation. In the water, counting until my brain went numb, my body not far behind, I outswam my problems. An F on my latest algebra exam or my dad's loneliness while I went away with my mom for a long weekend trailed me. They lingered by my heels lap after lap but never caught up. They remained in the water drowning as I got out, my body and mind mellow with fatigue. The workout felt so good.

But it never lasted. Although a hard swim temporarily washed away my stress, my problems refused to budge. Out of the water, my parents were still split and school kept up its stranglehold. My multiple practices each day became like a fix (even though all the hours I devoted to training also contributed to my poor grades). My morning swim dulled the terror of the start of school, while my midday one left me drowsy for afternoon classes. After my last practice, I slid right into dinner and homework until I fell asleep so fast and so hard it was as if I had been gassed.

So no, I wasn't nervous about swimming. It was getting out of the pool and the rest of life that freaked me out.

Nothing about swimming scared me, not even the Olympic trials in April of 1996. It was a really hard cut to make: usually only about six hundred U.S. swimmers nationwide make it to the trials. And though I had been swimming with the Novas for only about eighteen months and only one other person on our team made the trials in Indianapolis, I still felt everything happening to me was normal. I couldn't conceive of this not happening.

The only weird part was traveling with Jason Lezak, the Nova swimmer who had made the trials in the sprint freestyle, and my coach, Dave Salo. Once we got to Indianapolis, I spent most of my free time by myself. I hit gold when I discovered there was a T.G.I. Friday's *in* the hotel. (For eight days straight, I ate breakfast, lunch, and dinner there, indulging in my new culinary discovery—broccoli-cheddar soup—every single night.) I spent so much time in the hotel's video arcade that I became a Ms. Pac-Man champion and spent half my per diem on winning a race car key chain in one of those crane games. How else was I going to kill time out of the pool while traveling with a twenty-year-old guy and our coach?

Not that there was anything wrong with Dave, who had become my coach right before the Pan Pacific Championships when I turned thirteen and aged into the older group of Novas. Like Brian, Dave demanded a high level of commitment and attention to swimming. Never without a Diet Coke, including during morning workouts at 5:30 a.m., Dave patrolled the pool for dawdlers. If you didn't jump right in on time, he'd reach into his large fountain soda cup, fish out a piece of ice, and chuck it with alarming accuracy right at you. Extremely loud and passionate, he knew how to get the attention of his swimmers. He had an ear-piercing whistle that defied the laws of the universe and broke through the impenetrable quiet of the water. It's the only thing I've ever been able to hear underwater, and he used it all the time. It could mean practically anything, but usually it meant "Go faster."

I heard that whistle a lot when I first joined his group. With Brian, I had started out the slowest and worked my way up to one of the fastest. When I turned thirteen and started practicing with the older kids, suddenly I was back to slowest again. I had to start all over, only now with eighteen-year-olds who looked like humongous men as they passed me in the pool. The body hair and height and muscle mass didn't alarm me any more than my crazy breaststroke kick had. *Okay, I need to step it up. I can be faster.*

Dave was very motivating. Unmarried and without kids, he always told us we were his family. He devoted his life to making us better athletes and better people. Like a nice dad, he understood that we were dealing with a lot of pressures outside swimming, so he was cool with missing a practice every now and then for a dance or school trip. He got that we were young and should be able to have fun.

Also like a dad, he could get really mad. He was a hard coach, who required respect. Just like Brian, Dave kicked kids out of the pool for being lazy, unfocused, or late. However, Dave had his own particular method. Once after I forgot my kickboard, Dave ordered me to hold a plank position on the pool deck for the entire fifteen minutes of that particular set. My arms and abs burned, and my wet skin was covered in goose bumps, but this was nothing compared with his routine when a team member showed up late.

"Here, take this and fill it out," he shouted.

Always put together in a crisp polo shirt and nice Bermuda shorts (Dave never ever wore sweats, tracksuits, or swim gear like the other coaches), he handed the offending Nova a sheaf of light yellow papers. It was an application for a position at McDonald's.

"Sit here and fill it out, because with your attitude this is where you're going to end up working," he barked. "I'm not kidding. Fill it out!"

It was the kind and easygoing Dave who was by my side right before I competed against about eighty other swimmers in the 100-meter and 200-meter breaststroke trials that would give me a place on the Olympic team. He colluded with me in making the event just another meet, a simple act of swimming.

"You love racing, Amanda," he said, playing it cool because he knew that's what worked best for me. "Just jump off the blocks and show them what you can do."

My coach was completely right. I had a great meet in Indianapolis, winning both the 100-meter and 200-meter breaststroke events and breaking a pool record in the 100-meter. I was on my way to the Olympics.

Exiting the pool, I was super excited, but I didn't scream or jump up and down (thanks, Summer Sanders). Instead, I looked for my family in the stands. They weren't hard to find; they were the group of twenty or so grandparents, aunts, and cousins doing all the jumping. My sisters were high-fiving each other before hugging my mom and dad. Because they knew intimately how hard I had worked and how much I had dedicated to swimming, they were as overjoyed as I. It felt as if they had won too.

My mind wasn't on the Olympics ahead or the possibility of important medals. I couldn't think past the celebration we were set to have in a few hours. My family had rented a group of apartments in a complex where we would order pizza, maybe get in a little bowling at a nearby alley, and definitely act our goofiest. As I blinked the water from my eyes, my family, smiling and having fun, came into clearer focus. Swimming well was a good thing, because it brought us together again and made everyone happy. And I definitely wanted that.

chapter 4

All swimming meets are boring. Even the Olympics.

The 1996 Summer Games were no exception. It's not at all like what you see on television: eight long days condensed down into a few minutes, framed by heartwarming or heartrending vignettes of swimmers' lives created by producers to inject some drama into what's really an incredibly monotonous sport.

Try being there. That's a whole different kind of story. In Atlanta, our team began a routine that only made sense in the weird world of the Olympics. We woke up very early in the morning to swim preliminary races or warm up before beginning the real day, which was totally empty. The only thing to do was watch hours of races that could be exciting if there was a U.S. team member swimming. But with fifty Americans on the team and about a million races, there were only five minutes out of two hours that mattered. Finals started at 6:00 p.m. when we all returned to the pool, either to swim or watch, and after a couple of hours, we were back on the shuttle to eat dinner. Despite the endless hours of downtime, we didn't get back to the dorms until about 10:30. Sleep-deprived from getting home late and waking up early, by midweek I had turned into a zombie who would have been just fine not seeing another pool for as long as I lived.

We had too much time on our hands, and I was not good with any time on my hands. It didn't help matters that I had practically no friends on the team. It's not that I didn't like the rest of them; I didn't know them. To me, they were just a bunch of twenty-year-olds who, like most people way older than me, lived on another planet. At first I tried to act like an adult—adopt their customs of listening to music all the time and be sort of annoyed at everything. Still, I could tell that a lot of the people on the team knew the truth: I was young and dorky.

There were a couple of girls my age on the team—Jilen Siroky, a breaststroker out of North Carolina, who was three weeks younger than me, and Beth Botsford, a fifteen-year-old backstroker. But put us side by side, and anyone would have thought both had several years on me.

Part of it was physical. I was a late bloomer, a completely flat-chested prepubescent girl without an ounce of fat. Jilen and Beth had boobs and hips . . . and boyfriends. Having just graduated from playing with Barbies, I thought a boyfriend was Brian Wellikson, a boy from school whom I had never ever talked to but had "dated" for two weeks (which meant that through much back and forth among a network of friends, we showed up at the same movie, where we *didn't* sit together).

I was a very young fourteen-year-old, while Jilen and Beth had no problem blending in with the older kids. Like the other girls they hung out with around the Olympic Village, they had the typical look of normal teenagers—tight pants, little tank tops, push-up bras, mascara, eyeliner, and lip gloss, lots and lots of lip gloss.

With my plain, chin-length bob and makeup-free face, I was so excited about all the free crap we received that my wardrobe was head-to-toe graft. I had brought street clothes from home but thought I looked much cooler walking into the cafeteria sporting a Speedo T-shirt, Nike sweats, and Arena hat.

My teammates were friendly enough, but we just didn't click. The disconnect was apparent from the moment we arrived at our dorms for the Olympics on the Georgia Tech campus. I thought the clusters of four little bedrooms connected by small living areas seemed as though it was going to be the spot for a lot of fun, especially after the loneliness of our pre-Olympics training, where for two weeks, each of us on the team had our own room at a Marriott. I had hated going back to my creepy, anonymous room. After slowly opening the door and keeping my body out of the way in case any intruder wanted to run out the door, I would tentatively walk in. Then my nightly routine included checking under the bed that was big enough for six of me, behind the shower curtain, and in the closet. Still, I had to sleep with a light on and the TV on a timer. I was unused to being completely alone.

In the Olympic Village, I was happy to be surrounded by people again. With accommodations that were far more than I needed, I looked forward to camping out with everyone else. But I was alone in my assessment. People were not psyched about the close quarters and being forced to share rooms. When I ran into my room and threw my bag on the top bunk, shouting, "I want top!" my roommate Annette Salmeen looked at me as if I had a brain injury.

Soon enough I wasn't crazy about the dorms either. All people did when they weren't swimming or sitting by the pool was nap or listen to music. After a few days, it got so boring I thought I was going to shoot myself.

I had gotten into competitive sports in the first place because I had crazy energy. I liked to do stuff all day long: swim, go to school, play, swim. When the U.S. coaches at the Olympics told me to rest up for four hours in between practice sessions, I wanted to ask them if they were insane. Rest for four hours during the day? This was the Olympics, not an old-age home.

Bored and lonely, I started to miss my family, although I'd been away from them many times before for swim meets. We had been separated since training at Georgia Tech and wouldn't see each other again until after the swimming competitions, for a total of almost a month. Before I left home, it had been business as usual with my mom and dad. Even though they were divorced, they continued to act like a unit when it came to my swimming or anything else about me. If my going to the Olympics affected them, they never let on that it did. The world didn't revolve around the Olympics, or me. My dad and I would sooner talk about an episode of *Home Improvement* than my times for the 200-meter. There were no big talks or parties before I left, which was just fine with me.

Mostly, though, I missed being busy. I filled my days by wandering around and buying candy and soda (at the time, I thought Skittles and Dr Pepper were a delicious combo). Making my way through the Olympic Village was easier said than done. There was security everywhere. Bomb-sniffing dogs, metal detectors, and guards checking credentials blocked each turn and entrance. It was hard to predict how long it would take you to get places, which was stressful considering we had a strict schedule that was taped to our door every morning. Worried about showing up to my 8:00 a.m. practice late, I left over an hour early, while the dorm was still quiet with my sleeping teammates, and rode the shuttle alone to the pool.

Obsessively navigating the Village—to the point where I knew how many paving stones lined the walkway between my dorm room and the dining hall—consumed a fair amount of time. Eventually, however, I was going stir-crazy again and had to branch out.

I did any and every thing the Olympic Committee offered. I stopped by the free McDonald's kiosks, sampling favorites from their menu and expanding my palate with new things; I entered the spa, where I had my first treatment (a lavender wrap); and when I spotted a flyer to watch an indoor volleyball game with Al Gore and his entire family, I showed up at the allotted time and place.

After being sniffed up and down by a pack of dogs and thrown into one of a whole lineup of black shiny cars that drove on a freeway blocked from any other traffic, I found myself sitting next to the vice president's wife, Tipper Gore, during the game. She was like any nice mom, with her perfect blonde bob and smiling round face, asking me about swimming and school. I also talked with her kids and her husband, not in the least bit intimidated (I wasn't even sure what the vice president did). I was just glad to have someone to talk to.

In my quest for activity, I even ventured out to the Olympic Village's nightclub. I wasn't exactly what you'd call a club kid, but this wasn't exactly a club. Completely devoid of alcohol and closed by 8:00 p.m., the nightclub offered athletes the opportunity to get down while being closely monitored by officials. Fun. One night George Clinton, the very bizarre-looking star of a couple of famous funk bands, Parliament and Funkadelic, played the club, which a lot of people thought was a big deal. It wasn't my type of music, but I went along and danced (or at least goofed off) anyway because it was something to do.

With all of that, I still had time left over to kill. So when I wasn't swimming, watching swimming, eating McDonald's, clubbing, or getting spa treatments, I watched my then-favorite movie *Clueless*. A hundred times. (My sisters used to make fun of me for my film obsessions. If I liked a movie, I would watch it until I wore out the copy. One summer, I watched *Congo* at least once a day—not a movie I currently recommend.) From the top bunk in my room at the Olympics, I could, and often did, recite entire scenes from *Clueless*.

If one of my touchstones was Alicia Silverstone, then the other was Yvette, who I knew didn't care if I was the biggest dork in the world. When the dorm phone was free, I called her up. I could hear from the lilt in her voice she was excited to hear from me, which boosted my sagging spirits instantly. She wanted to know everything about everything, from my relationship with my roommate to the kind of food provided.

"There's free McDonald's everywhere," I said. "The athletes can eat as much as they want."

"That's so cool. You can eat whatever you want and don't have to pay anything?" she said.

Suddenly the boring Olympics seemed a little more interesting.

"I went to a health spa where you can get free facials and massages. I had a lavender wrap!"

"Awesome!"

"Yeah."

"What's wrong?" Yvette asked, detecting a hint of the bummed-out state I had tried to hide. "Aren't you having, like, the best time ever?"

"Not really."

"But it's the Olympics."

"It's actually kind of lame here. There's no one to talk to, and I'm not actually swimming that much. I got so bored one day I took a Jazzercise class in the Village."

"You didn't!"

"Yeah, it was a disaster. The teacher did some kind of kick-ball-change move to an awful Paula Abdul song, and I crashed into the girl next to me and killed her foot and probably wrecked her chances in the game."

"Classic. You're not exactly known for having a lot of coordination on dry land."

"Thanks a lot. There's nothing left for me to do in this Olympic Village; I've done it all."

"Aren't you forgetting something?"

"Like what?"

"Um, don't you still have a race?"

Four of us stood on top of the podium, and yet I felt as if all eyes were on me. Not because I was so great, but because I was sure I was about to do something stupid.

Beth Botsford, Angel Martino, Amy Van Dyken, and I had won gold for the 4×100-meter medley relay, my last event of the Olympics. The race had been particularly fun, which relays always are, because it's the closest a swimmer gets to being on a real team. The event is still very intense, but a little bit of the edge is taken off because you're not in it alone.

The first patriotic notes of "The Star-Spangled Banner" struck up and my heart went directly to my throat. It wasn't emotion. I had a hard-enough time accessing my feelings on my own time, with my own parents and best friends. I wasn't about to break down in tears, standing on a big pyramid under bright white lights, in front of thousands of strangers.

No, I was embarrassed.

I was proud of our win, but appearing like a statue atop a cake to mark it seemed absurd. I couldn't have been more insecure. Where should I put my hands? Was that a big cowlick on the left side of my head? How long was this song anyway?

The national anthem seemed to go on forever. I tried to block out the American flags waving wildly from the stands and all those eyes, staring right at me, in order to concentrate on getting the words to the song right.

At the pre-Olympic training camp we'd had a meeting entirely devoted to learning the national anthem because most of us didn't know much past "Oh, say can you see."

"We don't want you standing up there and messing it up," said one of the coaches as he passed around the lyrics printed on handouts. "If you are going to sing it, make sure you sing it right."

I had never been anywhere near great at memorizing in school, but while on that podium, I prayed for a few extra brain cells to get me through this moment.

"No refuge could save the hireling and slave / From the terror of flight, or the gloom of the grave."

I'm definitely going to mess this up.

"And the star-spangled banner in triumph doth wave . . ."

Then everyone will know I'm a dummy.

"O'er the land of the free and the home of the brave!"

Please just let this be over soon.

How did I get here? My races were like a dream, done before I knew it. As soon as they were over, I could hardly remember anything more than brief moments, and even those were hard to hold on to. I replayed them while wearing my medal. There was the moment right before my first event, the 100-meter breaststroke, when the coaches and other swimmers had gone quiet. Some even put on headphones so that they didn't have to talk to anybody else. I jumped into the warm-up pool feetfirst and started to joke around to lighten the mood.

"Think anybody's watching?" I asked.

My teammates did their best imitation of robots, not a trace of emotion on their faces.

"It's a joke!" I said, splashing a couple of them.

"What the hell, Amanda!" one of them replied.

"Get away," another said. "I need to focus."

Okay, so I wasn't hilarious. There was a sellout crowd of at least 15,000 people inside the stadium, and apparently billions more around the world tuning in on television. But you don't see faces when you're a swimmer. Once you dive into the water, you dive into your own world. Breathing forward in the most secluded stroke, I felt like nothing else existed but the wall ahead.

I touched the wall after the last lap and put my head up. On the giant scoreboard, I read, "Amanda Beard 1:08.09." I had come in second. Second! Lifting the goggles from my eyes, I scanned the stadium for the only people in it who counted: my family. It wasn't hard to find the group of thirty people smack in the middle of the stands going crazy and wearing matching T-shirts (brand-spanking-new white ones with the words "Team Amanda" in red).

The confidence of youth turned inexperience into validation. My silver medal proved to me that my attitude—swimming is for fun— was the right one. I had no idea what kind of pressures the older swimmers faced (for them this was no game), and no one thought it important to educate me.

On the contrary, my older teammates sheltered me. Instead of toughening me up, they took pity on me, especially the older ones, like the legendary freestyler Janet Evans, who ended her career after that Olympics. When most of the team was headed out to do laundry, she popped her head into my room and found me sitting on my top bunk with nothing left to wear.

"Come on, lazybones, everyone's going to do laundry," she said.

"I don't know how to do that," I said, embarrassed. "I've never done laundry in my life."

Janet didn't mock me or leave me there. Instead she did my laundry.

"Don't worry. Put all your stuff in a pile and I'll take it."

The next day, I found my clothes, clean, folded, and on my bed.

A few of my teammates did offer me a small glimpse into adulthood one night when they invited me to go off campus with them for something to eat. Because I was a pain in the butt to hang out with (my much-earlier curfew meant somebody would have to cut his night short to take me back to the Village), the invite was a rare opportunity that I didn't think twice about accepting. I got dressed in my best freebies, and we headed into a part of downtown Atlanta I definitely hadn't visited before. Darkly lit and run-down, the area had no recognizable chain stores, just head shops, bars, tattoo parlors, and other places I knew I didn't belong in. It definitely didn't look like Atlanta's center of dining.

Turns out, we weren't going into a restaurant. Instead, one of my teammates pulled open the door of a bar. I immediately tensed up. There was no way they were going to let me—a fourteen-year-old who looked like a ten-year-old—sidle up to the bar. I didn't have a fake ID, because who would ever believe it? I kept my mouth shut and walked in, doing my best imitation of invisibility. I was sure they were going to kick me out in about five seconds, and when they did, my teammates would be annoyed that they had to take me back.

Inside, the bar smelled like stale beer. The place was seriously shady, with a lot of old guys drinking beer and small shots of dark liquid at the bar. We moved to a table and I continued to wait for someone to throw me out, but nobody was even looking at us. These weren't folks who cared about legal drinking ages; all they cared about was their own buzz. My teammates ordered pitchers of beer and poured me a glass while we hung out and chatted. I didn't even want it; cheap, crappy beer is not delicious. But I took several sips so that I wouldn't stand out any more than I already did.

Later in my bed, my guilty conscience kicked in. I wasn't smashed, I didn't even have a buzz, but I couldn't shake the feeling I had done something really bad. Certainly, I would have gotten in huge trouble if any of the coaches, or my parents, had found out. As I replayed the events of the night, I questioned why I had put myself in a position that was so not me. I couldn't come up with a good answer.

The Village, where nothing was serious or real, at least not to me, was a much safer place. Not even a bombing later in the games could pierce my bubble of innocence. That night, with swimming over, a lot of the other team members were out partying when the sirens, the banging on doors, and the loud voices started around one a.m. in the dorms. But I was fast asleep, since I had an earlier curfew. One of the coaches knocked on my door and then came in. They were trying to find everyone who was out. What had happened? A pipe bomb had gone off in Centennial Olympic Park, the town square of the Olympic Village.

I understood the words but was still confused. Who set off the bomb and how'd they do it with all this security? I watched the managers and coaches trying to get ahold of everybody and taking head counts, but the picture never came into focus for me. I stayed on the sidelines of the commotion like a kid, overhearing snippets of conversation—Janet was apparently not too far from where the explosion had happened, doing an interview—but never learning any of the real facts. I didn't know who was responsible for the bombing or if anyone had been hurt (Janet returned safely). My uneasiness subsided as I watched the coaches murmuring quietly among themselves. Adults always worked everything out. And with that the bombing receded into a vague memory.

It was this same naïveté that made the rivalry the press cooked up between me and Penny Heyns, a South African breaststroker, seem like the biggest joke in the world. Our interactions had been limited to quick congratulations after races. Otherwise everything between us was in the media. Before the Olympics, the American press had built me up as the great hope for USA to bring home gold in all the women's breaststroke events, while Penny was getting the same coverage in her country. It turned out that her country was right. I came within half an arm's length of catching Penny in the 100-meter, but she won it and the 200-meter breaststroke event. I wasn't surprised—Penny's thick neck, broad shoulders, powerful thighs, and muscular chest made me look like a ninety-pound weakling—and I wasn't disappointed.

But that's not what the media wanted to hear.

"Are you upset that you didn't win gold?" a reporter asked me in the press conference after the 200-meter event.

Are you an idiot?

"Sometimes when I get second, I'm mad," I said. "This one I'm really proud about. Penny Heyns is pretty tough to beat. I'd rather get second to her than anyone else."

A couple of journalists cocked their heads like I was the most adorable thing in the world, but I didn't give my answer for cute points. Having raced as hard as I could and beaten girls ten years older than me, I was genuinely excited about silver. I couldn't imagine how anyone would view second in the whole world as a failure.

Celebrating my silver in front of all those reporters, I had felt on top of the world. But standing on the podium after the medley relay, with the gold that was so precious to the press around my neck, I wanted to die—or at least disappear. At fourteen, it was pretty unlikely that I was going to drop dead on the spot with a coronary. With my face as big as a blimp broadcast over the JumboTron, however, my disappearing was even more improbable. There was no hiding now.

Immediately after the Olympics, knowing that I needed to decompress, my mom packed Yvette and me into the backseat of her Camaro and drove us up to my favorite place in the world—the lake house. This summer would be no different from any other summer, which we always ended by spending a couple of weeks in Washington State at the cabin belonging to my mother's family on an isolated lake ringed by quiet freshwater woods.

As soon as we arrived at the small A-frame wood cabin and threw our sleeping bags down in one of the three bedrooms we'd cram into with all my cousins, all the interviews, accolades, and unwanted attention disappeared. I was thankful that my family, who had all been in Atlanta, didn't feel the need to rehash old news.

Instead we fell into our typical routine of days in the water and nights playing card games or building campfires for s'mores on the beach near the house. My grandma, aunts, and uncles kept the cabin filled with the delicious smells of all our favorite dishes, like Swedish pancakes (crepe-thin pancakes that I ate doused in cinnamon, sugar, and syrup) or crunch salad (a family invention concocted of sautéed almonds, sunflower seeds, uncooked Top Ramen, and lettuce mixed together with homemade vinaigrette).

One night Yvette, six of my cousins, and I decided to sleep out on the dock. We dragged our foam pads and sleeping bags and fit them together like pieces of a puzzle. Then we dragged Grandma out to tell us one of her stories. She indulged us by recounting our favorite: the tale of the fog. Sitting out on the balcony of the lake house as a younger woman, she had once seen a fog roll across the water, but when it finally reached her, it vanished. Grandma told the story in such a spooky, mysterious way that she left us dying to know the true nature of the fog and to hear the story again. Long after Grandma returned to the cabin to rejoin the other adults, we were still laughing and talking under a canopy of a billion stars, until one by one each of us fell asleep.

The only mention of the Olympics during our trip was when one of my cousins and I decided to swim across the lake and back. Whenever we would do this, another cousin would come along as a lifeguard, rowing the boat alongside the swimmers to make sure no one was mowed over by a boat. But when we got to the other side of the lake, the designated rower was so hot he wanted to swim back, so I tied the rope from the boat around my waist and towed it back to shore, where my uncle sarcastically commented, "Wow, look at the Olympic swimmer."

I thought that was going to be the extent of it: a little ribbing from my family and a couple of random interviews here and there. Otherwise, I imagined I'd put the medals away in my room and my swimming life would return to what it had been before—training and events. But the morning we got back to Irvine, I went with my mom to Ralph's, the local grocery store, and hanging over the electric double doors was a huge banner that read "Amanda Beard, Our Hometown Hero: Gold, Silver, Silver." I was so embarrassed, I didn't want to get out of the car. And I didn't—I waited very low down in my seat until my mom picked up the milk and eggs and we drove away.

I could stand in front of a room of reporters without the slightest trace of nerves, but parades, homecoming signs, or any other attention-grabbing displays made me ill. In moments like the Olympic awards ceremony, I had no idea what to do with myself or what kind of reaction people were looking for. The worst was when I had to endure a public display of cheesiness in front of my entire school right after winning the Olympic trials.

"Amanda, I've got to tell you something," Yvette had said over the phone when I had returned from Indianapolis. "It was supposed to be a secret, but I knew you'd freak out if they actually surprised you."

"What are you talking about?"

"You're not going to like it."

"Now *you're* freaking me out."

"The school is planning a welcome-back blowout for you tomorrow to celebrate."

My stomach tightened the way it did when Yvette asked me to do one of her awful algebra problems.

"I didn't want you not to know because of how much you hate things like this," she said. Then she added, "Um, there's more. They're picking you up at home in a vintage silver Bentley that's gonna drive you to school."

Who came up with that idea? I was a fourteen-year-old kid, not the president. I didn't even like it when dad dropped me off at school. This was certain social death. Yvette had to be joking.

"No."

"Yeah."

"Well, then you're spending the night here. I'm not going in that stupid car to school alone."

Sure enough, at 8:15 the next morning, Yvette and I, wearing jeans, tank tops, and our backpacks, walked out of my house and climbed into a waiting Bentley, the door held open by a man in the whole driver getup. Yvette tried to lighten the mood during the three-minute ride to school, but I was as quiet as if we were headed straight for my execution.

We pulled up to our school, where a couple of hundred people, including kids, local media, and administrators, were gathered. When I exited the car—not giving Jeeves a chance to open the door for me—they all started clapping, and then I went blind. Through the noise of the pep squad and jazz band, I was guided to a little podium where the principal—a woman I had never had a conversation with before but who would talk to me all the time from now on—made comments to the media about how proud my school was of me and my accomplishments. "Amanda, your life is never going to be the same," she said. It took everything inside me not to cry—and then I cried a little anyway, trying to hide behind a taller swimmer on the podium with me.

Even though I was the same as I had been before the Olympics, the way others saw me had changed. I shouldn't have been surprised when people back home acted weird around me; almost immediately after winning my medals, everyone began treating me differently. Fellow athletes in the Village started to approach me, asking if they could have our photograph taken together. *Me?*

I was going with the flow and wanted to fit in. But having won a gold medal in the Olympics would make fitting in even harder than it is for most fourteen-year-olds. Reporters, TV producers, and magazine editors from all over the country were calling my parents to see if I would do interviews, photo shoots, or appearances. Dave had to purchase a cell to keep up with all the calls from people requesting interviews.

My mom and dad put restrictions on the amount of time I spent dealing with the press, as they had done even before the Olympics when the *Today* show's Katie Couric and Oprah Winfrey both wanted me to appear on their shows in the lead-up to the Games. While I wasn't the demographic for either of these programs, I knew this was a big deal. My parents, Dave, and I had decided to decline their invitations so that my workouts and homework wouldn't be disrupted by travel to New York and Chicago. Oprah's people were persistent and followed up with a call offering me a late-night departure from L.A., an early-morning return two days later, and pool time in Chicago if I'd join other athletes for the two-hour June taping. But the answer was still no.

After the Olympics, there were a lot of things we said no to. For example, I was asked to write my autobiography. At fourteen.

"There's nothing exciting to write about." I laughed. "I get up in the morning, work out, go to school, work out some more, and sleep. The book would be, like, one page." I also got an invitation from Bob Dole to attend the Republican convention in San Diego, but I'm the least political person ever, so I didn't go.

Other opportunities were more up my alley. I did a lot of photo shoots, but my favorite was a spread for *Sports Illustrated for Kids* where the magazine went all out. They sank an entire living room set to the bottom of a pool, including a real couch, TV, recliner, and lamps. My job was to dive down, sit on the couch, and pretend to be on the phone, like I was lounging in my own home. Meanwhile, people swam above me. I couldn't believe the amount of work that went into getting one photo for a magazine.

Usually, though, doing press was a pretty tedious process. Over the course of many interviews, I got really sick of the same questions over and over.

How does it feel to be an Olympic swimmer and have all this attention?

I had a lot of fun doing it, but I'm happy to be home and return to my normal life, just hanging out with my friends.

What was it like to have a gold medal around your neck?

It's an honor to be a part of something like that. Now I'm excited to be back in the pool and win more medals.

What's up for you next?

School and training.

Do you want to be an actress or a performer?

No, hopefully I'll get a scholarship to college and swim on a school team.

Everyone seemed to ask the exact same stuff! So when my dad walked in to the family room one day to remind me that I had a phone interview with the *Star Register Herald*, *Tribune Post*, or whatever the name of the newspaper was, I told him point-blank, "I don't feel like it." I thought my brain would ooze out of my ears if I said the same thing one more time. He reminded me I had made a commitment, and I sank into my chair as if someone had told me my prison term in Siberia was about to start.

"I'll do it for you," said Leah, who was home from college.

It was a brilliant idea. My sisters and I sounded exactly alike on the phone, and they had heard me do enough of these that they could recite my answers by heart. But Leah did even better. Her answers were way more mature and polished than mine. So whenever Taryn or Leah were around, they did my interviews for me.

I didn't really have a problem talking to reporters, the questions the journalists asked were so easy to answer (much easier than anything I got in school). It's just that I thought I'd scream if I heard someone say "America's sweetheart" one more time.

Especially after Harold.

Jason Lezak, a Nova teammate, and his girlfriend Danielle had given me the stuffed teddy bear as a good-luck charm when we went to the Olympic trials the previous March. Harold, named by my friend Robby Honda, was super cute in his mini parka that matched one I wore, but he wasn't small. Still, I appreciated the gesture, so I packed the twenty-inch animal and dragged it all the way to Indianapolis.

I had planned on leaving the teddy bear in my room (I was fourteen, not three), but one night over dinner Leah and Taryn started in on me after spotting Harold in my room.

"Nice bear," Taryn said.

"Shut up," I responded cleverly.

"It looks like all that press about sweet innocent Amanda is going to your head," Leah said.

"It was a gift!" I protested.

"You should totally bring it to your race," Taryn said wickedly. "That would be hilarious."

"Oh my God, that's genius. You have to, Amanda," Leah piled on.

"Totally," I agreed, like a dope.

And so an icon was born. Taking my sisters up on their dare, I carried Harold to my event at the trials, dropping him at the starting blocks before racing. Right after winning, I grabbed Harold and someone snapped a picture of the two of us, grinning like idiots. Instantly, the picture was everywhere.

The image perfectly captured what people wanted to see: as my sisters put it, an innocent and her bear. The fantasy was of some mythical girl who could win the Olympics while still remaining pure and sweet. The driving competitive urges and the countless hours of willing my mind to bend around searing physical pain were annihilated in an instant by Harold's cuddliness.

Harold was such a hit that when NBC came to our house to shoot footage for my backstory, which they would air during the Olympics, producers asked my parents if he was coming with me to Atlanta.

"He doesn't have a plane ticket," said my dad in an attempt at humor.

"We really need him to be there," a producer said completely straight-faced.

"Enough with the bear," I said. He and I were no longer travel buddies.

"Looks like he's staying home this round," Dad said.

"Harold's a draw," the producer continued. "He's his own little celebrity. Trust me. You'll be thanking me later."

I refused to have any part of it, but my parents agreed to bring Harold and have him sit in the stands with them. They had no idea what a pain in the ass he was. Random people kept coming up to my mom and dad because they wanted to have their picture taken with Harold. It was bizarre.

Harold's fame didn't end with the games. When I returned from the Olympics, he was as big as ever. Anywhere I went to do media, they wanted the bear. It got really old really quickly. I wanted to shout at everyone, "I don't want to drag this stupid teddy bear with me. Stop the madness, people. I'm almost fifteen!" Instead, Harold's profile almost began to eclipse mine as he started to get his own press. At one point, we had to ship him to New York for a photo shoot for a story about famous people's good-luck charms. Before people wanted me *and* the bear; now they just wanted the bear.

Harold even got his own doll, sort of. One of the original Mouseketeers on the *Mickey Mouse Club*, Annette Funicello, made a line of teddy bears based on him. It didn't look like Harold or have a navy-blue and black parka. Instead these bears wore little gold medals around their necks. I was complicit in the whole farce when I gave one of the faux Harolds to Jay Leno during my appearance on his TV show.

Even though nobody my age watched *The Tonight Show*, it was definitely the highlight of my media tour—mainly because they sent a limo to pick up me and five of my friends to take us to the show. On the way to Burbank, we pressed every button available to us and blasted the radio like we were rock stars.

When we arrived, I was taken to my very own dressing room (right next to one for Crocodile Dundee), where I found a gift basket filled with exotic stuff like candied macadamia nuts, jasmine-scented hand lotion, and tiny purple candles. I was totally confident and ready for my appearance on late-night national TV. I had chosen an outfit I thought was cute at the time: a long-sleeved shirt covered in big sunflowers over a black dress.

I also liked being on camera. I've always wanted to act, but I'm not very good at it. So this was my way of having a tiny taste of it. I was never nervous about my appearances because, like an actress, I fed off the energy of the people around me. On *The Tonight Show*, I got so involved in responding to Jay Leno's questions and laughing at his jokes that I forgot a bunch of people were watching.

If I was able to get on network TV and have millions of people watch me give some Harold knockoff to Jay Leno, why did it bother me to be on a podium accepting a gold medal I had worked hard for or congratulations from a couple of hundred of my classmates? I was naïve enough to think I could separate swimming from life in my great desire to be normal. I was okay with taking a limo to *The Tonight Show* but not an old car to my school. I wanted to enjoy the novelty of my Olympic win and take advantage of the opportunities it afforded, without its affecting my private world.

With every passing day at home, it became more apparent that my idea about how my life should go was impossible. As people started to treat me like a circus freak on the streets of Irvine, I tried to pretend that it was no big deal. But when the Novas planned a parade in my honor, the attention became so oppressive, I could no longer ignore it.

I don't know whose idea it was to have me sit in a vintage convertible (what was with the old cars?) surrounded by my Nova teammates while we drove from one end of the Heritage Aquatics Complex, where we trained, to the other. Even though I dreaded it, I didn't feel as if I could say no. How would that conversation go? *You want to have a parade for me? Thanks, but no thanks.* I consoled myself by thinking that no one would show up. My teammates and I would have a good laugh at how lame it was after the fact.

I was wrong. The local media were, of course, on hand. (Weren't there any fires in town for them to cover?) And so were a crowd of young female swimmers from tweens to teens, and their mothers. Ninety swimmers had joined the Novas after the Olympics, which was a 200 percent increase over the year before. When I got out of the car, the crowd pushed toward me. They were thrusting paper, T-shirts, hats, and pens in my face as if they were trying to smother me with them.

Can you sign for my daughter? She looks just like you.
Amanda, Amanda!
Please make mine out to . . .
Amanda!
They said they loved me. They wanted my autograph. Then why

did it feel so bad? All of a sudden, I couldn't breathe. My heart was beating fast, as if I had just completed a tough swimming set. I was surrounded and the people were getting closer and closer. Everything was falling on me. I wished I could find a hole to crawl into and cry.

Instead of getting my hole, I got more parades. The mayor of Irvine decided to hold an event in my honor at City Hall. As my parents and I made our way downtown, I didn't say anything, but I felt like I was going to die. As we got closer, the streets were increasingly packed. News trucks lined up in front of the municipal building, where even more people were pressed up the stairs leading inside. In an unreal scene out of some TV show, reporters shouted questions at me while my mom, dad, and I pushed through the crowd and into the main lobby of the building, where the mayor planned to present me with a plaque and say a few words.

The ceremony went by in a blur of embarrassment, and then we were back outside again. Before I knew what was happening, a crush of people pushed toward me. They shoved many pens and pieces of paper into my face—I tried to keep up, signing and signing—until I found myself backed up to a wall. *Now I really am going to be crushed.* I started to hyperventilate; my mom grabbed me and pulled me inside the building, where I began crying.

"What's wrong?" she asked.

I regained my breath, but angry red hives broke out across my chest.

"I hate this," I sobbed. "I don't like doing this stuff. It's horrible. I can't handle it. I don't want to be here."

"Okay, we're done. I'm putting an end to the parades. I can't believe I let people convince me that this was a good idea."

This must have been my mom's worst nightmare. Although she never expressed it to me, I could tell the whole competitive sports thing made her worried. While my dad was Mr. Factoid, able to recite all my stats in a single sitting, she didn't know or care about any of that stuff. Mom tried her hardest to keep swimming a healthy activity in my life as opposed to having it *be* my life. Whether I swam really well or really badly at a meet, she ignored my performance and instead said, "You looked so cute out there." She was protective of my feelings, wanting happiness for me above all else.

"You can give this up at any time," she said, her words resounding in the large empty hallway. "Swimming is just for you, and if you don't want it anymore, don't do it."

chapter 5

The girl with blonde wavy hair gave the lanky guy next to her a big shove. He retaliated by snapping her swimsuit strap hard against her deeply tanned and fine-boned back. Then she doubled over in mock pain.

In the few minutes until practice began on this late-winter afternoon, most people were already stripped down, fooling around before jumping into the water. I, however, still had on shorts and a T-shirt, which I took off at the very last second at lightning speed only to cover myself up with a towel around my waist. There was no way I was going to hang out on the pool deck in my swimsuit and nothing else. That was something I definitely didn't want other people to see.

During the Games in Atlanta, the other girls on the Olympic team would make fun of me because of the way a normal training swimsuit used to fit me. I was so lanky and my hips so bony that the suit, instead of riding high on my hips as it did with most women, covered the tops of my thighs as if I were wearing an old-fashioned bathing suit you might see in a black-and-white photo. I didn't care how it fit. I never thought about that kind of thing as I ran around in my swimsuit as if it were a second skin.

Now I didn't even want to breathe in my suit, let alone run. I could feel every little despicable part of me jiggle when I walked across the deck to the blocks. My swimsuit rode up my hips, as their suits had with the older girls on the Olympic team, making me conscious about my thighs and butt. Right after the clock struck 3:30 p.m., but before Dave had a chance to hand me a McDonald's application, I dropped the towel from my death grip and jumped into the water.

Whose body is this?

At the age of fifteen, during my sophomore year of high school, I finally hit puberty. As if trying to make up for lost time, my body underwent such a massive and rapid growth spurt that within a year, I went from a height of five two and weight of 95 pounds to five eight and 125 pounds. Everything hurt—my hips, knees, and other joints ached for months—and I hated everything about the way I looked.

I was huge. I was pregnant. I was fat. I became convinced something was wrong when I could no longer fit into any of my clothes—or any of the clothes in the kids' stores where I used to shop, a discovery made during a trip to the mall to take advantage of the winter sales. The day started out ordinary enough, with my dad heading to Nordstrom, where he could sit on a lounge chair and read a book as he always did while a guy played the piano. I walked into Krazy Kids, where I had been buying my clothes ever since I could remember, and headed straight to the jeans section. I grabbed a few styles and went into the changing room to try them on. But none of them fit, and I soon discovered nothing else in the store did either.

The lady in Krazy Kids, who reminded me of my second-grade teacher, suggested I try Charlotte Russe. *Charlotte Russe!* I never thought I'd make it across the mall and to the much trendier and more grown-up store where all the high school kids shopped. Inside the boutique, filled with blasting pop music, I tentatively took a few of my usual staples—tank tops, jeans, and shorts—only these were without the usual rainbows and butterflies. I got a thrill slipping on a cool surfer T-shirt and a pair of rad overalls. The moment of retail euphoria came crashing down, however, when I caught my reflection in the mirror. I hated looking at myself.

I wondered what other people thought when they looked at me. While clinging to the side of the pool during afternoon practice, waiting for Dave to announce our first set, a few boys offered up the usual running commentary on which girls were hot and which were not.

"Dude, look at how big her butt is! It's huge," one kid said.

"I haven't noticed. I'm mesmerized by Mary's boobs."

"What about her cellulite? When she flips off the wall, her thighs shake so much, it makes me want to barf."

Boys and girls, raging with adolescent hormones and wearing tiny swimsuits, made training brutal. Add attitude to the mix and each week was a drama with different combinations of love and hate—or at least like and disgust. On a Monday, Rob might have a crush on Mary, but by Friday she was the biggest cow in the world.

Mary wasn't fat. None of the girls on the team were; they were all in great shape. But in trying to see what the boys saw, I turned their mean comments on myself. *If they thought she was big, then I must be ginormous.* I tried to shake off the thought as I pushed off the wall to start my laps. But when the fat on my thighs moved, as anything that isn't bone is going to do, I worried who might have seen it. I knew I was no longer excluded from the conversation.

I counted the lines at the bottom of the pool: one, two, three, four . . . and let my mind wander.

What did boys think of me? I didn't look anything like the girls whom all the boys had crushes on at school. Even John Bell, a slacker skater type in my circle whom I secretly liked, wanted to be with my opposite. I had found that out over lunch in the cafeteria. We were sitting with a group of friends when Kristin Riley walked in and John's guy friends started to give him shit.

"There's your girlfriend, man."

Kristin was the perfect girl: really skinny, big boobs, long legs that were always shaved and lotioned, blue eyes, tan, and perfect, perfect long blonde hair. Her expensive clothes fit her like a glove (her waist was so teeny!). I could only imagine what life was like for her inside her awesome BMW M5 and her parents' gorgeous home in Northwood.

John smiled shyly, and I could see his cheeks turn red even under a deep tan from skating and surfing religiously after school. I couldn't believe it. Even him?

"Nah, I don't have a chance with her," he said.

My heart sank. Of course he liked her. Why wouldn't he? Kristin was not only gorgeous but also smart, funny, and popular. If that's what guys wanted, I was never going to be that.

In my room that night, I fell into a new ritual of lying on my bed, staring at the ceiling, and spiraling into a litany of all the things that were wrong with me.

My smile: big and gummy. People always pointed it out because my teeth were abnormally huge.

My nose: pointy like a weird bird. It ruined my profile and didn't look anything like the little upturned noses of the most beautiful girls in town.

My skin: zitty, pore-filled, and gross. I had to wear tons of makeup and I still didn't look anything like those girls with flawless, porcelain complexions. I kept people at a healthy distance so they wouldn't see all my blemishes.

My hair: stringy and mousy. I wanted long, thick, shiny, flowing hair, which wasn't going to happen.

My body: fat.

I lay there for hours trying to conceive of one thing that I could feel confident about, only to return to my list over and over and over. There was nothing special about me, nothing worth being loved. Lonely, I retreated to my room more often than was normal even for the average moody teenager.

Withdrawing didn't stop this negative script from playing like a tape on a loop in my head. The only small escape from it came on weekends when I'd get together with my friends and go drinking. We were by no means big partiers. We didn't do drugs, which a lot of kids did, and we always appointed a designated driver even though none of us ended the evening wasted.

Getting a little buzzed from beer from a keg at a house party or a wine cooler we took from someone's mom, I finally felt a little bit confident, cute even. Cheered up, I was able to flirt, or at least talk to a boy (something I would be way too nervous to do when completely sober).

I knew it was bad for me to be drinking as an underage elite athlete. But I enjoyed the way I felt in those moments, which passed way too quickly. I wanted to be normal and hold a plastic cup around the keg like everyone else. That wasn't always easy at my high school, where people tried to mold me into the cookie-cutter role of the goody-goody swimmer chick (I had stood up on a podium with the principal, after all). All teenagers bristle at the thought of others applying labels to them, and I was no different. No one else was going to determine who I was—though they tried.

At one party, a couple of girls who sometimes got a kick out of being mean to me couldn't resist screwing with me when they saw me drinking. I was too easy a target to pass up.

"I'm guessing that isn't on your training diet," one of the girls said, pointing at my plastic cup.

"The Olympian is drinking," the other said, as partygoers started to stare. "Watch out. You're gonna get wasted."

That killed my buzz quick enough. I hated the swimming thing and would have rather had people make fun of me for just being me. Wasn't it obvious to everyone how many other aspects of me really made me a loser?

Mean voices, those of the girls and my own, followed me wherever I went, even into the pool. Over and over I tried to bring my mind back to numbers, the old calculations that used to soothe my brain. Twenty-five laps at twenty-five seconds a lap was . . . but my brain refused to cooperate and instead kept returning to that negative tape playing over and over: *You're fat and disgusting, unlovable.*

After practice, I no longer stood in the communal area to change out of my bathing suit and into my clothes but hid in one of the private changing stalls that almost nobody used except for me. From there, I could hear the rest of the girls comparing—what else—their bodies as they towel-dried their hair and got dressed.

"I am getting so fat. I need to go on a diet!"

"Look at my belly!"

"Are you kidding me? Check out these love handles."

"I'm not eating for a week. I swear."

Weight was by far the most popular topic of conversation in the locker room, beating out swimming and even boys. It got replayed almost every day, and yet each time I heard girls talking about how heavy they were, I thought, *But she's really skinny. I'm way bigger than her.* Unlike the rest of my teammates, I didn't express my revulsion with my body out loud. That was my private stuff, and I had no desire to address it with anyone. I especially didn't want other girls lying to my face, telling me that I was skinny when I knew I wasn't. Nobody wanted to hear my problems anyway. I just needed to be tougher and get ahold of these bad thoughts and keep my weight down.

But I was so hungry all the time. Before my monster growth spurt, I had a light appetite and preferred snacking throughout the day to eating huge meals. Now I started to devour bigger meals, and unfortunately a lot of them were junk. Lunch was always a disaster. In high school, we traveled off campus and that meant fast food: tacos, pizza, burgers, anything with grease. Ravenous after practice, I didn't order just Chicken McNuggets but also fries, soda, and often an apple pie for dessert.

At home, my dad continued to cook as if we were still part of a real family, making way too much food for two people. Although his meals were wholesome, it irritated me that there was always enough for seconds, thirds, even fourths. How could I stop eating when he had all this food lying around? Everything about my dad, even the sight of him, annoyed me these days. It seemed as if we had never been pals, though I knew we used to be close. Now he was just a total dork who embarrassed me. I couldn't even watch TV with him anymore. Instead, I'd go into my room after dinner and watch TV alone.

The last thing I wanted to talk about was swimming; my onetime safety zone was falling apart. If I felt disconnected from my new body in regular life, it was especially awful in the pool. Before puberty, I would have described swimming as easy, comfortable, and natural. Then all of a sudden, I was a completely different person in the water and swimming a completely different sport. I had to relearn how to swim carrying twenty-five pounds of extra weight. Unlike the first time around, however, the lessons were anything but easy.

Transitioning through puberty is tough enough for most girls, but when you're competing in a sport on the highest levels, it can be devastating. The bulk of female swimmers—maybe close to ninety-five percent—don't survive the changeup from a boyish figure to one with hips, breasts, and a downshifting metabolism. You see it all the time: little girls who swim really fast go through puberty and don't come back. Neither Jilen Siroky nor Beth Botsford, the young ones like me on the 1996 Olympics team, ever again achieved what they did in Atlanta.

A breaststroker wants to feel weightless in the water. Instead I was a sinking stone. My new giant-sized self could no longer glide forward like a little frog skimming the surface. Before, I'd jump into the pool and take off as if the water were carrying me. Now, the water fought me with every stroke. It pushed me down and pulled me back. My once-protective haven jiggled every ounce of fat on my body so that the solitude of swimming became a private torture.

I lost my rhythm in the water, and no matter how hard I practiced or focused, I couldn't regain it. It was beyond frustrating. As quickly as my times had gone down when first I learned the correct breaststroke, they seemed to rise back up again.

For a while, people who had seen me at the Olympics on television or in a magazine would show up at meets to watch me swim. They had heard all these amazing things about me and wanted to be close by when I won.

Six months after the games in Atlanta, I was at a swim meet in Long Beach, and even though it had been awhile since I slowed down, a crowd had turned out with signs bearing my name and paper and pens for autographs. As I stepped onto the pool deck, I could feel the energy shift. I tried not to pay attention to that kind of stuff, but there was no ignoring how the other swimmers grew quieter and eyed me intensely. They all wanted to beat me.

I was grateful when a swimmer from another team broke the tension and approached me, though it was to tell me how great I was. "Amanda, I'm such a huge fan," she said. "You are totally awesome."

"I'm not that awesome anymore," I said with a nervous laugh.

"Oh please. You're going to win this so easy."

Even though the girl was just trying to be nice, I wanted to tell her to shut up. While I struggled with the most basic elements of my sport, everyone continued to assume I would always win the race.

I proved the girl wrong by coming in fourth. While I was getting my stuff together to leave, I caught her glance. The swimmer quickly looked away. Deeply ashamed of the new slow me, a failure who crushed others' heartfelt expectations, I hated swimming more than anything.

Swim meet after swim meet, I continued to let everyone down. I was nowhere close to my normal times, easily adding four to five seconds to my 100-meter breaststroke, and by no means any longer a winner. Whereas before I had been in the top three, I couldn't break into the top ten American swimmers. That meant I still made it to the nationals and other big events in the United States, but I was no longer good enough for the international travel team.

People continued to turn up at events to watch me and ask for my autograph afterward, though each week there were fewer and fewer of them. The glare of the spotlight, previously a source of so much anxiety for me, ironically hurt when it faded away.

By the time I got to the Janet Evans Invitational in July of 1997, the fans weren't the only ones who had given up on me. Held at the University of Southern California, the event was a big meet with many of the biggest names in the sport. When I arrived at the arena, I approached the special desk for athletes and requested tickets reserved for my family.

"I'm sorry, we don't have any tickets under the name Beard," the official said.

"Um, could you check again? I always get at least two for my parents," I said, confused about what was happening.

"Nope, definitely nothing here. Sorry."

"Well, could I get two tickets for them anyway? They're here and need to get in."

"Walk down this hallway and make a left. There you'll find the ticket booth where they are available for purchase."

My ears reddened with embarrassment. Just last year at the same event, administrators couldn't do enough for me. "Amanda, do you need a special area to change in?" "How many tickets do you need? Seven. Not a problem." "Here, Amanda, we wanted to give you T-shirts for your entire family." I hadn't realized at the time how over-the-top and accommodating they were. I got used to the special perks without realizing that they were special or based on my performance.

I experienced the same rude awakening with my own peers. When I used to go to national swim meets, many people would sit with me and be super friendly in the downtime between races. During the couple of days of the Janet Evans Invitational, which dragged on for what seemed like weeks, hardly anybody said a word to me. Even the coaches and staff, adults, gave me the cold shoulder. Sitting in the stands, I was relieved to see a friendly face when I spied a coach with whom I had gone to the Olympics. I waved enthusiastically but he didn't move any closer. "Hey, Amanda," he said in a strained voice. "How're you doing?"

"Okay."

"All right then. Nice seeing you."

That was it? The man who wanted to be my best friend in Atlanta acted as if he didn't even know me. The message wasn't subtle: you aren't fast anymore, so you don't matter.

I definitely wasn't fast. I came in a humiliating seventh in the 200-meter breaststroke and eighth in the 100-meter, where I was beaten by a twelve-year-old Nova. In a rare moment of defenseless honesty after the event, I told a reporter, "Look, in ten years, there won't be anybody who will remember Amanda Beard."

A year after the Olympics, I ranked twenty-third in the world in the 100-meter breaststroke and twenty-sixth in the 200-meter.

My parents did their best to shelter me from the unanimous criticism of public opinion. I didn't need anyone to tell me how bad I stunk; I knew that already. The harsh numbers of my ranking told the whole story. At least that's what I thought until I got acquainted with a whole new kind of low.

I had come into the living room of our house to find the newspaper because I wanted the movie listings; I needed to find a flick I could lose myself in. After looking on the couches and coffee table, I sat on the recliner chair where my dad read the newspaper and all his books. I saw a piece of newsprint sticking out from in between a stack of books. Thinking it might be the paper, I lifted up the four or five volumes on top. Instead I found a hidden stash of clippings and knew immediately they were about me.

Since the start of my career, my dad was my own personal archivist, clipping any and all articles about me so that I could have them later on in life. But after carefully cutting them out, he always put them into the big red scrapbook he kept in his room.

Reading the dozen or so articles in my lap, I saw clearly why these hadn't made it into the book. Sportswriters called me fat, washed-up, and finished. I'd never do anything good in swimming again, they wrote. There it was in black and white, a complete validation of the negative voice playing on a loop in my head. It was true, I was a fat loser. The words I attacked myself with stared out at me from the page, causing a kind of sweet dread. I had suspected that everyone was talking about me, and they were. The shame—this wasn't just a couple of mean girls at school but the whole world—hurt so much it almost veered 180 degrees into pleasure. I wrapped myself up in sadness like a martyr, then tucked the clips back in their hiding spot so my dad wouldn't know I had found them.

I didn't talk about what was happening to me with anybody—not my dad, mom, friends, or coach. Everyone knew that I knew I sucked, but we all ignored it. *Hop into the pool, do your sets, dinner, homework, bed.* Business as usual. At the time I was grateful for the normalcy. The last thing I wanted to do was draw more attention to myself. Not addressing something, however, doesn't mean it goes away.

I was completely beaten down, even if I refused to discuss it. The moment that sent me over the edge, though, had nothing to do with swimming. It started with an incident at practice. Before the team got in the pool, we always had about half an hour of training on land—running, doing push-ups or sit-ups. On this day, Dave had come up with an exercise where we had to shimmy up a football goalpost, across the top, and then down the other side. While the girl in front of me was on the top of the goal, she lost her hold and fell. It was really scary and she ended up hurting her shoulder pretty badly.

That night, her father called my house to find out what had happened. "I want to know your side of the story of what went down," he said. I wasn't sure what he meant by "my side," but I told him what I saw.

"We were going across the football goalpost and she fell."

"I know that, but what did you do?"

"I didn't do anything."

That was all it took for this man to start screaming and cursing, blaming me for causing the accident and hurting his daughter. Even though he was a psycho swim parent, always on the pool deck talking to the coach or giving his daughter a hard time for not doing better at meets, I took his accusations to heart. He was an adult, after all. Maybe I had been going too fast and she fell because she was nervous? Though I stayed silent as he continued to yell over the phone, a whole conversation was happening in my head.

I did it because I'm a horrible human and can't do anything right. I'm poison and now other people are getting hurt because of me.

I didn't go to swim practice for a whole week after the altercation. Nothing could overcome my embarrassment at what I had done—not even swimming, which until then had always been my coping mechanism. Whereas in the past I could put my face in the water, not talk to anyone, and get my aggression out through energy, now the pool had become another spot of despair. My safe zone was now a place where my brain constantly battled itself. While I was trying to pretend that other things, such as the swim parent yelling at me or my horrible ranking, didn't exist or weren't such a big deal, I didn't have mental energy left over to quiet the voice berating my body. Every time I did a flip turn and felt my butt and thighs jiggle, I yelled at myself to forget it and just swim. But the next flip turn came too quickly.

So, right after the New Year in early 1997, I decided to stop training permanently. Fed up and exhausted, I had become too discouraged to fight any longer. Swimming, which I had loved so much, was now solely a source of stress and anxiety. Heading to the pool felt like a drag. I decided to give it up and become a normal high school student and do whatever normal high school students were doing.

My parents were both incredibly supportive of my decision, which wasn't a surprise. As my mom had always said, "If it's not fun anymore, stop doing it." They treated the end of my career as no big deal. More shocking was that Dave had the same attitude.

My coach, a firsthand witness to my frustration in the water, felt bad for me. I've heard horror stories of other coaches really ragging on swimmers who start tanking, but Dave never got on my case. He knew that I had been a teeny tiny thing who would one day have to grow. His giving me a hard time would do nothing to change the facts of life. Although he still acted tough in practice, at swim meets, he had a sad expression on his face, like he wished he could flip a switch and I would swim well again.

I didn't want people to pity me, so when Dave came over to my dad's house to talk to me about leaving swimming, I didn't want his concern. He didn't try to talk me into staying on the team. "I respect your wishes," he said. "If you ever want to come back, the door's open. And I want you to know that I am always here for you whether you are a Nova or not."

Despite Dave's kindness, I didn't give much in the way of a reply. I was so sick of having the swimming discussion. *Can I have one conversation where people don't talk to me about swimming? It is so annoying. It's just something I do, not who I am. I'm moving on.*

On my first official day as a regular teenager, I returned home from school and watched TV for four hours, until I got a headache and had to stop. In my room that night, exhausted from doing nothing, I fantasized about the cool things I was going to do with my friends now that I had all this free time. We'd probably head to Brad's house later in the week and play pool in his basement, or maybe take Lisa's Jeep out to the beach to watch the surfers.

But I discovered no one did *anything* fun after school. People didn't even hang out; they just returned home, did their homework, ate dinner, watched TV, and went to bed. As it turned out, being a regular teen meant sitting on the couch. A lot. The most exciting thing I did that week was to watch *Saved by the Bell* with Yvette while we were both on the phone. This was not what I thought I would be doing if I wasn't training all the time. And I definitely wasn't looking for any extra time to do homework. By week's end I was bored out of my mind.

Even worse than the boredom was the feeling that I was getting fatter. Although I wasn't working out anymore, I still maintained the same eating habits. Now when I indulged in cheeseburgers and greasy fries at lunch, the food just seemed to stick to me. My jeans started to feel tight, and flab that I'd never thought I'd see on me poked over the waistband. The guilt mounted but I didn't change my diet. If I thought I was fat before, now I was a monster. When I returned home from school, I was in a foggy state. Even though training was exhausting, it also energized me. Without any change of pace, I felt like a lazy lump.

After about a month and a half away from the pool, I realized that my levels of stress and anxiety were actually getting worse, the negative loop in my head getting louder and louder. I couldn't believe it, but I had to go back. I was like a character in one of those Lifetime movies I'd seen where the woman who is abused by her husband goes back to him because she has nowhere else to go.

I used my best tool for getting through uncomfortable situations: pretending they were no big deal. Yes, I was going to rejoin the Novas, but not as the old intense Amanda. I would use the pool as a healthy activity. I made a shift in my own mind that competing and racing trailed far behind exercising and staying in shape. Dave was equally nonchalant when I asked him if it'd be okay for me to work out at the pool again. "Sure," he said. "See you Monday."

The getting-in-shape part turned out to be harder than I imagined. In swimming, if you take a couple of days off, you feel incredibly blah in the water. After taking two months off, I needed a whole month to get back in the swing of things. Once my heart no longer felt like it was going to explode after a set, I continued to struggle. My time away had done nothing to improve my speed. The descent that had started at the end of my sophomore year followed me through my whole high school experience.

Instead of trying to regain my former fourteen-year-old glory in the breaststroke, I focused on other events, like the 100-meter freestyle, races where people weren't there to watch me and certainly didn't think I'd win. Mixing it up reduced my stress because it allowed me to hide out in plain sight.

I was way beyond worrying about the faded attention from fans and the media. The pronouncements that I was old news, which had upset me at first, also made meets easier. As expectations fell away, a sense of freedom filled its place. Without the weight of other people's opinions, I got back to improving in my own time and my own way.

With the pressure gone, my competitive juices, which had been driven down to a place hidden within me, began to run again. I started to get bored with meeting my own goals for conditioning in the pool and began to eye faster swimmers like prey. I started to race people training in the lane beside me every day, even if they didn't know it.

I kept to my program of downplaying myself and my efforts. *I just want to work out and stay healthy.* It was the only mode of protection I had. But in the back of my mind, I wanted to get back to the Olympics. I wasn't satisfied with what I had done as a fourteen-year-old or the idea that that one time was my only shot. I wanted to be great again.

I worried about the judgments of others, but I should have been more concerned about how hard I was on myself. Becoming good, let alone great, felt far off at best, totally unrealistic at worst. Still, I refused to give up. The wrestling match that my relationship with the water had become was not over.

chapter 6

The smell of the pine needles and the fresh air added to my good mood. I love camping no matter what, but it's absolutely the best when you're in the middle of pine trees. They make everything feel clean and new.

All the members of the University of Arizona's swim team had gathered on Mount Lemon, forty minutes and worlds away from the school's campus, located in the desert terrain of Tucson. Up on top of the mountain, at an elevation of nine thousand feet, it was actually freezing and the stars filled the sky. This random getaway transported me to trips with my family and other past moments of sheer happiness in the woods.

The one-night camping trip was an opportunity for members of the Wildcats to get to know new recruits, like me, in a relaxed, informal setting off campus and far away from the pool. I had already bonded with a few people on the team and was excited to spend a night outdoors with my new friends. Sitting around the first of many campfires that night, I recognized that I was among peers. No longer the swimming freak, I had a chance for a fresh start.

I was grateful for the chance to be a part of such a prestigious swimming team. Even though through the rest of high school I had never gotten my times down to where they had been during the Olympics, winning gold as a freshman and still being a top high school breaststroker in the United States secured me a full scholarship as an NCAA swimmer.

As a high school senior, I didn't know exactly what kind of college experience I wanted to have. That I would swim in college was not in doubt: it meant a scholarship, plus I still wanted to swim. But because I was uncertain about my abilities, I didn't know how seriously I wanted to take it. Should I go to a big-time swim school, where I'd still get to feel the thrill of competition, or to somewhere a little bit more relaxed, where I could try again to be a normal kid? The issue wasn't my future, since I didn't consider swimming to be a big part of that. I was going to get a regular job, get married, and have a family. My ultimate idea of success was opening my own clothing boutique that catered to my style: jeans, tank tops, and anything else for the California beachy type of girl. Being my own boss and in control of my own place sounded like heaven.

The University of Arizona was on one extreme side of the spectrum. With one of the most intense hard-core swim programs in the nation, it has always been one of the top five swimming schools. The program expected a lot out of its swimmers, and the coaches were known for giving really hard, long workouts. Favoring lots of distance, they thought nothing of filling a Saturday-morning practice with a five-hour workout that started with a spin class, followed by ten thousand meters of swimming, and ending in weight training.

Since I'd told myself for so long that I was swimming only as a healthy activity, the program seemed like the opposite of what I was looking for. But on my recruiting trip, despite all the defenses I'd put up around myself, I fell in love with the school, the swimmers, and the coaches.

The head coach, Frank Busch, trained the men's and women's teams together (an anomaly for the sport at the college level) in a way that fostered camaraderie, respect, and healthy competition. This was totally different from the scene at a lot of other schools, where the men's and women's teams hate each other. The Wildcats were like one big family.

And the best part, this was a family I fit into. All of the swimmers, beyond being really cool, sweet, and easy to get along with, were really fast. They didn't think I was special because I was a good athlete. At a team dinner during the trip, they asked me stuff like what kind of music I liked and if I had any cool summer vacation plans. There were no freaky swimmer girl questions. I blended in easily with the group.

That's how I felt on the camping trip, just another swimmer hanging out with my kind. I was more relaxed than I'd been in a long time, even when Ryk Neethling, an Olympic swimmer and UA legend, sat down next to me.

A South African swimmer who had enrolled at Arizona in 1996, following a fifth-place performance in the 1500-meter freestyle event in Atlanta, Ryk had expanded his reach under Frank's tutelage as a champion long-distance freestyler and a world-class sprinter. Those two completely different skill sets made him a larger-than-life figure.

"Hey, welcome to Arizona," he said, giving me a big hug. "I'm so glad you decided to come to school here."

Really? Ryk Neethling was glad I was here? I couldn't believe he even knew I was here. Of course I knew *him* from meets over the years because he was a really great swimmer. And on the UA campus, he had a major presence. Even though swimming was far less popular than basketball or football, he was someone everybody recognized because he was the model athlete: social, successful in his sport, and very handsome.

"Thanks" was about all I could think to say back to Ryk, who didn't seem like a college kid at all. This guy was a man. He was huge at six foot five but also incredibly lean. His blond hair, blue eyes, and very tan skin were the appropriate complement to his perfect swimmer's build. And now he was flirting with *me*.

At first I couldn't even process the fact. Ryk was the popular guy on the team, the hottie. There was no way in hell I could ever get someone like him. I wasn't nearly pretty enough, so even though he was giving me his full attention, I didn't entertain the thought.

As the night wore on, it became clear that Ryk was not leaving my side. Sitting around the campfire, he kept his focus trained directly on me as if we were the only two people on the trip. I don't remember what we talked about, since the voice in my head—*This is so not happening*—was way louder than anything he said.

He jumped up to refresh my cup from the keg whenever he saw it was getting low, just like guys did in movies. The more I drank, the more I settled into the situation. When the alcohol drowned the harsh voice telling me I wasn't good enough for this, Ryk's attention added to my high. In high school, I couldn't even get losers to take me out, and here the alpha dog was acting like I was the "it" girl. I still didn't imagine that we would ever date or anything like that, but our flirting was further proof that I had come to the right place.

Perhaps sensing my mellowing out, Ryk started to hold my hand and eventually put his arm around me. I just went with the flow, drinking in the smell of pine and fire, the warmth of Ryk's broad shoulders, and the image of my new teammates joking around and laughing.

When the temperatures dipped to the point that sitting around the fire was no longer fun, everyone retreated to their tents. In a hazing-light ritual, freshmen weren't allowed to bring a tent or sleeping bag on the trip, which meant we had to find someone who'd let us into one or both. By that point, it was a given that I was going into Ryk's tent, where four other people were sleeping as well. In his sweatshirt and sleeping bag, I kissed him. But that was as far as it went, because being packed in with a group of drunk people passing out all around you isn't exactly romantic.

The next morning everyone was a little the worse for wear and I was no exception. My hair was stringy, greasy, and limp, and my breath smelled like something had died inside my mouth. When Ryk said he'd give me a ride down the mountain, I wanted to say, "No, thanks. I'm going to walk." I didn't want him to see my real skin, without the benefit of makeup or even a wash, in the bright light of day. Of course, I got in the car; it was Ryk Neethling.

As the scenery passed from pine trees and boulders to cacti and dust, Ryk casually asked, "Can I take you out for dinner this week? I've got to show you my favorite Mexican place."

Really, you are asking me out on a date when I look like this?

My instinct was to say no. Insecure thoughts on reasons he was asking me flooded my brain.

He's just a typical senior looking to prey on an innocent freshman.

I'm going to be one of twenty chicks he's dating.

He's never going to be totally into me, so we'll have some fun and then I'll get dumped.

Part of me wanted to stop this thing in its tracks before something bad happened to me. But instead, I did what anyone would do in my position and said yes.

Everything about college was new. Even the desert terrain of Tucson was to me a whole new kind of beauty. Its flat lands dotted by cacti and a vast crystal blue sky unbroken by a single wisp of cloud blew my hometown away.

The Wildcats' approach to swimming was also new to me. I still had the same number of practices, nine a week, as I had in high school, but the workouts were a lot harder than what I was used to. Every coach has his or her belief about what's the most beneficial way to train swimmers, and Dave and Frank were on completely opposite ends of the field. The Novas' approach to swimming was all about speed and sprinting. In practice, Dave would have us do four or five thousand yards, which wasn't a lot. Frank wanted endurance and lots and lots of yards. We did seven to ten thousand yards per practice.

The first couple of months were a hard adjustment for me, as I was often swimming twice the distance that I was used to in a practice. To stay at a high level of output for such a long time was simply physically exhausting. Exhausting doesn't even do the feeling justice. It sucked every molecule of energy out of my body.

After one of Frank's marathon sessions, I was starving to the point where I couldn't make it to a convenience store, let alone my room to eat. Still dripping wet, I opened the fridge on the pool deck, grabbed a nutrition bar, and gobbled it down. My body was screaming, *Feed me!* Walking through campus back to my dorm, I was a zombie, bumping into people and pissing them off. I hardly noticed, I was so zoned out. Climbing the five stairs into my dorm building nearly broke me. My legs felt like they were filled with lead and my head with water. I wolfed down some food and banged out a short email to my dad ("We did ten 200m freestyle sets today! Can you believe it? I'm dying. Seriously.") before crashing on my bed for ten hours. And this was only a Tuesday.

As I got in better shape, the workouts became easier for me to cope with, and then I actually fell in love with that way of training. I thrived on getting into the groove and pushing myself to an extreme level I had never before contemplated achieving. Long-distance swimming got me back in the zone I had lost during those difficult high school years. I realized I now needed more time to get into a meditative state where my problems on dry land washed away and all that remained was the way the sun's reflection sparkled at the bottom of the pool.

I hadn't realized that part of my problem in high school was that I was burnt out on the Novas. A fresh environment gave me a jump-start. It wasn't only the new approach but also my new teammates. While I was the best breaststroker on the team, I was surrounded by amazing swimmers, who provided an instant group of friends that warded off the typical loneliness of freshman year with group activities like carving pumpkins, bowling, or preparing family-style dinners.

If on dry land we acted like a family, in the pool we were competitive siblings fighting for the attention of our coaches, who naturally gravitated toward the best. Everyone wanted to be the winning swimmer, making points for the team. All the other breaststrokers saw a target on my back, hoping to catch up and be the favorite.

There was no doubt that Frank was a father figure to everyone on the team. He was a combination of stern and sensitive that made you want to work extremely hard for him. He knew exactly what to do to motivate me during the slow process of getting my swimming back to where it should be.

"Beat the boys, Amanda," he screamed at the tail end of a particularly grueling breaststroke set.

I could beat all the girls, but Frank reached out for my competitive jugular, challenging me to push myself a little further. I felt my energy spike and went after them like a dog after a stick. This was fun. Then he took it up another notch.

"Come on, guys, don't let Amanda beat you!" Frank shouted.

Oh, it was on. I went all out and ultimately beat two of the men. I was smiling ear to ear (even though any inch of me that wasn't on fire had begun to cramp) when Frank started ribbing them for getting beat by a girl.

"Amanda doesn't count as a girl," one protested.

"I'm a chick," I said, loving every minute. "It counts."

The only thing that was less than awesome when I arrived at UA was my dorm room, which I'm pretty sure was the smallest one on the college's vast campus. It consisted of two single beds, two desks, and that was about it. There was no sink, but we did have a mini fridge and microwave. Between sleeping, hanging out, doing homework, and making food, it was a lot of life for such a little room.

My roommate was also a freshman swimmer, but we didn't really have anything to talk about. Our jail cell didn't help matters. Mainly we tried to stay out of each other's way, as many college freshman roommates do. If I went back to the room and she was there, I often headed right back out. My dorm wasn't so much a home as it was an inconvenience.

Luckily I had lots of other things to keep me occupied, the main one being Ryk.

On our first date, he took me to the Mexican restaurant that he'd mentioned in the car on the way back from Mount Lemon. The way he held the car door open for me or touched the small of my back while showing me into the restaurant made me feel like I was in someone else's life. Up until now, getting drunk at a party and making out was the closest I'd come to a date.

I could feel the attention he got while walking to our table. His height made him stand out, but he also had the stride of someone really strong. Suddenly my clothes felt too tight and I didn't know where to look. I reconsidered my decision to come on this date. What was I thinking? I wasn't anywhere close to Ryk material. If I felt awkward, it suddenly got a whole lot worse when we ran into one of our swim coaches.

Although Ryk gave him a manly shake, the assistant coach looked at us with a pained expression as if he really wished he hadn't seen us. He didn't want to know his swimmers' personal business.

"Okay," he said matter-of-factly. "I'm going to sit somewhere else."

I thought I was going to die, I felt so embarrassed. I didn't want it getting around that I was some dumb freshman, the slut of the team, one of Ryk's chicks.

I had no idea what I was doing because I had basically no experience with boys. I didn't start dating until I was about sixteen or seventeen, and when I did, it was nothing serious. The longest I ever "dated" a guy was about a month—maybe because I was very much a prude in high school. Kissing was as far as it went. I was so insecure about my body, the last thing I wanted to do was be intimate with a guy and have to reveal it. I didn't see my burgeoning curves as a sexy thing; they made me sick.

I lived through my first date with Ryk, which was followed by a second and third. Without talking about our status, it became apparent to us and everyone we knew that we were in a relationship. From that car ride on, we hung out all the time, inside the pool and out. He did everything that a real boyfriend is supposed to do, taking me out, being sweet, making me laugh, and caring for me.

At any one of the house parties happening on every night of the week at UA, he stayed glued to my side, holding my hand and putting a protective arm around me. I didn't create a lot of strong bonds with people, so it was nice to have someone to watch out for me on a campus of almost thirty thousand undergrads. When we came up on a group of Ryk's friends from Europe at the party, he went out of his way to include me in their conversation, even if it was a stretch.

"Amanda and I threw around the rugby ball today," he said. "After I taught her how to toss it properly, she was good."

The guys looked at him like he was crazy.

"No, really. She is."

Sweet.

Toward the beginning of school, when I was still getting used to Frank's grueling practices, I got so dehydrated and weak that I had to go to the hospital. My idea of hydration was drinking about four to seven Dr Peppers a day, but that doesn't cut it in the desert. Right before I drove myself there, I left Ryk a message that I was going to the hospital without specifying which one. I was nervous about going on my own when I had never even gone to the doctor without my dad.

The nurse was about to administer the needle into my arm for an IV drip, when out of nowhere, Ryk appeared in the doorway. He filled up the whole frame.

"How did you find me?" I said, surprised and impressed.

"I figured you would come to this hospital because it was the closest one," he said. "Then I asked around and it wasn't too hard to track you down."

Sweet and capable.

I started to like Ryk. A lot. I was seventeen years old with a twenty-one-year-old swimming god for a boyfriend. Yvette, who came out to visit me and met Ryk for the first time, pretty much summed it up when she said, "Oh my God, he is hot. You are so lucky."

I was lucky. He was kind, good-looking, a great swimmer, and totally attracted to me. What more could I ask for? As far as I was concerned, nothing. By November, two months after we started dating, I decided it was time to lose my virginity.

Ryk had been really nice and patient about the difference in our experience levels. Experience, however, wasn't really the problem. I was so insecure about my body that I never thought of it or anything I could do with it as sexy. As a swimmer, I was used to being half-naked all the time. Wearing a bra and underwear when we were fooling around shouldn't have been all that different, but I hit a new level of self-consciousness. While we were together, I couldn't stop imagining what Ryk was thinking, none of it good. When he put his hand on my hips: *They are so fat.* When my shirt came off: *My boobs are so small.*

Perhaps sensing my unease, Ryk wanted to make sure I was ready to do it. Was I ready? I had always wanted to lose my virginity to someone important, someone special. I really, really liked Ryk and wanted to do it for him. I couldn't imagine being more ready than that.

The fact that I went all the way with Ryk was a testament to my feelings for him, since I had hit a new low with my feelings about my own body. My growing self-hatred had nothing to do with swimming, which was slowly improving, and everything to do with college.

In high school, my girlfriends were beautiful but not overtly sexy. They didn't parade around in heels and short skirts. But at college, it seemed like every day was a fashion show for a lot of the girls, and the purpose was to show off their wares.

During my first Halloween at UA, I had naïvely dressed up for the night as a flapper with a 1920s-style dress, kitten heels, and a feather in my hair. I thought I looked totally cute until I walked into the party, where every single girl was a sexy version of something. There were sexy nurses, sexy vampires, sexy witches, sexy cats, sexy stewardesses—even a sexy mail carrier. Suddenly my dress was transformed into a shapeless sack.

Then came the pièce de résistance: two girls who walked into the party wearing nothing but skimpy white underwear, matching push-up bras, wings, heels, and halos. Every guy and girl in that room had their eyes on them, which made sense. Not only were they naked but they were perfect. Their boobs were big, their waists tiny, their legs long, and their butts perfectly round with not a trace of cellulite.

"What are you guys supposed to be?" asked a boy, as he practically drooled on himself.

"We're Victoria's Secret Angels," one of them giggled.

I was disgusted and jealous. I would never have been able to wear anything like that in public, because I didn't have the body or the confidence. The more I looked around at the girls at the party, with their perfect figures and perfect makeup, the more I felt like a failure. I didn't measure up. How was I going to keep Ryk when he had so many better options right in front of his face? I had to work harder to be prettier. Even outside the pool, I saw the world as a competition. And if I wasn't winning, I completely failed. At the Halloween party, all the other girls were better-looking than me and my stupid granny outfit.

The perfectionist drive that made me a star athlete in the water, out of the water tore me apart. As I nitpicked every little aspect of myself, I discovered over and over again that I wasn't good enough.

As soon as I arrived at UA, problems with eating started to arise. For the first time in my life I was in control of my meals—no more home-cooked chicken, broccoli, and salad put in front of me by Dad. However, while living in the dorms, getting good, wholesome food was not a straightforward operation. Instead of a traditional cafeteria, the college had a food court in the middle of campus filled with several options, including Mexican food, Italian food, sandwiches, and typical fast food. That worked for about a week, but after that it felt like eating at a highway rest stop every meal of every day.

Students were able to cook their own food in one of the two kitchens, shared by the entire dorm building that housed hundreds of students. It was the biggest pain in the butt to carry all your stuff—from plates to cooking utensils to ingredients—up or down to one of the kitchens, only to find a few people already waiting to use it.

The school provided a microwave and a mini fridge in each room to pick up the slack. Determined to figure out how to feed myself, I drove to the supermarket to do my own grocery shopping. But what should I buy? I reached for a jug of milk, which I'd seen my dad do a million times, but immediately put it back. That wasn't going to fit into the mini fridge. A salad? Forget it. Way too complicated.

I had to keep the perishable items to a few small ones that would fit alongside my roommate's food, and everything else had to live on a shelf. I bought a loaf of white bread (that stuff never goes bad), a few packages of nonfat processed cheese singles, mustard (better than mayo since it doesn't have fat), the economy-size Chewy Chips Ahoy! cookies, and an enormous container of Goldfish.

Other than bean and cheese burritos after late nights drinking and nutritional bars after swim practices, cheese sandwiches, cookies, and Goldfish were the components of my extremely limited diet (at least it didn't stink up the room like my roommate's most common meal: nauseating tuna out of a bag). I thought I was being so resourceful and smart, but eating like this, I felt both fat and hungry.

I didn't look at nutritional value or caloric intake but instead had a vague idea that one or two sandwiches and two cookies was what I should eat. I would come back from swimming for three hours, make my two pasty sandwiches, and before I knew it, they and the cookies were gone. They hardly made a dent in my appetite but I didn't want to become a heifer. So I tried to limit myself to that.

I'd do anything to distract myself from the gnawing hunger and keep myself from eating more. I took a walk around the campus, did my laundry, took a shower. Sometimes the only thing I could do to stop myself from plowing through more food was to go to sleep.

This wasn't a long-term plan. A couple of weeks into it, I was so tired and weak, I could no longer resist food. If someone put a plate of nachos in front of me when we were out at a bar, I'd devour it like an animal. In my room, I'd grab a handful of cookies and eat them, only to return over and over again until the whole bag was gone. Whenever I pigged out like that, I got so pissed at myself. Why couldn't I control myself? Why was I so hungry all the time? I couldn't understand it, especially since I seemed to be getting fatter by the second.

A month into my freshman year, I went out with a few swim team members for dinner. I had ordered a typical burger and fries and eaten every last thing on my plate. But when I finished, I was overcome by a sense of guilt over eating so much. I confused the sensation of being full with being fat. And it sickened me. Walking back to my dorm, I became more and more disgusted with the way my stomach strained against my jeans. I wanted a perfect flat tummy with defined abs, not a paunch.

In my room, I got an overwhelming sensation of needing to get rid of whatever was in my stomach. *I can't have this food in me. I need to get it out.* As logical as it was to eat when hungry, it also seemed logical to throw up when full. I walked to the dorm's communal bathroom, and after checking that it was completely empty, I put a finger down my throat and threw up my dinner. And it worked. I felt lighter and had a sense of satisfaction.

I found something that felt good, something that finally told the voice calling me fat to shut up. Chasing that feeling, I began throwing up once a week, slowly graduating to two or three times a week.

My purging didn't really have a pattern or schedule. If I was distracted, I didn't think about it. But if I was alone, or hungry, or angry, then I thought about it a lot. Mostly it was chaotic. The urge could come over me at any time, and it did.

There were extreme periods when I would throw up multiple times in a day. Lots of different things could set it off: a pretty girl talking to Ryk at a party, a failing grade on a paper. Some days it would be bad just because I had woken up. You know those days when right from the moment you open your eyes, you're in a bad mood and pissed off? *The day is going to be shitty, and nothing will make me happy.*

Those days were a battle to stay in charge of the one thing that gave me a sense of control. Anything I put into my body, I had to get rid of right away. *Get it out. Get it out.* Once I threw up seven times in one day. Hanging over the toilet bowl, I saw dark red blood mixed with my puke. I had wrecked my throat so badly that I was vomiting up blood. *That's not good.* Visual evidence of how I was hurting myself on the inside scared me. But the fear wasn't as powerful as the benefits of purging. I took a couple of days off, giving my body a little time to recover, but slowly I gravitated back to it.

The blood was only one aspect of the inner struggle I had with my newfound habit. I knew what I was doing was a problem. But I chose to push any thoughts about how I could be harming my body right back down. I didn't enjoy throwing up; it's not a fun thing. You can't breathe, and it burns your throat. It's uncomfortable, and depending on what I'd eaten, it could be downright painful. Once I threw up cashews, and it was awful. But the pain was for the payoff. After I had wiped the snot from my nose and gargled with mouthwash, I felt better. *I got that shit out of me.* When I was putting the food in my body, I felt out of control; when it was coming out, I regained it.

I didn't want anyone to know what I was doing, so I made sure to carefully cover my tracks and never get caught. Sharing a bathroom with sixteen other girls meant I had to be discreet and aware of what was going on around me. I couldn't just walk into the bathroom while one girl peed and another curled her hair and start puking. I always made sure nobody was in the bathroom before I started. If somebody came in when I was in the middle, I would immediately stop throwing up and wait for her to leave before I finished. If I was sure my roommate was gone for a while, in a class or somewhere else, I would line the trash can with a plastic bag, throw up, tie the bag up, and take it out to the Dumpster before she returned. Only once, when I was throwing up at night, did a girl that I was unaware of overhear. She approached me the next day to ask if I was okay. "I heard you throwing up. You must have been pretty drunk," she said.

"Oh yeah, I had a rough one," I replied.

No one suspected anything, not only because I kept it quiet but also because I wasn't losing any weight. I had mixed feelings about my lack of weight change. In one way I was frustrated because I wanted to be thinner. On the other hand, I could keep getting away with purging. If I wasn't wasting away, no one would say to me, "Amanda, what's happening to you?"

I was excited to go home for Christmas break. Not only did I look forward to having some real home-cooked food, sleeping in my bed, and seeing my parents, sisters, and all my friends, but this holiday I was bringing home a boy. The swim team only got a week off for Christmas, which was too short a period for Ryk to fly home to South Africa, so we decided he'd come to Irvine with me. I was excited and nervous, having never come close to bringing a guy home. But mostly I was elated to show my family that I was a real college student with a boyfriend and everything.

My boisterous family greeted Ryk with open arms and a lot of chatter. But the louder and friendlier they became, the stonier he got. If they noticed, they didn't let on. My very social family continued to hang out night and day. And they weren't the only ones. A re-volving door of my friends came through the house wanting to catch up, joke around, and meet Ryk.

Ryk retreated into his training. After his long morning workout, he returned to the house to take a nap, and when he woke up, he'd work out again. He didn't have a single conversation the whole time he was at my house. He was sleeping, exercising, or being antisocial.

One morning toward the end of the week, I woke up to find a note on the part of the bed next to me where Ryk should have been.

I read it in amazement. After meeting my skater and surfer friends with their Southern California style and lingo, he decided that he could not possibly be my type if these were the people I hung out with. "We don't have anything in common," he wrote. "I'm driving back to Tucson. I'll see you when you get back from break."

At first I was confused. Not with the message—that was clear; he was breaking up with me—but about the kind of person who would take off before dawn like a criminal, and for no good reason. I didn't cry or get angry but reverted to my usual line of thinking. I should never have barraged him with my family and friends. From our very first kiss, I predicted that he'd dump me. He might have written that he wasn't good enough for me, but I knew what that really meant: I wasn't good enough for him.

I walked downstairs, where my dad and sisters were having breakfast in the kitchen.

"He left," I said to no one in particular.

"What?" my dad asked.

"Ryk and I broke up, and he just wanted to leave."

After a beat to process the information, Leah said, "He didn't seem like he was having a fun time."

"Yeah," Taryn said. "All he did was sleep."

After the break, I returned to UA and the weirdest situation ever. Ryk and I still saw each other all the time—at swim practice, par-ties, team dinners, or events—but we didn't talk to each other. We never talked about what happened in Irvine, the note, us, anything. The only consolation to the abrupt ending of our relationship was that I didn't have to talk about it with him.

After a couple of months of silence, Ryk approached me at a party. I could see from the soft focus of his pupils that he was already tipsy.

"I still like you and think about you all the time," he said.

Unexpected and out of the blue, his comments, for some reason, didn't surprise me.

"I don't get it. You left me," I said.

"I just didn't feel like I was cool enough for you after meeting all your friends, who dress and act so different. I'm not like that."

He didn't make any sense to me. Ryk could have been with anybody, and my friends weren't cooler than him. I couldn't fathom that he suffered from the same insecurity that plagued me. I didn't say anything. We just left the party together and picked up where we had left off.

Except this turned out to be a whole new relationship.

The Ryk who had wooed me with romantic dinner dates and squired me around parties as if I was precious cargo completely disappeared. In his place was a volatile person who, though he said he wanted me to be his girlfriend, rejected me at every turn. Now when we went to parties, which we seemed to do all the time, he gave me a stern and bizarre warning when we arrived: "I'm going this way. You go that way." Then he took off, ditching me for the entire night until it was time to go home. I was so shocked and hurt that I didn't know what to do with myself.

The first time it happened, I tried to talk to him when he finally found me to leave the party. I've never been good at saying how I feel, but facing Ryk's clenched jaw and steely glare made it near impossible. "I need to have my space," he said angrily.

Soon I got used to the drill and didn't need to be told to get lost when we walked into a party. I'd wait around for him to be ready to leave so that we could go home together. Ryk was always one of the last to leave any party. At a Halloween party in Phoenix with lots of costumes and drinking, I found Ryk because it was past two in the morning and we had to be up in a couple of hours.

"I'm not ready to leave," he said.

"I'm tired and don't want to go home alone. You've had enough," I said.

"I'm not done."

Ryk was never done. It didn't matter that I had to fend for myself far from home.

I should have called him a dick, left him on the spot, and never looked back. Instead, I just shut down. I didn't stick up for myself, but even worse, I turned his meanness on myself. I not only took it, I ran with it. *I look bad, that's why he doesn't want to be seen with me.*

The parties were just the start. Soon Ryk didn't act as if he wanted to be with me even in private. Watching TV at his place, I snuggled up to him on the couch as I always did. But he untangled his arm from mine and moved a few inches away from me without ever once breaking his gaze from the set. Walking out of swim practice, I absentmindedly went to take his hand, but again he pulled away without explanation or pity. I was dying for his attention, and he didn't want to touch me.

Our sex life became equally unsatisfying. Ryk seemed to never want to kiss me or do anything else unless he had been partying. Then, if he still had any energy before totally passing out, he began groping and kissing me. Sometimes I was relieved he finally noticed and wanted me. Other times I was tired, and the smell of alcohol annoyed me. But I always did what he wanted.

The terrible turn my relationship had taken validated every negative thought I had ever had about myself. Now I was convinced of my ugliness. I saw the way that he looked at other girls, especially when we went out and got drunk. He flirted with them but not me. If only I could have looked more like the small pretty blondes, then

I'd be worth more than an occasional lay in the dark of night when he was blinded by alcohol. It didn't matter that people often complimented us. ("You guys are so perfect for each other." "It's cool that you are both really fast swimmers.") Maybe those were the ulterior motives for putting up with me, even though he wasn't proud to be my boyfriend.

When I complained about my flaws in front of Ryk—my body, my face, my hair, my teeth—he told me I was crazy.

"Why would you even think that? You are so stupid," he said.

But we were very much alike; he thought the same things about himself. Ryk had a body that any man would kill for, but he never seemed to believe it either.

"I've gained so much weight," he complained, after weighing himself for the second time that day. "Look at me. I'm fat."

I stared at him, his rippling six-pack and long, lean legs. Even though I struggled with getting an accurate image of myself, I didn't understand how he could ever call himself fat. I didn't identify with him or his body issues—perhaps because we had different ways of expressing our lack of confidence. When he was down on himself, he was hard on me. And when I was down, I was hard on me.

I just felt that there was so much about me to be unhappy with— including school. Academics never got any easier. Still struggling to keep up, I didn't outgrow my old problems with reading, tests, and writing papers. As an athlete, I had to take a full load made up entirely of general education courses required of freshmen, including math, English, and history. I thought in college I was going to learn stuff I wanted to know about; instead it felt exactly like being back in high school. The only change was that if I didn't hold a certain GPA, I would lose my scholarship. So there was a lot more riding on my lousy grades.

Competing on the NCAA level, it was nearly impossible to juggle school with swimming. I was always playing catch-up but could never win. Traveling for meets or shoehorning homework around practice and classes, I consistently found myself two steps behind where I was supposed to be. At first I was overwhelmed by the situation, then defeated.

I took a history class on the Civil Rights Movement where we were assigned to read a five-hundred-page book for an exam within three weeks. Most college students wouldn't blink at an assignment like that. My classmates were able to skim their reading or do only part of it and still do well on tests. Meanwhile, even if I read every single word, I barely passed. Three pounds of reading combined with all the work for my other courses and the fact that I'd be on the road competing for almost half the time was too much for me to handle.

I called my dad in tears.

"There's no way I can do all of this," I wept. "How can anybody do this? I'm going to fail the class and lose my scholarship. I know I will. Then what'll happen to me? I'll have to move back home and work at the Krazy Kids."

"Don't get ahead of yourself, Amanda," he said patiently. "Just focus on this one exam and do the best you can. I know you can do it."

A couple of days later, a package arrived containing several cassette tapes. My father had checked the book out of the library and, after putting in his own full day as a professor, stayed up through the night for several nights and read the entire book out loud to record it for me. The tapes came with a note: "I know you're reading this, but I thought being able to listen to it in the car or while you're on the road might help too."

Deeply indebted to my dad for always caring so much about me, I passed the test and the class. But as with everything else having to do with school, I got through on a wing and a prayer.

Depressed, lonely, and stressed out, I started drinking more to drown it all out. When I was drunk, I still wasn't up to Ryk's standards or doing any better in planetary science. The difference was,

I didn't give a crap. I wasn't seeking anyone's approval after three screwdrivers.

UA was a big party school with plenty of opportunities to get drunk. It is so close to the Mexican border that underage kids could drive about forty minutes to a country where they could drink to their heart's content. But even in Tucson, getting alcohol was beyond easy. Three times a week I would go out to bars or house parties where we did serious drinking. This was not sipping a Chardonnay in a lounge; this was doing shots of disgusting things. We weren't drinking because it tasted nice; we drank to get wasted.

I got the operation down to a science. When I went to a party, I wore a small black backpack where I'd stow a fifth of vodka or tequila. This was my own stash that I didn't have to share. Getting my buzz on was a lot easier when I didn't have to fight crowds around the keg. I usually tried to keep the contents of my backpack quiet, but a lot of times people wanted to know why I was wearing it at a party.

"It's more comfortable than a purse."

"That's dorky."

If someone saw me take the bottle out of the bag, I got a very different reaction.

"That's genius."

No matter how much I drank, I never got wildly out of control or made a huge fool of myself in front of others. I never was that person dying of embarrassment the next day because of what I had done while drinking. I didn't do wet T-shirt contests or make out with other girls.

I always wanted to be able to hold my own. I needed to be in control and take care of myself, because nobody else was going to do it. Even if I wasn't really in control, I was good at faking it. I put on a sober face with as much skill as I did a happy face. The purpose of my drinking wasn't to draw attention to myself by doing something incredibly crazy. I wanted to take a break from my insecurities by feeling less.

Getting drunk became more of a goal every time I went out. A lot of times I ended the night by getting sick. If I wasn't throwing up, then I was helping somebody else throw up by holding back her hair. Then I'd head home and pass out.

My drinking, late nights, and purging, combined with my hard-core training, started to take a toll on my body—just as my swimming was turning a corner.

Swimming was the only thing going well at college. Slowly it started to click over that first year. In addition to the long-distance practices, I also spent time in the weight room, something I had never done before. My growth spurt hadn't been all muscle, so part of the problem was that I didn't have the strength to pull my new body through the water. After building muscle mass through weight training, I felt stronger in the water. Swimming became less of a struggle. Each month I got a little better. It was slow and steady, but it was progress. I almost began to feel like myself in the pool again.

Even though I was abusing my body, I still trained hard and continued to improve. But I started to feel sick at least a couple of times a week during practice. In the half hour of dry land work before swimming, my stomach already wasn't feeling good. As soon as I jumped in the pool, it got steadily worse. I just wanted to get out of the water, I was so uncomfortable. I thought about food a lot (*Boston Market for dinner: turkey with three sides, applesauce*). Imagining my dinner under the water made my mouth water and killed my drive. I felt like I couldn't swim another lap. I needed to eat. I looked up at the clock, thinking we were near the end, and only a few minutes had passed.

Time moved excruciatingly slowly, because my body was so pissed off at me. Yet I could still produce results. But the suffering involved in the process was huge. Even if my purging had hurt my swimming, I wouldn't have stopped. I wanted to be a great and fast swimmer, but more than that I wanted to be pretty, skinny, and perfect. Those hazy adjectives were squashing my will to swim.

Toward the end of my freshman year, I arrived at practice with such a bad stomachache that I couldn't get into the pool. It wasn't just that my stomach hurt or that I was devastatingly hungry. I had zero motivation to jump into the water. I just wanted to go back to my room, get into bed, and do nothing. Totally empty inside, I had nothing left to give.

"I'm really sorry, but I can't train today," I told Frank. "I have to go back to the dorm."

"What's going on? Are you sick?" he asked. A nurturing and inquisitive father of five, Frank saw instantly from my demeanor that something wasn't right; I wasn't the type to bitch or skip practice.

"Yeah, I'm nauseous."

"The flu?"

"I'm not eating right."

"What do you mean? Tell me what you ate before coming to practice."

"Well, I'm having trouble figuring out when to eat. If I eat too close to practice, I get cramps. But if I wait too long, I'm hungry."

"Just tell me what you're eating."

"I'm having issues with food staying down."

Frank didn't say anything, but his look said, *Please explain.* The two of us sat on the pool deck watching the rest of the swimmers raking the water with their continuous strokes. He heard in my tone that more was going on than a simple illness.

"I've made myself throw up a couple of times. I don't know what I'm doing."

I hadn't planned on telling Frank anything close to that. It just sort of came out, surprising both him and me. I guess it was because he was the only person who ever really asked anything about what was going on with me. And I answered truthfully. The poor guy had no idea what to say.

"Let's send you down to the doctor to get your stomach checked out. And then let's work on this together. What you need is better eating habits. We can deal with anything. You just keep me in the loop."

I didn't tell him a lot, even though I felt like I could. His ears were open for me to say whatever I wanted, and he showed concern for me as if I were one of his own children. It felt good to have someone worry about me, and I was relieved he didn't think I was totally pathetic.

On Frank's orders, I went to the campus doctor, who asked me about my eating. I told him the truth about what I ate and what I threw up. "You will burn a hole in your esophagus if you keep this behavior up," he said. "And your teeth will rot out."

I think the doctor was trying to scare me straight, but his teeth comment sent me on an unhelpful spiral. I already hated my huge teeth; the idea of having huge and nasty teeth was unbearable. While he was talking to me about setting up an appointment with the campus nutritionist, all I could think about was big rotting teeth sticking out of my face.

Still, I followed the doctor's orders and went to see the school nutritionist, a mousy little woman with posters of the food pyramid and kids eating fruit on the walls of her depressing office.

After asking me to sit down, she put her reading glasses on and began reading from a piece of paper.

"We're going to go over what you should be eating on a daily basis," she said without looking at me. "In the morning, you need protein. So eggs are a good idea, peanut butter . . ."

Was this lady serious? She had no idea who I was or what my issues were. She didn't even use my name or say the word *bulimia*. If she wasn't going to bring it up, I sure as hell wasn't.

"A good idea for a snack is a handful of almonds . . ."

Did she even know I was an athlete? As she continued with her generic rundown on what I should eat, I was getting more and more frustrated.

"For dinner, choose a lean protein, like chicken or pork, with a side of steamed vegetables."

Oh yeah, that was a perfect meal for me to cook up in my microwave.

After two minutes of her talking, I tuned her out. What she was saying was totally useless. At the end of our session, she handed me the eating plan she had been reading from as a parting gift. I walked out of her office and threw it away.

chapter 7

In the summer of 2000, Frank and I worked hard to fine-tune my stroke, maximizing the strength of my kick and the efficiency of my pull, as we headed into full Olympic trial mode.

My times were steady but my confidence rocketed up that winter when I competed in the Pacific-10 Conference. I had already been winning my events at dual meets for much of the year, but those didn't compare with the big meet that included the best swimming schools on the West Coast. Going into the competition, where all the fastest swimmers in the league were raring to go, I felt pressure from all sides. Every race counted for points toward the goal of making the Wildcats number one; I didn't want to let my teammates or myself down. Personally, there was more riding on the meet than just the division title; if I couldn't handle this, then I had no hope for the Olympics, which were right around the corner.

Right before the 200-meter breaststroke, I was so anxious that I was buzzed from my own nerves. Sick with waiting, I paced around until it was my turn to go. Then I flew to the blocks like a racehorse scratching at the ground before the gate is lifted. I was desperate to get in there and get it over with. I came from behind in the final stretch to claim my first Pac-10 title with a time of 2:10.41, missing the Pac-10 record by less than nine-tenths of a second. My amazing female teammates and I won Arizona's first Pac-10 Conference championship, beating the Stanford women's team, which had won every conference title in the event's thirteen years.

Things were really coming together in the ultimate proof that my swimming truly had improved. I no longer had any excuses for why I couldn't do this. I let my mind wander to the outer limits of my capabilities. Could I actually swim in another Olympics, something that I wanted deeply? Maybe I wasn't as washed-up as most people thought.

Winning at Pac-10 was one thing, but getting a spot on the Olympic team was quite another. For that I would have to be one of the top two swimmers in my event out of the whole country. Achieving that seemed like a fantasy. Although I didn't have a lot of faith it could happen, I brought my old laser-like focus back to my swimming while I trained with Frank. And though I continued to throw up and suffer from my stomachaches sporadically, my eating had significantly improved ever since I had moved out of the dorms.

My dad proposed buying a house in Tucson after months of listening to me bitch and moan about how much I hated living in the dorms and how miserable the lack of privacy and space made me. He wanted to invest in real estate, and Tucson, where the property values were low, was a great place to start. He needed someone to live in the house, so why not me? Dad to the rescue again.

Once I had moved out of his house in Irvine, I rediscovered my old appreciation for my dad. Resuming our relationship, as if I had never been that moody, sullen teen who couldn't stand it when he breathed around me, we talked on the phone at least once or twice a week. A lot of times it was practical or academic stuff, like activating my new debit card or identifying the thesis statement in an essay for English class, but my dad had returned to being my rock. He was the first one I called whenever I had a question about money, school, or swimming.

Buying a house in Tucson was a classic move for my father. He always wanted to feel needed, and he loved to help me and my sisters in any way he could. If he bought a home, I wouldn't have to pay rent, and he could continue to take care of me. I was relieved and grateful to accept his help, as I did time and time again.

In April, a month before the semester ended, he bought a five-bedroom ranch-style home a few minutes from campus. I didn't wait for the electricity or the hot water to be turned on before I packed up all my belongings into a handful of crates and moved in. I slept on the floor in a sleeping bag and used a flashlight at night to find my way to the bathroom.

Two of my female teammates moved in with me, and with a lot of help from my dad, we turned the place into a perfectly comfortable home. It was nice to have my dad around; he came all the way from Irvine on weekends to be our contractor and handyman, putting in light fixtures, giving the place a fresh coat of paint, and building a carport. There wasn't anything fancy about the house; it didn't have a dishwasher or garbage disposal, and the freezer wasn't self-defrosting, so we often had to chip our way to the food. But there was so much space. With a laundry room, dining room, kitchen, big front and back yards, it was a pretty awesome spread for a few college kids.

Unfortunately, no amount of space could make living with my new roommates easy. I found the atmosphere in the house—filled with constant cattiness and drama—incredibly stressful. The source of the turmoil was always the same: boys. Someone always seemed to be breaking up or getting back together with her boyfriend, and I wasn't exempt. Ryk was not their favorite person. They hated it when he hung out at the house and spent the night; they bitched about everything from how he ate all our food to how much his car sucked.

"His car is always parked outside the house. It's such an eyesore," one of them complained.

"It's a Saturn," I said, confused since Ryk's car wasn't some clunker with a rusty hood and hanging tailpipe.

"It's embarrassing," the other said.

The friction that was there from the start worsened as the Olympic trials neared. Beginning in April and running through the summer, swimming picked up to a nerve-wracking pitch. The workouts weren't that much different in terms of sets and length, but the undercurrent of pressure we put on ourselves made the swimming harder.

This chance only comes around every four years.

Everything was fine-tuned, no detail ignored. Every time I dove into the pool, it had to be a perfect dive; every time I turned, it had to be a perfect turn. Elements that I would normally be lazy about and take for granted became crucial.

"Only seventy-five more days to Olympic trials! No time for slacking," Frank yelled at us. We were constantly reminded that time was flying by really fast. Only fifty days left. Now forty.

The closer I got to a big meet, the more psycho I became. My patience wore thin. I got annoyed if I didn't get enough sleep, eat well, or do exactly what my regimen required. I became overly sensitive, with a short and fiery fuse that could blow up in any unsuspecting victim's face. I wasn't a very fun person to be around. Anything I had to handle that wasn't about swimming was too much of a burden.

When one of my roommates, a good churchgoing girl, had her parents come stay with us, and it became our job to cover for the fact that she had a serious boyfriend who she was basically living with, I thought I was going to murder her nice mom and dad so I wouldn't have to deal with them. We censored our conversations and talked in code when he called. I didn't have the bandwidth to be thinking about this right before trials, so when she asked me to drive to her boyfriend's house to pick up some of her clothes, I bit her head off: "Go get it yourself!"

The pressure didn't help my bulimia. Being hypersensitive triggered my purging. I had more meltdowns per day, and so more times when I found myself throwing up. My new home was a blessing and a curse. I definitely was eating better now that I could make meals and stock healthful foods like granola, yogurt, and fruit. Returning to the menus my dad had made for me as a kid, I prepared chicken on my George Foreman Grill, little salads, and broccoli. So much broccoli. But just as I had access to a kitchen and homemade food, so I also had my own room with my own bathroom. Now there was nothing stopping me if I had the impulse to purge. It was as easy as entering my bathroom, locking the door, and throwing up.

The months leading up to the Olympic trials in early August were a battle with my brain and body to stay positive and healthy. I knew I was a long shot in both the 100-meter and 200-meter breaststroke events. It had been a very rough year personally, and though my swimming was coming together nicely, I still wasn't totally confident in the water. It was easy to get subsumed by doubt. I had to be first or second in the whole United States to make the Olympic team. I had worked hard, but I was not first or second. Not by a long shot.

My broccoli-and-cheddar soup had congealed in its bowl, and now my chicken fingers were starting to go cold too. I didn't have an appetite, not even for my favorite T.G.I. Friday's meal. Overcome with a host of bad emotions, I didn't want to eat; I wanted to cry and hide.

My self-confidence was in the gutter. Earlier that day, I had my first event, the 100-meter breaststroke, at the Olympic trials in Indianapolis. The swimmer to beat was sixteen-year-old Megan Quann, a big, muscular high school student from Washington State who had been on fire in all the important meets leading up to the trials. Through her times, her press, and her attitude, she let every swimmer know this race was hers.

Megan hadn't been wrong. She won the 100-meter easily and went on the record as saying a world record might be hers in the 200-meter. I, on the other hand, finished eighth. When I looked up at the scoreboard and saw that I had come in last, I put my goggles back on to try to hide my tears.

I hadn't thought I was going to do well, but I also hadn't thought I'd do *that* badly. Dinner at T.G.I. Friday's that night with my mom, dad, and sisters was like a funeral. I kept on replaying the devastating loss in my mind. Finally Leah broke the silence.

"You looked miserable out there," she said.

I didn't look up from my plate of untouched food to acknowledge her comment. Yeah, I looked miserable. I *was* miserable.

"You walked up to the blocks and you didn't have a smile," she continued. "You seemed pissed off to be there. It wasn't very much fun for us to watch you."

"We didn't fly all the way out to Indianapolis to see you upset," Taryn added, "and go to the blocks like you had already lost before you'd even touched the water."

So now this was a pile-on?

"What do you want from me?" I replied. "I'm just not that good anymore. I can't win like everyone wants me to."

"That's not what we're saying," Leah said. "We love to watch you do what *you* love to do."

My sisters could have cared less if I won; they wanted me to enjoy something into which I had invested so much of myself. They continued to get on my case, keeping their younger sister in check, until I agreed that I would walk out to my 200-meter event with a smile on my face and try my best to enjoy it.

Sitting in the little ready room with the seven girls that I was going to swim against in the 200-meter finals, I remembered my sisters' advice—don't take anything too seriously. But the tension in the air was suffocating. I didn't want to give in to the pressure, but these seven women were living reminders of the obstacles ahead of me. The worst thing I could have done is look at my competitors, literally face that they wanted this just as much as me, maybe even more. So I didn't. Instead, I did my stretches, made sure my cap was on right, watched the swimmers racing before us, paid attention to the details I could control.

As we paraded down the side of the pool toward the blocks, I kept my gaze fixed ahead of me and stuck a smile on my face. I waved to my family and gave them my best I'm-having-fun expression. At first it was a facade. I didn't really feel happy or ready to go. But while I was walking down the side of the pool, all the coaches and athletes lining our path started to smile back and offer me enthusiastic high fives. Their energy changed mine. The outward led the inward until I thought, *This is fun*.

Then came the real fun. For the first half of the race, Megan was out front with Kristy Kowal, a swimmer from Georgia who had just been named NCAA woman of the year, close on her heels. I didn't try to keep up with Megan, who always started out like a rocket, but thought if I could just stay close to Kristy, I might have a chance.

One minute Megan was bobbing up and down decisively ahead of the rest of the field, the next she was no longer visible. She had run out of steam, which meant the only person in front of me was Kristy. I dug in hard and pressed on, knowing that if I held steady until the second hundred meters, then the Olympics could be mine. I've always been a strong back-half swimmer, but Frank's training had turned me into an endurance athlete.

When I came to the surface, I wrapped my arms around the lane line and looked up at the scoreboard: Kowal 1, Beard 2. I'd done it! I'd made the Olympic squad for 2000. I threw my head back in disbelief and joy.

That race meant a hundred times more to me than winning gold and two silvers in the 1996 games. I had to push myself to such extremes, both mentally and physically, to get to this point, never giving up on myself, even after a lot of others had. I wanted to say to all those who had lost faith in me, *To all of you who didn't believe, I'm still here*.

"I knew you'd be able to do it," Ryk said. "You are good at surprising everyone." When it came to swimming, he was a terrific partner in that he could fully empathize with my situation. He knew exactly how much stress, pressure, and effort had gone into passing those trials.

He had already made the South African team, so I was relieved I'd made the American team—for the sake of our relationship. I felt that if I didn't go to the Olympics, we were definitely over. I assumed he'd go there and hook up with a bunch of other girls and that'd be the end of us. When we eventually got to the 2000 Games in Sydney, Ryk and I were totally separated. Because we were on two different teams, we didn't train in the same place or time or live anywhere near each other. Still, we were at the Olympics together.

Being a swimmer at the Sydney Games was an amazing experience. In Australia, they love swimming. They are a water country and they treat their swimmers like celebrities, so our sport always got top billing. Every day the newspaper and TV had some article or spot about swimming. It makes everything more fun and exciting when the crowd is into your sport and understands it.

The only pressure I felt was whatever I put on myself. There weren't a lot of eyes on me since nobody had expected me to be here in the first place. Unlike four years ago, when I was the great American hope for gold, now I was a dark horse with a lousy world ranking. I wanted to win a medal but gave credence to the naysayers. I had the same feeling as I did going into trials: *There's no way I can pull this off, but I want to pull this off.* I laughed thinking back to the 1996 Olympics, when people used to ask me all the time, "How do you deal with the pressure, being so young?" My youth was an advantage, not a liability. I had been oblivious to the intense environment and opinions that I now had to work so hard to ignore.

The push and pull of my mind-set made me incredibly grumpy. My short fuse revealed itself as it always did before a big event. My sisters got burned by it on their very first day in town, when I joined them for lunch outside the Village.

"How's the swimming going?" Leah asked.

"Good," I said, immediately tensing up.

"Is your calf okay? Is it giving you any more problems?" she asked.

"It's fine."

I started to chew on my lower lip to keep from screaming.

"What's *your* problem?" Taryn asked.

"When I'm not underwater, I'm living with fifty swimmers and going to a million swim meetings and races a day. The last thing I want to do when I'm with nonswimmers is talk about swimming."

"I'm so glad I traveled halfway around the world to have you bite my head off," Leah said.

"Sorry," I replied. "Can we just get lunch and do a little shopping?"

As long as we weren't talking about swimming (which we didn't do again), my family and I got along great. Being with them was always a reprieve from the seriousness of a once-in-four-years shot to prove your worth as an athlete to the world.

I couldn't say the same about Ryk. Suddenly, in Sydney, our both being swimmers was not an asset. For the entire Olympics, we were grumpy with each other. During the swimming competitions we were mostly apart, but when we did hang out, there was so much anxiety in the air that we bickered constantly. Not a single day went by that we didn't have some kind of argument that usually started like this:

"Want to hang out at two o'clock?" I asked him.

"I was going to go to the pool then to work out," he said.

"Fine, then we'll never hang out!"

And—*bam!*—a ready-made fight.

I had enough adversity without adding Ryk as an enemy. In the preliminary rounds of the 200-meter breaststroke event, I squeaked into the finals in the very last of the eight available berths. I was going to the finals but in the outermost lane, away from the fastest swimmers (during races, swimmers are arranged in a pyramid by speed, with the fastest one assigned to the center lane and slower ones radiating from there). I wouldn't be able to track my toughest competitors. Instead, I'd be up against the wall and the gutter, swimming through their riffles and wakes, racing only myself and the clock.

I sat in the ready room, using every ounce of energy to fight my nerves and stay zoned, not to be defeated before I dove in, as my sisters had put it. Right before we were going to be called out onto the pool deck, I felt a hand on my shoulder and looked up; it was Frank. He had been hired as a coach for the South African team, so he was at the Games although the two of us hadn't talked before this moment. He motioned for me to come out of the room and sit next to him on a pair of folding chairs.

"Forget everything we've been working on," he said. "Forget about any kind of strategy. I don't care if you have a stronger finish than start. I just want you to go all out, Amanda. Go for it.

"And when you're done," he continued, "leave it all in the water. Don't get out with any regrets or excuses. No I-should-have-done-this-or-that. Know that everything you had went into the pool. You race your heart out and walk away, happy with just that."

I didn't know what to say. Frank, like my dad, was another pillar there to prop me up no matter where or what.

"Pin your ears back and go flat out," he finished. "You have absolutely nothing to lose."

I went down to the blocks, and when the starter sounded, I pierced the water, rode my glide to the surface, and went for it.

I forced myself not to let my gaze drift to the left in an effort to check on where the rest of the field was. I swam against myself and for myself. When I made the turn into the final hundred, the crowd began to roar. The unexpected sound was dull, but I knew what was happening and that it had to be really loud if it could reach my ears. It didn't mean it was for me, but something exciting was definitely going on in this pool. Regardless of who it is for, the sound of a crowd going wild is energizing. In the outside lane and unable to see the front-runners, I pretended it was all for me and used that to drive myself harder.

The final fifty meters, the homestretch, I pushed harder still. I worked my legs and lungs until they were on fire. Then I touched the wall and shot out of the water to take a look at the scoreboard: Hungary, USA, USA. Hungary's Agnes Kovacs, who'd set an Olympic record in the preliminary race, had touched in for the gold; Kristy Kowal, my teammate, was a tenth of a second behind her for the silver; and in third, for the bronze, just a second off the winning time, A. Beard, USA. I couldn't believe it.

I had pinned my ears back as Frank had asked, going all out for it, but I'm not sure if I could have left everything in the water if I hadn't medaled. Luckily, I didn't need to worry about it. I had given a good show for my family (who had spent a ton of money to buy tickets to Australia last minute after I'd won the trials) and my fellow teammates.

Ryk, who put on a good show as well, didn't medal. He made it to the finals in the 1500 freestyle but then placed fifth, which sent him into a dark mood. He had been in the opposite position from me before the games, because the spotlight had been on him as a top contender. At the end of the 1999 school year, he was named the NCAA swimmer of the year and also received the award for University of Arizona's Athlete of the Century. Ryk was the great South African hope for gold, and the team put a massive amount of pressure on him. Fifth was a huge disappointment. Adding to the stress, Ryk had graduated from college the spring before the Olympics; swimming was all he had left.

I wanted to be happy for myself, but in light of Ryk's loss, I felt as if any celebration was rubbing his face in it. I stayed away from any talk about my medal and concentrated my energy on trying to cheer him up.

My humble success winning bronze was nothing compared with Ian Thorpe's mind-blowing Games, and the anger that triumph inspired in Ryk was also pretty huge. The seventeen-year-old Australian native shattered three world records to win three gold medals at his first Olympics. He also won two silvers, establishing himself as the greatest men's swimmer in the world. I secretly loved to see him swim (Ryk would have killed me if I'd said anything like that). When someone does something so perfect it seems effortless, it's a joy to watch.

Ian was one of Ryk's main competitors and the guy was unstoppable. Not only that, Ian was the best swimmer in a country crazy for swimming. He was a big celebrity in Australia, with his face all over billboards, magazine covers, newspapers, and television. Gossip columnists followed his movements like he was a movie star. Everyone knew who he was and what he was up to.

Ryk despised that Ian was covered in medals. I understood the feeling of wishing you could be that person, and when you can't, the jealousy turns into hatred. Everything about Ian, even his swimwear, rubbed Ryk the wrong way. "Look at that swimsuit," Ryk said, about the full-body suit Ian was known for wearing. "He looks like a seal."

After collecting all his medals, Ian walked into the cafeteria where Ryk and I were eating, and everyone took notice. A very big guy and an even bigger winner, Ian had a presence. Athletes from countries and sports all over the world began to approach him for his autograph or a photo with him. With every camera flash, I could feel Ryk's anger rising.

"Why do they want to take their picture with that guy?" he said, full of venom.

I wanted my photo with Ian. But I kept my mouth shut.

Ryk wanted to forget about everything and move on, and for him moving on was going out to clubs, lots and lots of clubs. In his usual fashion, Ryk knew where all the action was even though we were a hemisphere away from home. After the swimming events finished, we went out all the time. Every night there was a different bar, a new club, an impromptu party.

One night, we headed out to a party for all the athletes at a club close to Sydney Harbour. The city was electrified like a giant theme park during the Games; the Olympic sign made out of hundreds of lights decorated the Harbour Bridge. The enormous club's two stories of multiple bars, dance floors, and lounges were filled with athletes and their entourages. You could spot the athletes from the civilians right away. Big or compact, these muscular, intense people looked awkward dolled up in their hair, makeup, and normal street clothes. It was like a freak show night at the club.

Everyone was blowing off steam like crazy in the dark, hot, and crowded club that was so loud it erased all thought. All of us had been cooped up in such a confining, pressure-filled environment where everyone is on your case all the time, telling you what to do and when to do it, that we went crazy once let out. It's just nature that humans who have been babied for so long will rebel and swing wildly the other way. The fittest, most focused folks in the world were knee-deep in hedonism. With low body fat and long periods of abstinence, they were drinking as if someone was about to take the alcohol away. That meant people getting seriously wasted, dancing on tables, and hooking up with each other in plain sight.

I was loving it. While sipping Midori sours, I checked out the scene with a deep sense of celebration. As an eighteen-year-old, I didn't need to dance on banquettes. Enjoying my win and all the work that went into it with a few cocktails and my fellow teammates was all the crazy I needed.

By midnight I'd had my fill of celebrating. Tired to the point where I wasn't having fun anymore, I searched out Ryk. My toes had gone numb from standing too long in heels, and I had nothing left to say to anyone. I'm not a dancer, so I'd sat down and watched everyone else, which I didn't mind for a while. But now the only place I wanted to be in was my pajamas.

"The night's just getting started," Ryk said.

I could feel my temper rising; Ryk never wanted to go and I had no idea how to get back to the Village alone.

"You always do this to me," I started.

"Come on, Amanda, just stay a little bit longer."

What? Ryk also never tried to convince me to stay. Something had to be up. A guy at the club put his hand into his pocket, pulled out two pills, and held them out to me.

"Look what I got," he said.

"What is that?" I asked.

"It's ecstasy."

"What does it do?"

Losing control was not high up there on my list of favorite things to do. Whenever I drank, I never went so far that I couldn't get myself home.

"It is not a big deal," he said. "It's a light fun pill. You'll be yourself but you'll like everything. It'll relax you. Don't worry."

I had a quick debate with myself in my head. Drugs were not my scene. As athletes, we were drug-tested all the time. Since I'd been thirteen years old, an official could show up anytime or anyplace to find out what was running through my bloodstream. Usually, the tests were right after a race, and they were looking for drugs that would make a better athlete, not something that would get me to dance. That's what I told myself. Plus, Ryk was there. He wasn't going to let anything hurt me. He loved me. So I went for it.

"Sure, why not?"

I felt good. When the drug hit my system, everything lightened up dramatically. Suddenly, I didn't mind the crowds and my feet no longer hurt. I got a second wind and everyone I knew was interesting again. There was so much to talk about and do. I danced for a while, feeling the beats from the music in a way I never had before. And Ryk turned into an awesome boyfriend. He paid attention to me as he had when we first met. We danced, laughed, and just had fun together for hours. I felt gorgeous and loved. Ryk had been completely right; this *was* fun.

Our curfew was at 6:00 a.m. (we had to check in with the coaches for them to make sure we weren't dead), so we left the club a few hours earlier to get back in time. Even on drugs, I'm the kind of person who spirals into a bad mood when I'm out late enough to witness the sun creeping up. As the light grows, so does my anxiety about the day ahead and how I've screwed up with the night before.

Getting back to the Village was a nightmare. As I came down off the ecstasy, we tried to catch a cab, unsuccessfully battling throngs of tourists in town for the Olympics. Traffic was so chaotic and slow that it looked as if we might not make it back by curfew. Ryk grew surly under the stress. I tried to hold his hand in the cab, but he withdrew it, and I went from a huge high, a pretty girl with a boy-friend who dotes on her, to a huge low, a stupid and lonely loser who takes drugs.

We made it back with only a few minutes to spare, and I headed directly to bed, exhausted from the stress and chemicals in my system. But lying in my small room, I couldn't get the music to stop playing in my head. My hands and feet were fidgeting out of my control, and my teeth were grinding against each other. *What is happening? Why can't I sleep?* I had never been so agitated in my life.

Ryk and I landed in South Africa with the bitter taste of disappointment still in our mouths. Because I, like most college swimmers who made the Games, had taken the fall semester off for the Olympics, I decided to use my free time to spend a couple of months with Ryk in his home country. When we got into the waiting car and began the long drive to his home in Bloemfontein, a city in the middle of the country, I was more than willing to leave the Olympics behind. My mind raced to meeting his parents: Would they like me; would I like them?

Not long into the silent drive, I spotted a billboard on the side of the road with an enormous picture of the two of us, smiling and happy.

"Oh my God, Ryk! Check it out," I said, tugging at his arm and pointing at the billboard. "That is hilarious. I've got to get a picture of that to send to my parents. Nothing like that would ever happen back home."

Ryk didn't even look up. As one of the country's top athletes, he received a lot of attention here. For our trip to South Africa, we not only had billboards but requests for major interviews and invitations to official dinners. Before we'd left Sydney, he translated a gossip item from the South African press written in Afrikaans. "Swimming's golden couple are coming to South Africa. The best-looking pair at the Olympics will return to Ryk Neethling's country so his girl-friend Amanda Beard, who won a bronze medal for the Americans, can meet his parents. Is a walk down the aisle next for the king and queen of the pool? They would certainly make some perfect little water babies."

I laughed at the article, but most of what the South African press wrote about Ryk wasn't funny. Angry that he didn't bring home a medal, they were hard on him about his performance. People easily forget that athletes are human and not a public commodity to be tossed aside when the dividends on everyone's emotional investment are disappointing. "My country wanted gold," he said. "I'm such a failure."

We arrived at his home, a beautiful old house that backed up to a game preserve, and after dropping our bags headed straight out to dinner with his family. His father, mother, and two sisters, excited to be reunited with Ryk, talked in their native tongue, Afrikaans, the language of most educated South Africans. Even though they spoke English pretty well, it was their second language, so I understood why they were talking in what felt most comfortable.

After a little while, however, his mother, a kind and proper woman, interrupted her family. "Let's try to speak English so that Amanda can feel included," she said.

"Sorry to be so rude," his dad apologized.

I shook my head in protest and said it was no big deal, but it was nice to understand what everyone around me was talking about. His dad asked about a particular race in Sydney in English, but when Ryk responded, he spoke Afrikaans. Soon his mother followed up with a comment about a childhood friend getting married, again in English. When Ryk replied, he returned the conversation to Afrikaans.

"English," his mother reminded him after a few minutes.

It didn't bother me that Ryk continued to gravitate to Afrikaans the entire night. I figured he was so used to speaking to his parents in that language, he couldn't break the habit.

Back in South Africa, Ryk was definitely at home. I now understood why he was such a slob, never went to the grocery store, and didn't know how to cook a single dish. It all made sense when I met Angelina. She was the family's full-time housekeeper, nanny, and chef all rolled up in one little black lady.

She did *everything*. Angelina would bring Ryk and me breakfast in bed—anything we wanted. For me, that was a breakfast sandwich with egg, cheese, and bacon on a biscuit with fruit salad and coffee. She also washed and ironed everything, even our underwear. It was insane. If I left a sock on the floor, she picked it up and cleaned it. At first, I felt extremely awkward. When Angelina went to make our bed, I said, "No, no, no. I can do it." I didn't feel right having someone else take care of that. She and I spent a little time tugging at the sheets until Ryk intervened.

"It's her job," he said. "She loves it."

After about a week, I started to let her take care of me. It never seemed normal, but it was definitely nice, a pleasurable break from reality like being on a luxury vacation. Angelina, who had her own living quarters on the property and had worked for the family for twenty-three years, cooked full-on, sit-down feasts for every single meal—and they were never the same meals either. There were roasted meats, side vegetables, fresh pies, cookies, tarts, and handmade doughnuts, even for lunch.

Every day Ryk's dad came home for lunch. He left his law office in the middle of the day to sit down at the dining room table prepared with perfect place settings. Then after a delicious lunch (which always included a fruit salad that Angelina made especially for me because I loved it), he'd return to the office. What a weird little world.

Their house was literally an oasis with a huge front yard filled with lush flowers and trees (tended by a staff of gardeners) and a pool in the back, which opened out on an expanse of dry desert that was a nature preserve. A big back fence divided the green around the house from the backdrop of roaming zebras and gazelles.

Everything about this life was foreign to me. It wasn't just Angelina pouring me my first coffee of the day from a silver pot or the giraffe poking its head above the fence to watch me in the pool. It was also the old-fashioned dynamic of Ryk's family. His dad was the provider and his mother the stay-at-home mom with a lot of help. In my world everyone worked inside and outside the home—even kids. A friend of Ryk's mom told her I wasn't a proper girl because I didn't wear a hairdo and makeup. I hadn't received the memo that it was still 1950 in South Africa.

As if to highlight the fact that I didn't fit in, Ryk spoke Afrikaans when anyone other than me was in the room. His mother finally gave up her reminder of English and let him speak whatever language he wanted. This was supposed to be a big moment for us: the first time I was meeting his friends and family and staying in his house. Instead, I felt as though I didn't exist.

He didn't do a very good job of helping me to fit in. My outsider status was a constant no matter where we went. When we went out to dinner with a bunch of his friends, after he introduced me around and we exchanged a few pleasantries, Ryk launched right into Afrikaans. I sat there, looking like such a bitch, but I couldn't pretend to involve myself. I would have loved to join in, but I didn't understand a single word anyone was saying. No one minded my bored, angry expression. Ryk talked over my head as though I weren't there, and his friends followed suit. I felt unimportant and lonely.

It seems like the only times Ryk and I bonded were when I was on drugs. I was willing to live with the comedown from ecstasy because I loved being on it when I was with him. That altered state was like traveling back in time to the first months of our relationship. He told me I was beautiful and held me tight. By swallowing a pill, I felt like the center of his universe, and I liked it there.

I had pharmaceutically induced love adventures on little trips around South Africa. In the two months I stayed in the country, Ryk and I traveled about half the time, going away to different cities for a few nights and then returning to the homestead to be revived by Angelina and her cooking. While away, we didn't check out museums, parks, or any of the normal things tourists typically do. Mine was a tour of the nightclubs of South Africa.

Whether in Durban or Johannesburg, the nightclubs were pretty much the same as they are anywhere else—dark places with booming music that is usually unsettling or grating, unless, of course, I was on drugs. We made new best friends everywhere we went. Whatever group assembled around us was made up of the best people on earth, until we went back to our random hotel and completely forgot who they were.

In our trip to Cape Town, I was introduced to cocaine. "Try it. You'll like it," a new friend said nonchalantly. I didn't know how to take the white powder, so he showed me. He held one nostril and sniffed up the stuff with the other.

I liked it. Cocaine was an insecure control freak's dream drug. Ecstasy lasted way too long, but coke was a short buzz during which I felt hyper-able. It focused me and took away my shyness so I could chat with strangers. Cocaine seemed to give me whatever I needed in the particular moment. Wiping away my insecurities. I was good, smart, and pretty, and Ryk seemed generous, sensitive, and happy.

I partied two or three nights a week, doing whatever drugs were on hand. I went from a regimented Olympic medalist to a foggy club kid in one short plane ride. I became nonchalant about what went into my body. I was so laid-back that while lying on the beach in Durban, I agreed to take acid.

I was given a little piece of paper and instructed to put it in my mouth and suck on it. The drugs always seemed to magically appear. For the first half hour, I didn't feel anything and assumed nothing would happen. Then I started seeing things, really creepy things.

There weren't a lot of people on the wide sandy beach. But I spotted an older white couple in their late fifties. When the heavy-set man and woman came into closer view, their jowly rich faces morphed into those of hideous demons. My heart raced and I clutched Ryk, who simply stared at the milky-white ocean. Had he seen what I'd seen?

More beachgoers passed and all revealed their true devilish selves, but only to me. I started to freak out. I didn't want to see what I was seeing but I had no control. Everything was so messed up and I was powerless to stop it.

"I don't like this," I said to Ryk. "I want it to stop."

"Oh shit," he answered. "Well, it's going to last for a while."

"Well, get me the hell out of here," I begged.

Ryk got me off the beach and we found our way back to his friend's cliffside house where we were staying. Nothing, not even the beautiful view of the ocean, could calm me. I was plagued by nightmarish visions and spent hours in the throes of the scariest experience of my life. When I came out of it, I was exhausted and pissed. How could I have taken something like that? I should have known better. I was angry at myself. Doing drugs like a mindless idiot was not how I ever pictured myself. As much as I loved breakfast in bed, I needed to get the hell out of South Africa.

Not long before I was set to leave, Ryk and I took another trip to a little town called Margate. Again, we were staying in a friend's country house, but this time in a quiet beachy town without a club or anything like it. We went out for an early dinner, and afterward Ryk suggested we drive up the coastline so we could enjoy the view. I immediately was on edge. A romantic drive up the coast? That was completely uncharacteristic of him. He had to be up to something.

At a certain point, he stopped the car and said we should get out to savor the moment. He helped me out of the car and was holding my hand. Now I was totally weirded out. Why was he being nice and sweet? *We don't sit and look at the city lights together. We're not that kind of couple.* He had a plan, and I needed to figure it out.

"I'm tired. I just want to go to sleep," I whined, saying things I knew would piss him off so that he had to reveal his true intent. But Ryk kept it up.

"You're not going to be in South Africa for much longer," he said. "I just want to enjoy this moment with you."

"Do you think I'm pretty?" I asked, since Ryk hated that question more than anything.

"Yes."

"No, you don't. You wish I had bigger boobs."

"What are you talking about? You have a perfect body."

"Is that why you never want to touch me?"

"Shut up."

"Seriously, what do you wish you could change about me?"

"Forget it. Let's just leave and go back to the house."

Back in the car, Ryk was furious.

"You know, I was actually going to ask you to marry me back there. But you ruined it," he said.

Marry me? So that was it. But why would he want to marry me? We had so many issues and only got along when I was on drugs. I thought his proposing was seriously crazy. He didn't have a ring, so I wasn't sure how genuine he was about his proposal. But I also didn't want to find out. I told him that at nineteen, I wasn't ready to get married to anyone. Now I knew I really needed to get back home and back to reality.

chapter 8

After almost three months in South Africa, I returned to Tucson in the winter of 2000, but reality was not as healing as I'd hoped it would be.

Ryk and two of my male teammates moved in—after the two women I had been living with moved out—and overnight it became a guys' house. I didn't mind that at all. I liked being in a houseful of boys; it was much less complicated emotionally and easier for me to find privacy whenever I needed it. The two boys were really sweet and easy to get along with. They didn't have any complaints, needs, or drama. They liked to act like I was their sister, alternatively protective or teasing.

Best of all, they weren't messy or disgusting. I loved having my own place off campus because I could keep it neat and relatively organized. With roommates, I could never achieve perfection, but at least the house was always clean. The dishes were put away, pillows remained on couches, and people's clothes stayed in their rooms. I was grateful the guys didn't live up to stereotypes of their gender. Instead they cleaned up after they ate and kept the common areas tidy.

Ryk, however, was a freaking disaster. His process of moving in was to pull clothes out of his bags, wear them, and throw them on the floor until everything was dirty. Then they were laundered (by me), put away in drawers (again, by me), and the bags stowed in a closet (that's right, me). Almost instantly, his stuff was everywhere, since picking anything up was apparently against his religion. He never ever went to the grocery store to buy food and cooked even less. But he still ate my food. And wherever he ate—at the kitchen table, in bed, or on the couch—there his plates stayed.

I had known before that Ryk was a slob, but living with him was a whole different level of knowing. It was one thing to walk into the room in his old house and be disgusted for a night. It was another to share one with him. I felt bad for him, though, now that he was no longer in college and struggling to make it as a swimmer.

He continued to practice with the UA team in the afternoons before he coached a swim club. That meant he had swim practice from 2:00 to 4:30, then went straight into coaching from 4:30 to 6:30. After practice he returned home unbelievably cranky and depleted because he was starving. So I took to rushing home from my practice and classes to cook him a meal, package it in Tupperware, and drive it over to him while he coached, before returning home to eat my own dinner.

It didn't take me too many days of washing and folding his clothes and cooking and delivering his food to feel like Angelina. I don't mind cooking, shopping, or cleaning (I'm so OCD, I can't walk by a huge pile of laundry on the floor without doing it). But Ryk hardly seemed to notice, let alone appreciate all that I did for him, which turned everyday chores into huge grievances. I didn't like that he began to expect me to do it; I wasn't his wife or his maid.

"I'm so sick of this!" I said, slamming the refrigerator door shut after finding the cold cuts I had bought that morning gone.

I walked into the living room, where my two other roommates were watching TV; Ryk was still at the pool coaching.

"Every time I go buy food, I come home and it's gone," I complained.

"So stop going to the grocery store," one of them said.

"Ryk's never going to do it if you keep doing it for him," the other said. "Don't do it and see what happens."

I tried, but the experiment didn't last very long. It was kind of like giving the silent treatment to your boyfriend who doesn't notice you've stopped talking. When Ryk opened the refrigerator and found it empty, it never dawned on him to go food shopping. Instead, he drove to the nearest takeout place and picked up food for himself. And his laundry piled up until he had nothing to wear. That's when I spied him picking a shirt out of the pile and putting it back on.

That was the last straw. I went back to my routine, because I needed food in my stomach and the house clean. My father let Ryk live there for free, and I bought all the food, so basically, as a sophomore in college, I was supporting my boyfriend. I am very much like my dad in that if someone needs me, and I can help, I'll do absolutely anything. We Beards like to be needed. I've taken advantage of that trait many times with my dad. ("Can you drive down to Tucson tonight because the garage door doesn't work?") Now Ryk was taking advantage of me. The only difference was that I didn't get anything in return.

When I first started catering to Ryk, I thought he would be really sweet because of it. But all I got in exchange was moodiness. Ryk seemed to be more pissed off than he'd ever been before because of the situation he found himself in after graduating from college. Armed with a very ironic degree in psychology, he had no idea what to do next. He wanted to continue swimming but needed to figure out a way to fund it, and lucrative endorsements weren't happening, particularly since he hadn't medaled in the Olympics. Under pressure to figure out his future, Ryk hardly interacted with me, and when he did, it wasn't pleasant.

Like the captain of the football team who shows up to his high school reunion a used-car salesman twenty pounds heavier, Ryk was no longer top dog. He wasn't alone in this predicament. Like so many college athletes, he'd put everything he had into his sport during his years as an undergraduate. That's what an athlete has to do if he wants to be competitive. But it left no room to think about anything else. Now he was done and without a plan or any financial reward.

Because he was a foreigner, Ryk had the added problem of needing to get a working visa after his student visa expired, so that he could stay in the country to train at UA. He knew the owner of a commercial real estate business in town who was kind enough to hire him and pay for his visa. He got his real estate license and fell into a career that he hated.

Every day, he woke up and went to morning practice, then returned home to put on one of the suits I bought for him. After working all day, he went back to the pool to swim at night. I didn't see him much and when I did, he was angry.

"This dinner is terrible."

"These suits are so uncomfortable."

"I was so slow today in the pool."

"The deal I've been working on for weeks fell through."

Everything sucked because he had to work instead of supporting himself through sponsorships and endorsements. The whole situation was really depressing, but the lowest moment came when I was emptying the pockets of his suits to take them to the dry cleaner (he would have worn them until they could walk away themselves) and found two different lunch punch cards to local strip bars.

"What are these?" I asked him.

"Oh, they're for the lunch at the strip clubs," Ryk said without missing a beat.

"You eat there?" I asked, not believing him, since Tucson strip joints rank up there with some of the most disgusting places on earth. "That's like when guys say they buy *Playboy* for the articles."

"No, they have really good buffets. Rich and Jason from the office and I go."

I couldn't think of anything more desperate than going to a strip club for lunch with your coworkers.

"You are going to catch something from eating the salad," I said, dropping the membership cards on the dresser.

Ryk may have wanted to see girls get naked, but if so, I wasn't one of them. Ever since he moved in, our relationship had hit a new low. We didn't have sex for months; we didn't even hang out together. Ryk went out all the time now, coming home around two a.m. before passing out, but he never wanted me to come along.

"I want to go out with my friends," he told me one night when I finally protested. "I just need a break from you once in awhile."

"They're my friends too," I said. "I'd like to go out too. I don't want to sit at home all the time. Is it really such a big deal? I won't talk to you."

"This is a guys-only night. Next time."

After angrily watching his car lights fade out of view, I tried to find a movie on TV to lose myself in. But suspicion set in and gnawed at my concentration. Why did he protest my going out with him all the time so much? He knew I wouldn't bug him if I went out. I called Ryk's cell phone but he didn't answer. Instead of giving up, I kept calling and calling. But he never answered. It was a psycho move on my part—but unfortunately not the worst one of the night.

I decided to track him down at the bar he told me he was meeting "the guys" at. I walked into the place, which wasn't Ryk's usual kind of dive bar but a more upscale restaurant with a little lounge, and my heart fell into my stomach. From the front, I could see into the lounge, where Ryk and two other guys were sitting with three women I didn't know. This wasn't a guy thing at all. He was out with girls, and really pretty, skinny ones that were way girlier than I could ever manage. Ryk was sipping wine (wine?) while a blonde laughed at something he'd just said. I wanted to take the wine and throw it in his face, but the hostess interrupted my fantasy. "Uh, did you want a table?" she said quizzically, eyeing my messy bun and sweats.

I ran out of the restaurant without answering her and drove home, crying all the way. When Ryk got home and crawled into bed, I was wide awake.

"How was your night?" I asked.

"Good."

"Who was there?"

"Just a couple of guys from the team."

"You're lying! I know you were out with girls."

"They were nobody," he said, too drunk and tired to be concerned with my accusation.

"Am I so disgusting and ugly, you don't want to go out with me? Is that it?"

"No, I love you. They came with the other guys. They're just friends. It's not a big deal . . ."

Ryk fell asleep while I was kept awake for hours by my anger at him, myself, and life. We were never what one would call a stable couple, but now that Ryk and I were under the same roof, all our worst tendencies were impossible to hide. When we clashed, our differences took on a violence neither of us understood or knew what to do with.

We fought on average three times a week—full-on loud, screaming, mean fights.

"I hate you."

"I never want to see your face again."

The biggest fights would end with our breaking up, which sometimes meant he packed up all his stuff (still not more than a couple of bags), moved out, and slept on someone's couch until I begged him to come back. When he returned, there was the brief rush of the reunion. We said we loved each other so much and that we could work through the drama and jealousy. But we didn't work through anything. It was just something we understood people should say, so we said it.

Even though we couldn't resolve our problems or communicate in any way other than through anger, Ryk and I refused to call it quits. We were both competitive athletes uncomfortable with giving up and losing. Instead of accepting that we were horribly wrong for each other and moving on, we looked at breaking up as a failure.

We powered through the pain as if it were one of Frank's grueling sets, digging deeper and deeper into the relationship. I was trapped. I didn't know how to make the situation better, but I couldn't emotionally disengage either.

One night Ryk and I were having a fight—one of so many, its start is totally unmemorable—when I felt as though my feet had been bolted to the floor. I couldn't find my voice or escape the crushing sensation. While Ryk continued to scream and I to cry, I didn't know what happened, but all of a sudden I felt something wet on my hand. I looked down to where I had dug my thumbnail into the webby flesh between my thumb and pointer finger. While angrily but unknowingly rubbing my nail back and forth along the skin, I had opened it. There was so much going on in my body, I hadn't realized I had cut myself.

The sight of the small patch of blood didn't freak me out. Oddly, it came as a relief. I took a breath and walked away from Ryk and our fight. I went into the bathroom and looked at my hand. The skin was ugly and raw and scratched, but I liked looking at it. It didn't hurt. Something had escaped through the tiny cut. I had no way of explaining it, but in that moment it made complete sense. The anger built up inside me had been released through the opening.

I took a Band-Aid out of the medicine cabinet and covered the cut. I wasn't worried about it becoming infected—it was so small— but I didn't want Ryk or anyone else to see my secret and powerful outlet.

After that first time, cutting became my cure. Whenever Ryk and I got into an argument, it was such an easy go-to that it became automatic. Like my purging, which I continued to do sporadically throughout my freshman and the start of my sophomore year, cutting came naturally. I didn't give my actions labels or consequences. It seemed like a no-brainer that if something worked, I should do it. And cutting worked for me. The initial release allowed me to mellow out. I'd return from the bathroom and calmly sit down next to Ryk, who would be obliviously watching sports on TV by that point, and we'd move on without talking.

For a while, I used my finger as I had done that first time. Standing in front of Ryk midfight, I grabbed my arm and dug in. Or if I was sitting down with my knees up to my chest, I dug around my ankles. I quickly graduated to walking into the bathroom during the middle of a fight to find something sharper and more effective. In a rush of pain and need, I grabbed whatever I could find, which was at first a pair of tweezers. I pushed them together to create a point and raked them across my arm in a quick back-and-forth motion like using an eraser to rub out something.

The whole thing happened quickly. About five or ten seconds after I found the tweezers, I was done. My arm had a small red patch with tiny beads of blood, as though I had been scratched by a cat. It didn't hurt because I didn't feel anything. With my system shut down, I pulled the sleeve of my shirt down and returned to the living room composed.

I only had the urge to cut myself in moments of extreme stress, which at that point was only when I was fighting with Ryk. I didn't cut to bleed but rather to soothe. It wasn't for the effect or result of the cut. Once it was done, so was I. Although the process was so short, that's where I found the relief. If I could have made the blood and cut disappear right after the incision, I would have.

That's part of the reason I turned to an eyebrow razor as my preferred tool. I had bought the paper-thin blades set atop a handle that's designed for precision cutting to use on my eyebrows—at least that's what I told myself in the drugstore. When I took them out of their package, I discovered the little knife-like objects were surprisingly sharp.

Although I didn't consider it at the time, this was definitely an escalation. There was a dosage factor involved: tweezers were too little, large razors too much, eyebrow razors just right. The tweezers made thick red marks that looked messy. With an eyebrow razor, I could make a deeper and cleaner cut. One little slice and my skin opened up. The satisfaction of these cuts, so tiny as to be unnoticeable, was immense. They were so small, they healed really well, closing up almost right away. In this way, they were completely private.

I liked to cut across my arm in the meaty section between my elbow and wrist. Sometimes I did one little slice, sometimes three or four in a row. It varied. There was never any thinking, just instinct. After I'd finished, I took it all in, allowing myself to breathe and enjoy the clearheadedness that dried up the darkness sloshing around and threatening to drown me from the inside. I always left the bathroom feeling better than when I entered it.

The finesse of the eyebrow razor allowed me to cut myself more often. But unlike with tweezers, I had to be really careful while I was making the cuts. If I put too much pressure on the razor, it could make the cut too deep. In the out-of-body moments when I cut myself, it was hard to stay in control of my hands doing the work. Luckily, I never went too far.

I wasn't trying to kill myself; it wasn't about that. I wanted the satisfaction of the tiny slice, not the harm of a deep cut. I was trying to figure out how to live in a bad relationship. I didn't want to commit suicide. I desperately wanted attention and approval from someone who refused to give it to me. No matter what I did—drinking as a party girl, winning medals as an Olympic swimmer, or cleaning up as a Stepford wife—nothing worked. Ryk never noticed the scratches or Band-Aids on my arm. When I walked out in the middle of an argument to go to the bathroom, he didn't know if I was cutting myself or getting away from him. And he didn't care.

Usually I only cut myself once a week. It was the same thing as when I threw up; my urges came in waves. There were bad times, and really bad times. After a month-long trip Ryk took to South Africa, I went to pick him up at the airport and couldn't wait to see him because I had missed him so much. My happiness didn't even last the car ride home, during which he told me he had kissed another girl while he was away.

But he won't kiss me.

That time I fell into my own dark world where I cut myself every day for three days straight. I was so enraged, it came to the point where I couldn't be near him without wanting to take a blade to my arm. I felt emotionally and physically sick. I called the only person I knew who would rescue me without any questions: my dad.

"I need to get out of Tucson now," I said. "I need to come home."

My dad bought me a plane ticket, so I could chill out for a few days at home where everyone I was closest to still lived. At school, I had a whole swim team of friends but no best friends. That term was only for those I had made in high school, like Yvette, who had no clue about anything going on but still offered me a necessary break from my crazy life back in Arizona.

I got my cutting spiral under control not only because I didn't want to hurt myself; I also didn't want anyone finding out my secret. I never wanted to cut myself so much or so deeply that people might notice. Being in a swimsuit all the time made hiding my habit harder. When I still used tweezers, people were naturally curious about the scratch when I arrived at swim practice. There was no way I could ever tell the truth.

What happened to your arm?

Oh, I scratched it because it feels good to me.

I knew that was crazy talk and didn't want to get close to having a conversation like that. So instead, I blamed the cuts on my rough-and-tumble lifestyle. I was mountain biking and a twig scratched me. Or a dog did it. I was playing rugby with Ryk. People didn't think twice about it. I had fooled everyone again. Just like my purging, I kept my cutting a controlled secret.

I never planned on telling anyone about this new habit. It wasn't a burden to have this secret. I've always been a very private person who has kept a lot to myself. Telling Frank about my purging had been an anomaly—and a mistake, since it didn't do anything but worry him. If I was concerned about what he'd think of me after hearing that I threw up, I couldn't imagine talking about this thing that was a lot weirder.

Cutting was my own revelation. Through it I could finally solve something.

By the spring of 2001, I was ready to give up college swimming. I had started thinking about going professional right after Sydney but kept going back and forth on the pros and cons of that decision. If I went pro—which meant I would get paid for my sport through sponsorships, prize money, public appearances—I gave up my full ride through college, where you can't take any kind of compensation while competing in the NCAA.

It was a huge risk since I didn't have any endorsement deals lined up or guarantees that I would get any. This wasn't like after the 1996 Games, when I was all over the media. People weren't knocking down the door of a bronze medalist. If I gave up a college scholarship to realize that I couldn't make money, I would be screwed.

However, there was also a risk in my staying in college swimming. I had witnessed case after case of amazing athletes swimming all the way through college and finding nothing for them on the other end. They worked their asses off to have no financial reward or future of any kind. These people, who didn't get any love from the outside world for the dedication and training they poured into winning, wound up in entry-level positions. One swimmer from UA, who was an Olympic gold medalist, went to work on the floor of Victoria's Secret after college.

I wanted something more for myself, something to show for all the hard work I put into my swimming. I would be giving up the college experience and competition with a team I loved, but the idea of going pro sounded appealing. I wanted to become financially independent and wasn't worried about dealing with the media or marketing executives. I never had a problem doing a job. My dream was to be in control of my life, and I was sure—well, pretty sure—that going pro was the best path.

The first thing I needed to do was get an agent. In the world of swimming, there are not that many agents to choose from, so I narrowed down the options quite quickly. One of them was Evan Morgenstein, a straight shooter completely unafraid of honesty in a profession where most people will just tell you what they think you want to hear. We had a series of phone conversations where he talked about my capabilities as a professional swimmer and how to "brand my image." "Sure, we can get you swimming clinics. Then there's the whole swimsuit catalog market," Evan said. "But I don't see why you wouldn't be able to branch out to hair care products and makeup."

As much as I enjoyed Evan hyping me up, I took everything with a grain of salt. I wasn't going to get excited until I had a signed contract in my hand and the project was moving forward. My goal, outside of actual swimming, was to land one big sponsor who would pay me more than what it cost to go to college—so basically $15,000 a year. That wasn't the highest goal in the universe, but I had no interest in setting myself up for failure.

My parents were both on board, which I appreciated immensely. Even though they had been by my side since I entered the sport as a small kid, the concept of a professional swimmer wasn't entirely intuitive. Most people have no clue that professional swimmers even exist, since we're not like basketball or football players who go on tour and play each other. Plus my parents are both teachers, and education is huge for them. Giving up a scholarship was not something they took lightly. But they heard my fears of graduating without a future and my desire to turn my talent in the pool into a career. So with their blessing, in April of 2001, I called Evan and told him it was a go.

Now the only thing left for me to do was tell Frank. Standing outside the door to his office, I had that old feeling of my feet being glued to the floor. This was not a conversation I wanted to have. I thought it highlighted every aspect I tried hard to diminish in myself: selfishness, thoughtless ambition, being a general letdown. I hated abandoning my teammates and, even worse, Frank.

I fought back my nerves and knocked on the door. When I entered, Frank looked at me surprised. I didn't often pay him an office visit. I had blurted out my news before I had a chance to sit down.

"Are you mad at me?" I asked.

"I'm not mad," he said. "I can't say I'm not disappointed. You're an asset to my team, and not just because you are a great swimmer."

Frank always knew exactly what to say to get you.

"I just feel that there is something more out there for me, and I don't want to miss it."

"Okay, if you believe this is the right thing to do, I support you."

Just like my dad, Frank has always been there for me. Strong and constant, he remained part of my backbone in swimming and life. He didn't let my choice to go pro affect our relationship. In fact, he was kind enough to let me continue to train with him and the other members of the UA team—a gesture I'll always be grateful for.

Just a couple of months after my decision, Evan landed me my first deal: a four-year contract with Speedo. That meant I got paid to wear anything the swimwear company made, from goggles to caps to T-shirts, whenever I appeared in any kind of photo or video. I would also appear in the company catalogs and promotional material as well as do autograph events for them.

Not too long after I signed the contract, I had my first photo shoot for the company in Phoenix. A week before, I started to get nervous. I had no idea how to prepare myself for it. I was used to training for things in a very specific way. Doing nothing while waiting around for the shoot to happen set me on edge. In a Phoenix hotel room the night before, I did what I could, which meant make sure my bikini line and legs were shaved. Unwanted hair was an easy target. I also washed my hair and let it dry straight so that the person styling it the next day didn't have to deal with a nasty mess.

I still felt anxious the next day when I got to the set. I wasn't very chatty, trying instead to observe what everyone else was doing so that I didn't get in their way or have to ask too many questions. It wasn't a big-budget shoot. We were taking pictures at an ordinary swimming pool with me wearing typical training one- and two-pieces. I was at home in the environment and used to being photographed in this kind of bathing suit. So my nerves weren't about my body or how it'd look in pictures but rather about doing a good job. This was my first time working for Speedo and the contract with them meant everything to me. I wanted the photos to be amazing, but I didn't have the first idea what that took.

When the photographer, who was really generous and mellow, started taking my picture, I tried to clear my mind and not think about anything so that I wouldn't have an awful expression on my face.

"Amanda, put your chin down," the photographer said. "Look over here."

"Relax your face."

"Hand on your hip."

"Great, now give me a smile."

He talked me through everything, helping me to learn the ropes of taking a decent picture. Taking direction on how to move my body was easy for me. I did that all the time in the water. By giving me constant physical instructions, the photographer made the awkward experience of being photographed completely natural.

When I got my first paycheck, I deposited it straight into my bank account and instantly became the richest person in the world. Coming from being a college kid, living for free in my dad's house and eating ramen noodles, I thought the sum was a fortune. More important than the actual dollar amount, I no longer had to ask my dad for money, which I hated doing. At that moment, I became self-sufficient. I hadn't given up college for nothing. The money I earned off the bat was enough for me to pay my expenses, purchase a new car (a Lincoln Navigator that I still drive), and put a little extra away to buy my very first house, which I did when I was twenty years old.

I felt better about myself than I ever had in my life. There was just one problem: my immediate success in going pro, which brought me so much confidence, was the very thing that Ryk wanted for himself but couldn't achieve. Despite his day job as a commercial real estate agent, he wasn't paying rent. Not only did he have to work a job he hated, but he still wasn't making enough money to support himself and his swimming. He tried so hard to get to that point, but it never came for him. And then here I waltz in with my Speedo deal and suddenly I'm doing what he thought he should have been.

"It's not fucking fair. People are just throwing things at you," I recall him saying to me. "You are living *my* life."

On top of his jealousy of my being able to swim full-time, there was also a cultural dynamic at play that made him totally uncomfortable. He had grown up with a traditional stay-at-home mom and a father who provided. That was the relationship Ryk expected and wanted to have. He couldn't accept that there had been a power shift; I'd gone from struggling freshman to working woman. It made him feel like less of a man on a daily basis that he was living in my house and taking my money. "I want to be able to support my family," he said all the time. "One day I'm going to be the one taking care of you."

Because it bugged him so much that it wasn't working out that way, I never talked about my career even though I was excited about everything happening to me. When Evan called me a month or so after my Speedo contract with the news that I had landed an endorsement deal with Red Bull, I wanted to jump around like I had just drunk three of them. Instead, I got off the phone and quietly returned to the couch, where Ryk was watching TV. I knew he didn't want to hear it.

I decided we needed to get away and forget reality for a weekend. So I booked a flight to Las Vegas and a room at Caesars Palace, because there is no better place to leave reality behind than Vegas. I knew Ryk, who had never been there, would love the overstimulated crazy place, and I wanted to treat us to some fun.

I hadn't been wrong. Ryk did love it. We walked down the strip and into all the hotels, soaking up all the action. When we had our fill of fake world wonders, ice sculptures, and drunken bachelorettes, we returned to Caesars Palace to lie out by the pool and swim under the hot desert sun. Ryk still had plenty to look at; he checked out every chick, his head moving in line with each pair of fake boobs barely concealed by two little triangles of material. The girls he liked (big boobs, bikinis with more sparkle than material, and long, styled hair) were the opposite of me, my flat chest, sporty two-piece, and hair up in a bun. In a rare moment of self-control, I kept my thoughts to myself and let Ryk look. What happens in Vegas stays in Vegas.

That night we had dinner and then went to a club. Our trip was having the exact effect I'd hoped for: Ryk and I weren't fighting. When he was feeling good, Ryk was great to be around—fun and caring. That night, as he held my hand and gave me small kisses on my cheek, he charmed me with the side of him I loved.

Almost as soon as we entered the club, Ryk suggested that I amp up the sentiment by finding some ecstasy.

"You need to do it," he said to me.

I panicked. I had never purchased drugs before. I didn't have the first idea of how to do that. Whom would I go up to and what would I ask?

"I can't do that. I'm scared," I said.

I pictured someone overhearing me ask for ecstasy, recognizing my face, leaking it to a gossip column, it hitting the press, me losing all my sponsorships and endorsements, and Ryk and me living the rest of our days both working commercial real estate together in misery. I didn't care about taking drugs. I just wanted to spend a night with my boyfriend. There was no way I would risk everything to get some pills.

"I don't want to."

"Fine, then we're leaving."

He stalked out of the club, with me in tow, and turned to face me as soon as we got outside.

"I'm sick of this," he yelled. "You go do your thing, and I'll do my own thing. See you later."

There I was, standing on the strip, my boyfriend having just ditched me because I wouldn't score some ecstasy. It was pretty sad.

I returned to our room and broke down in tears. Then I washed my makeup off, got into my pajamas, and literally cried myself to sleep. When I woke in the morning, Ryk was next to me in the bed. We both got up, showered, changed, went to breakfast, and didn't discuss what had happened the night before. We went about our last day in Vegas like some beaten-down couple who've been in a loveless marriage for twenty years.

I had financial stability but lacked emotional maturity. Even though I was now making more money than Ryk, I continued to seek his approval. I was in love with him and didn't want to give up on us. My cutting still followed on the heels of bad fights with Ryk, yet I didn't put two and two together. I wouldn't allow myself to think ours wasn't a healthy relationship. I wasn't ready to let go even if it meant my slicing myself open to stay.

Something small, though, did shift that night in Vegas. When Ryk suggested that I buy drugs, perhaps unconsciously trying to sabotage the night and my career, I drew a line in the sand. I told him no.

I pushed through the water and into the noisy roar of the stadium. Scrolling up to the top line of the scoreboard, I found my name and then my time. My mouth fell open in disbelief, and I squinted to make sure I was seeing right: 2:22.99.

I had matched the world record time for the 200-meter breaststroke.

No one on that warm July night at the 2003 FINA World Championships in Barcelona was more shocked than me. Not only was the record set by China's Qi Hui two years earlier thought to have been untouchable but my usual times had been nowhere near it. I had dropped two and a half seconds from my best time in the race, which was ridiculous. You do that when you are a ten-year-old kid, not a twenty-one-year-old who's been swimming for seventeen years.

I had gone into the championships feeling good. Since going pro, I had continued to train with Frank at the UA pool, where things hadn't changed much for me. I had the same coach, same workouts, same times. They were solid and similar to what I had done at the 2000 Olympics. The only difference was that I was making money off races, but when you are swimming, you aren't thinking about that. It's a nice bonus but totally irrelevant in the water.

Barcelona was beyond a career high. It was a miracle. I won the 100-meter breaststroke as well, but I had no explanation for what happened in the 200-meter. In that moment, I tapped into the potential I had had within me this whole time.

When I got back to my hotel room, which I was sharing with a roommate who was resting, I went straight into the bathroom to use the phone in there to call Ryk, who was also staying in the hotel to compete in the championships (finally that phone they put by the toilet had a purpose). I had looked for Ryk after the race but couldn't find him anywhere. Still buzzing from the high of my amazing win, I was dying to talk to him.

"Hi!" I said.

"Hey."

His tone didn't sound like that of a boyfriend super pumped that his girlfriend just had the race of her life. I could hear he was upset.

"Sorry I didn't get to talk to you after the race."

"I got out of there pretty quickly."

"Okay. Well, what did you think?"

"Not much."

What the hell? This conversation was like pulling teeth.

"What's wrong?"

"Nothing. I'm trying to get ready for my race."

"I don't get it. Aren't you happy for me?"

"Don't give me that shit. I saw you with Ian after the race, and *he* looked very happy. You don't need me anymore. He'll be happy for you."

Then he hung up. I put the receiver down and began bawling. I raced from the top of the world down to a loser crying on the toilet. Ian Thorpe, whom I had gotten to be friends with after the last Olympics, had been genuinely excited for me after my race and gave me the warm congratulations he offered any of his friends. I didn't understand Ryk's anger at all. Ian was a terrific guy but the last person Ryk should have been jealous of.

My relationship with Ian was solidified when he took me as his date to the 2002 Australian Swimmer of the Year awards about a year after going pro. I was already in Australia for a World Cup swim meet when Ian asked me to go. "I need a date," he said in his easygoing way. "I'll change your flight back home if you want to stay an extra day. I'll buy you a dress and handle everything."

I said yes, because it sounded fun. But I had no idea how fun Ian could make things. He made good on his promise of the dress, sending me to a designer that he thought I'd like. He was right; the dresses were gorgeous. The saleslady told me that Mr. Thorpe said I could pick out anything I liked. It was a wonderful Cinderella moment. I chose a black halter top dress with lace on the top and tulle around the skirt. Very Cinderella.

The night was a blast. The guy goes above and beyond. Never once leaving my side, Ian introduced me to everyone and made me feel a part of every conversation. He pulled my chair out at dinner and didn't let me pay for a single thing. I was stunned that someone who is a superstar in his own country could also be so down to earth. His generosity didn't stop with the awards evening. I had been bummed out because I missed Thanksgiving while in Australia. At some point, I must have mentioned to Ian that the thing I missed most was pumpkin pie, because he had a chef make me one (he couldn't find pumpkin pie in any bakery) and sent it to my room. There is a level of nice, and then there is Ian.

Our relationship was hard to describe. We were very romantic and affectionate, holding hands and hugging. But it never went beyond that. There was no passion between us. We had our chances to hook up—sometimes I slept in his room during swim meets—but we never got physical with each other. Ian wooed me like a boyfriend, better than a boyfriend actually. He sent me designer dresses for Christmas and my birthday, paid for all our meals together, bought me a gold ring, and arranged for me to borrow jewelry to wear to events. He took pleasure in giving me things, and I was happy to receive them. Still, we never took our relationship to any level other than friendship. We never talked about us dating, and there was no undercurrent of desire. We were just very good friends.

Even though Ian and I weren't romantically linked, he opened my eyes to the fact that Ryk, while he might have been my boyfriend, wasn't my friend. When we were together, Ian put my needs first, and we weren't even sleeping together. The day after I hit the world record, Ian sent a huge bouquet of flowers to my room. It wasn't just the size of the arrangement that made me happy but also the fact that it was filled with gerbera daisies, my favorite flower. That someone caring and nice thought I was special enough to mark my success lifted my spirits. The flowers brought me back toward my initial high after Ryk had sent me crashing down. But they also highlighted how wrong things were with Ryk and me.

Returning to Tucson, Ryk and I swept our argument under the rug with countless other unresolved fights and got back to life as usual. Nothing changed. He worked at the real estate office and swam; I swam and did whatever gigs came my way; we fought and made up.

Then one evening in early 2004, we were having yet another random fight and Ryk shouted that he was moving out, which he did all the time, and instead of crying and begging him to stay, I was okay with it. Normally my role was to tell him things like "Please don't" or "We can work it out." But this time, I didn't have it in me. I wish I could say I was finally standing up for myself, but in truth I was simply exhausted. I was twenty-two years old and couldn't go through the drill one more time. I was so beaten and broken down that I could no longer put up a fight.

I left the house while he packed up his stuff (he still had so little, he could do it all himself in only a few hours). If it got this far, then our ritual usually involved me calling him at his friend's house after a few days and pleading for him to come home. I don't know if Ryk left for attention and the satisfaction of my coming after him, but now I didn't. I was just fine alone in my home.

A week or two later, I packed up every little thing of his that he'd left behind, probably thinking he'd be back soon anyway: every trinket from South Africa, every piece of memorabilia from the course of our relationship, and every single photo with him in it. I was so done that if I saw another picture of Ryk, I'd burn the whole house down. I threw everything into a box, drove it over to where he was staying, and handed it to him, saying, "I don't want this stuff in my house." His expression was one of total shock. He was surprised to see me standing up for myself and to know that he wasn't going to be moving back in next week.

Like a light switch, I was ready to move on, but the rest of the world needed a little more time. At the start of the summer of the 2004 Olympics, Evan called me with exciting news. *Vanity Fair* wanted to include me in its Olympics issue. There was only one catch: they thought Ryk and I were still a couple and wanted us to pose together.

It was an honest mistake made by Bruce Weber, the very famous photographer who looks like a funky Santa Claus, when he came to a swim meet to shoot swimmers for the issue. He had met me and

Ryk separately but wanted to photograph us together when he heard we were an item.

Ryk and I agreed to it immediately. While it was annoying to pretend I was his girlfriend, it was a no-brainer in terms of business. Leading up to the Olympics, you couldn't buy the kind of publicity appearing in a huge mainstream publication like *Vanity Fair* offered. For the shoot we flew together from Arizona to L.A., where they had so considerately booked us one room at the Standard on Sunset. Of course a real couple would only need one room in the sexy boutique hotel. We didn't want to chance the *Vanity Fair* people's finding out, so we didn't get another room. Instead, I ordered two martinis from room service to prepare for the shoot.

It wasn't hard pretending on set, since we had never been a lovey-dovey couple. We just didn't tell people that we weren't together—even when they made the comments everyone always did when we were together. "Oh my God, it must be so fun going to the Olympics as a couple," said a makeup artist making conversation. "Your kids will be *so* athletic!"

Enduring annoying comments and a night with Ryk was a small price to pay for the gorgeous photograph (where our heads are together but we are tellingly looking off into separate directions) that appeared in the magazine with the caption "This year marks the second time that Ryk Neethling, who's been described as the 'endurance machine,' and Amanda Beard, who won a gold and two silvers in 1996 at age 14, will be traveling to the games as a couple."

Relieved *not* to be with Ryk at the Athens Olympics, I was extremely confident with myself and my swimming. I was a twenty-two-year-old who owned her own home, paid all her bills, and had *broken the world record in the 200-meter breaststroke at the 2004 U.S. Olympic trials*. I'm not big on records or stats, but it felt pretty amazing. Everything was looking up. I was single and perfectly fine with that. Without the distraction of those crazy emotional blowout fights Ryk and I used to have constantly, all I needed to concentrate on was my swimming. Easy. Despite the pressure of the international event, I felt a kind of peace because I was in control of my world. No matter how many unhappy times I'd had with Ryk, I hadn't realized how much I was suffering until it was over.

I won silver in the 200-meter individual medley and 400-meter medley relay, and my first individual gold medal in the 200-meter breaststroke. Standing on top of the podium, all by myself, I still felt a twinge of self-consciousness. But any awkwardness was no match for the pride I had in myself and the awe of the moment. All those early mornings, meters logged underwater, pain I pushed through— everything finally paid off in one overwhelming instant. With that gold medal around my neck, I felt like a winner for the first time.

Outside my family, the only other person I really wanted to share my win with was Ian. He and I hung out all the time during the Games. We were best friends, who walked around downtown Athens on our time off, shopping and dining out. He was so easy to be around; we never ever fought. There was nothing for us to fight about. We quickly got into a rhythm, doing a lot of media during the day, grabbing a bite, and then heading together to whatever party was happening that night.

Ryk's attitude toward Ian never let up, not even after we broke up. It made him incredibly upset that we were spending so much time together. If he saw me standing next to Ian at a party, Ryk refused to say hello, preferring to glare at us from the other side of the room. I sensed Ryk was mad that Ian continued to beat him at swimming, and my allegiance with his enemy felt like a betrayal. He was jealous and uncomprehending of our friendship.

I couldn't really blame him for being confused. Rumors swirled in the media and online swimming forums that Ian and I were a couple—especially after our trip to Las Vegas together two months before the Olympics. The entire Australian team had been training nearby, so Ian thought it would be fun to blow off some steam in Sin City and invited me along. I bunked with him and two other guys, all of us smushing into one hotel room as if it was camp.

As usual, Ian made it his mission to spoil me. He gave me money to gamble with and wanted to take me shopping. While we were walking through an arcade of boutiques in one of the big hotels, we passed a cheesy jewelry shop with an array of blinding cubic zirconias in the window. There were all kinds of engagement rings for those who impulsively decide to get hitched in Vegas but don't want to make too much of a financial commitment.

Ian turned to me, his face beaming, and said, "Let's buy a ring!" At first I thought he was making an out-of-character bad style choice, but he explained his thinking: because no one could figure us out, it would be fun to really confuse them with a fake engagement. And what better for that than a fake engagement ring? I was all aboard for pulling a prank, so we went inside and bought a big old honking ring with black diamond baguettes surrounding a huge fake cushion-cut diamond. It was a brilliant choice since Ian loves black diamonds, giving the ring an air of authenticity.

That night for dinner, we met up with about twenty members of the Australian swim team (including his coach and top swimmers Grant Hackett, Michael Klim, and Geoff Heugill), when Ian stood up to make a toast. "Amanda and I have a big announcement. You are about to enjoy our reception dinner," he said, as jaws around the table dropped, "because Amanda and I got married today."

Everyone believed him and started freaking out. Red-faced, giggling, and showing off my "engagement ring," I waited for Ian to tell the truth and give everyone a good laugh. But he kept going and going. He had a whole story about how we went to the courthouse and got the papers and then found this cute wedding chapel.

"Amanda doesn't love the ring setting but she loves the stones," he said. "We are going to have it reset."

Who knew Ian had such a good imagination and acting skills? Although eventually Ian came clean that the whole thing was a joke, someone at the dinner had already made a phone call and leaked it to the Australian press. Later we were both bombarded by media requests wanting to know if it was true and if we would grant interviews about our new marriage. Ian's mom didn't think the prank was so funny. Seeing the reports in the Australian press, she freaked out and thought her son had gotten married without consulting her.

I wasn't sure what Ryk had read, heard, or believed. But at a party in Athens after the Olympic swimming events were over, a good friend of Ian's made a comment to one of Ryk's teammates that "I was with the Australian boys now." Ian, Ryk, and I weren't at the party, but the Australian and South African swimmers came to blows.

When I got back to Tucson, Ryk was sick of me and America. He called to get mad at me one more time. He expressed his supreme contempt that Ian and I had become so close.

"I can't believe it," he said. "To think I was looking at wedding rings online and was going to propose right after the Olympics."

We hadn't been together for months. I couldn't understand how Ryk's brain worked. It was the last insane moment in a long string of them between us. After that, he moved back to South Africa for good.

chapter 9

I knew my hair wasn't great, but I had no idea it was that bad. The photographer and hairstylist argued about the problem on top of my head as if I weren't sitting right there.

"This is not sexy hair," the photographer said.

"I know. We have to put in the extensions," the hairstylist replied. "Otherwise it'll be a disaster."

"We don't have time for that. We've only got the studio for two more hours. We won't have time for the shot. You'll just have to make do with what's there."

"You're kidding me, right?"

The photographer walked away, meaning yes, she'd have to work with my crappy hair. The stylist fingered the hair that fell an inch below my ears as if it had just been retrieved from the garbage. Apparently short hair is not sexy, and for this shoot for the men's magazine *Maxim*, I had to be sexy.

I felt terrible as the hairdresser began to apply her products. I had never thought about my hair in the sexy sense until right this moment. (For a swimmer, whose hair is always wet, a short cut is the only practical one.) I felt stupid and worried that the entire shoot was screwed because of my ignorance. My hair, which no one had ever paid too much attention to before, including me, was a monumental catastrophe.

I had been surprised when Evan first told me that the magazine, which featured hot women seductively posing in barely-there bathing suits or lingerie, wanted me in their 2004 August issue featuring Anna Kournikova on the cover.

"They want to do a photo shoot with you," Evan said. "It'll only take three hours while you're in New York anyway for your meetings about the Olympics."

Immediately my mind went to the gorgeous blonde tennis player who guys lusted after; I didn't want to be compared with her. *I don't match up. I'm not bad, just normal.* Whoever thought to put me in their magazine had the wrong idea about me. Sure, as a fit athlete who'd accomplished a lot in the pool, I could take photos for Speedo or Red Bull. But I was far from supermodel material. The misconception that I was some hot swimmer chick who hung out in skimpy bathing suits made me uncomfortable. I wished they knew what I really looked like. Then I doubted they'd want me for the photo shoot. I pictured my walking onto the set and the collective response being, *Oh crap.*

Despite my fears, I wasn't going to turn down the offer. There weren't a ton of swimmers who got opportunities to be in a popular magazine like *Maxim.* For what I was trying to accomplish in my sport, I had to raise my profile, and for that I had to do anything that came my way. If I got to New York and they were disappointed, that would be their problem, not mine. I had to put my pride aside and take a chance, because this was business. More exposure meant more opportunity.

"Great," I said to Evan. "Just tell me where I need to be."

If I wanted exposure, that's what I got in the New York photo studio, where the bright white light streaming in from the huge windows exposed every little bump, pore, and stray hair. I actually didn't mind the tiny string bikini that I had to wear (the hallmark of the magazine), because I'm not shy in swimsuits, which I wear all the time. It was everything else that bothered me.

If they thought my hair was unsexy, I couldn't imagine what they were going to make of my super hot posing style—or lack thereof. The sexiest thing I'd ever done in a picture was cross my legs on a diving board, still giving my best all-American-girl smile. When the photographer called me over to start, I was more nervous than I had been for my last Olympic race.

"Okay, Amanda, I want you to put your shoulders back and put your hands on the front of your thighs."

I did exactly what he said.

"Lower your head, look up to me with your eyes."

"Relax your face and your lips."

"Take your left thumb and push the top of your bikini bottom a little bit. A little bit more. A little bit more. Too much. Perfect."

As the photographer told me how to move my body, I realized being sexy for these magazines was achieved by the same mechanism as any look in any magazine. Whether wholesome or vixen, it came through the photographer's direction. I didn't have to be sexy or think about being sexy (in fact, it was better if I didn't think about anything at all because it led to that awful thinking face). I certainly didn't feel sexy, but that didn't matter either. All I had to do was follow direction. Like a mannequin, I was created purely through another person's vision of how I should look.

The photographer knew what he was doing, because I made it into *Maxim* and, on the heels of that shoot, was offered another pictorial for another men's magazine, *FHM*. This time I was in the running for the cover of their September 2004 Sexy Olympic Special, also featuring pro volleyball player Logan Tom; track stars Amy Acuff and Jenny Adams; and another pro swimmer, Haley Cope.

The magazine agreed to photograph me in Orlando, where I was competing in a swim meet. The location scout had found the perfect place for the shoot—an outpatient hospital-style clinic not currently in use. No sleek pool with cocktails to put me in the mood. Nope, instead I had a rehab pool with an apparatus to lower in people who used wheelchairs. Hot.

I strode past the oxygen tank on the wall in a white bikini and heels, feeling like a massive fool. I know heels make legs look longer and leaner, but everything felt out of proportion. My bathing suit was tiny and my hair huge. The poor hairdresser had spent hours putting in extensions so that I would finally have sexy hair in a place where people tried to overcome life-altering accidents. This was for a chance at the cover (a lot, a lot of exposure), however, so I had to shove my self-consciousness aside again and get down to business.

The all-day shoot, which started with a 6:00 a.m. call time and didn't wrap until after 8:00 p.m., was the longest I'd ever done at that point and beyond exhausting. I was antsy and irritated by the end— partly due to the fact that I didn't eat very much when I was on the set. The last thing you want to do when you're being photographed in three triangles of fabric is to chow down on a big meal, or actually put anything more than a carrot in your stomach. Mostly, however, I was worried the pictures were going to be bad. I really, really, really wanted to be on the cover, because it would be huge for my career.

Thanks to hours and hours of hair and makeup, great photography, and some serious Photoshopping, the pictures came out awesome and I landed the cover alongside Logan Tom. I'm not sure if it's sexy or not, but Logan and I have these expressions on our faces like we'll tear the head off any man that gets near us.

Apparently, guys like it when you look like you are about to kill them, because that cover got me a lot of attention from them. I was genuinely surprised by how many people saw it, and how many out of those told me directly, "You look *hot*." I knew the photos were supposed to be sexy, but having someone say it to my face made me really uncomfortable—especially when they were guys I hardly knew or hadn't heard from in a hundred years.

Dudes from as far back as high school crawled out of the woodwork after the magazine hit the newsstands. I got texts, emails, and even phone calls from them either pretending to catch up or getting directly to the point and asking me out because they wanted to date the girl in the photo, or at least be seen out in public with her. The most annoying call came a week or so after the magazine came out.

"Amanda. Hi!" an anonymous male voice said.

"Hello. Who is this?"

"It's John from high school."

John Bell, the scruffy and shy skater who broke my heart with his crush on Miss Perfect, Kristin Riley, during those dark days of high school. He was the last guy on earth I thought would call me.

"How've you been?" he asked.

"Pretty good, I guess."

"When are you going to be back in town?"

"Christmas, I guess. I'm not really sure."

"It'd be really cool to hang out."

"Yeah. I'll call you. But I gotta go now. Sorry. I'm kind of in the middle of something."

"Sure. Cool. No problem. It'll be awesome to see you. By the way, I checked out your photos in *FHM*. Man, you look great. Really great. Heh, heh."

I couldn't have been more turned off. There was no way I would call him when I went home. In fact, if I saw John by chance, I planned on running the other way. I didn't care if someone was a friend, old crush, or possible new love interest, if he acted like a slimeball about my photos, he was an instant write-off.

My new sexy image made dating even harder than it already was. I couldn't be sure of a guy's motive when he asked me out. Did he want a sex kitten or arm candy to show off, or did he actually like me? Because I was neither of those things, I took a risk on a cute University of Arizona basketball player who was part of a group I still hung out with even though I no longer went to school there. I liked him, and we had a lot of fun together, but it was short-lived. I quickly realized that he only wanted to hang out with me in public. He asked me to attend his basketball games or to hang out at crowded parties and bars, but he never wanted to go to the movies or spend a quiet night at home. Finally it dawned on me: *This guy doesn't like me.* After that I stopped giving any guy a chance because I didn't trust any of them. I would have to be top-to-bottom impressed with someone and absolutely sure that he wanted to be with me and not a *Maxim* girl the next time around. Until then, my friends were all the companionship I needed.

After appearing in *FHM*, I got chopped from one of my sponsors—a huge American corporation that felt my pictures weren't "the way they wanted their company to be viewed, and I wasn't the kind of person they wanted associated with it." They weren't the only ones who didn't want to be associated with me anymore. A clinic where I was scheduled to hold a four-hour workshop for a hundred kids looking for pointers on their strokes was canceled because the parents felt I wasn't a good role model. Their reaction was absurd. I was in a sport where I was half-dressed all the time. Swimming, however, is typically reserved for the conservative country-club set, and they didn't want their kids to be around the likes of me.

There was also the group that thought I was degrading women in sports by posing in men's magazines. I don't know how many times I'd seen the cover of health, fitness, or fashion magazines with male athletes topless and preening. Yet nobody was bothered by their showing off the bodies they got from working so hard at their sport. Why couldn't I do the same? A female runner on a magazine cover in a revealing outfit was ripped apart for a million different reasons, but put a shirtless football player on one and the general reaction is *He's buff!* The double standard angered me.

At first I was really angry. I couldn't stand that people I didn't even know judged me based on a couple of magazines. It seemed so unfair and superficial. After ranting to Dad and Yvette, who listened patiently, I took a deep breath and recognized that I was the one who chose to put that image of myself out there. The only way the public knew of me was through the media and the way I participated in it. I had to take my personal feelings out of any backlash. I made business decisions, which opened some doors while at the same time closing others.

Happily, I didn't get any grief from the really important people in my life—my friends and family. All the folks I knew from growing up in Southern California, where hanging out in bathing suits was second nature, thought my pictures were awesome. Even my seventy-five-year-old grandma, who also happens to be my number one fan, loved them. Knowing that in real life I was anything but a slut, she commented, "Ooh. That is a little scandalous. But you look very beautiful. As always."

Most important, I was happy. Appearing in those magazines had been a successful career move for me. It's hard for a swimmer, whom most people only see once every four years at the Olympics, to get any name recognition. It's even harder to get people to know your face, because in the water everyone looks the same. Whatever anyone thought about those images, they had a big impact. They put a face on a swimmer otherwise hidden by a cap, goggles, and swimsuit identical to every other swimmer's in the world. In the quest to make myself as recognizable to the public as possible, and in turn bring in more sponsorships, those shots were invaluable.

My *Maxim* and *FHM* pictorials opened doors for television work, such as stints as a commentator for Fox Sports, ESPN, and VH1, which increased my fan base and contacts in the industry. There was a growing number of people who had no idea what I had accomplished in the pool but liked my image. In 2004 I supplanted Anna Kournikova as the most downloaded female athlete on Google, MSN, Yahoo, and Lycos. Not too long before, I had thought I didn't come anywhere close to her, and now I had surpassed her, according to the Internet?

When Evan called to tell me the news, I was happy but also confused.

"What the hell are people downloading?" I asked. There wasn't that much stuff of me out there.

"What do you think? Your boobs."

My boobs? I had always been hard on myself, particularly my appearance, but there's nothing like having your picture taken professionally to make you feel really bad about yourself. From my boobs to my feet, I never knew just how many things were wrong with the way I looked until I started modeling. As my career picked up and I did more photo shoots, I became intimately acquainted with all my flaws, thanks to the host of professionals on set to pick them out.

"Your eyebrows are awful!" a makeup artist said. "You look like a drag queen. Did you do these yourself?"

"Are you a heavy smoker?" another asked. "You're not? Really? I totally thought you were because the skin on your upper lip is ten shades darker than the rest of your face. Weird."

"Jesus, what are we going to do with that pimple in the middle of your face?"

"Do you *ever* wear sunscreen? Your skin is so damaged."

"Your cuticles are really rough."

They picked me apart, looking at every detail, each of which had its own issue. I grew a thicker skin, but even an elephant's hide couldn't completely protect me from the barrage of complaints. Some days I could block everything out and some days I couldn't. I began to see myself through the critical eye of a professional who works with the most beautiful women on earth—and the results were harsh. I didn't complain or argue, because these people knew what they were talking about and I wanted to succeed in this job. I was lucky to be in this position. So I took what anybody said very seriously and did my best to fix it. The list of things I needed to do to look better was endless:

Grow my eyebrows out and have them done professionally every two weeks.

Apply skin-lightening cream to my upper lip.

Purchase a two-hundred-dollar anti-acne serum.

Slather myself with SPF 600 even in winter.

Get a manicure every week.

It was universally agreed that my hair sucked. In almost every photo shoot, they had to go through the long, expensive, and annoying process of filling my head with fake hair. I knew it bugged everyone (including me), so I made it my mission to get long, thick hair. Ever since I was a kid, I had worn it short for convenience. For a swimmer, it's extremely annoying to have long hair. Not only is it a pain in the ass to shove it all under the tight rubber of the cap and it's heavy when you're in the water but you wind up spending ages getting the knots out, and it always seems to be wet. But I didn't want people to be upset with me every time I showed up at a shoot with my short, unsexy hair. For a whole year, I wore hair extensions and grew my hair out until it was long enough that only the occasional hairstylist complained it wasn't thick enough.

Modeling helped my confidence level in my business and swimming life. It made me feel special to be able to make money from being an athlete, because I understood how rare that is. But it didn't do anything to improve the negative vision I had about my physical self. When I looked at myself in magazines, I wasn't looking at me. There were two different Amanda Beards. There was the one on the page, who had undergone four hours of hair and makeup, expert styling, professional lighting, and Photoshop. The reality of me was not so pretty; in the flesh, I was an ugly version of the *Maxim* and *FHM* girl. I wasn't a *real* model, who did fashion shows or ads. I booked jobs because of my abilities as a swimmer. Advertisers wanted me for my medals and times, not my looks.

I couldn't stand when others misidentified my job. At a cocktail party in New York that I attended to meet industry people, some corporate guy looked confused for a split second after Evan's introduction. When the confusion disappeared, he smiled, and said, "Oh yeah, you're that model."

I wanted to shout, *No, I'm not!* I hated when people would say I'm a model. I was an athlete who did photo shoots. Putting the label "model" on me set an unrealistic standard for me to live up to; a model is gorgeous and that is not how I felt.

I definitely wasn't skinny enough to be a real model. Stylists accused me of having love handles or got frustrated after I couldn't wear half the suits they'd chosen because of the way the bottoms cut into my hips.

My worst fears about my body were realized after a photo shoot in 2005. A day or two after the shoot, Evan called me and atypically beat around the bush.

"This is so stupid," he said. "I can't even believe I have to say this to you. It's absurd."

"What?"

"It's about the photo shoot. It's really dumb."

"What!"

"They weren't happy with the photos."

"Why not?"

"They want you to slim down."

"Okay."

"And they want you to lose the weight before the next photo shoot."

I waited until I hung up the phone to start crying. The people on the photo shoot thought I looked so fat and ugly that they had to do something. I was so humiliated.

I didn't wallow in self-pity for long. I didn't have time; I had to lose enough weight to make a visible difference in less than two weeks. That's when the company was paying for another big, expensive shoot. I couldn't risk their losing money on me and cutting my sponsorship. So I went on an intense crash diet that involved a lot of black coffee and TrimSpa pills (the ones that employed Anna Nicole Smith as a spokesperson) and not much of anything else.

After two days of black coffee in the morning, raw vegetables for lunch, a salad (no dressing) for dinner, and TrimSpa throughout the day, I had no energy and a serious case of the shakes. But I didn't give up, and it worked; I lost 10 pounds in two weeks and got my weight down to a wiry 120 pounds.

I was still nervous when I got on set for the second shoot. There was the same crew as the last time, which made me totally insecure. I kept on sneaking glances at their expressions or listening to hear any comments. Shaky, starving, and exhausted, I was desperate to know what they were thinking. I read lots of meaning into the littlest details, paranoid from too little food and too much caffeine. I slipped off my robe and stood in front of the camera.

Halfway through the shoot, while we were on break, a representative, whose job it was to make sure the photo shoot stayed on message and produced the images the company wanted for the campaign, approached me. Dressed in a crisp polo tucked into a pair of khaki pants, he stood out from the sea of jeans and black or white T-shirts worn by everyone else.

"You are looking really good," he said with a smile. "Really fit."

I represented the ideal athlete, super slim and defined. Only, this type of definition came from lack of muscle as well as a lack of body fat. My look was completely unrealistic for anyone truly competing in a sport. It put me in an impossible situation: be skinny *and* be strong.

I returned from the shoot and slumped on my couch. I could feel one of my down moods start to wash over me. I had no idea how to talk about the things I was feeling and going through: the end of my relationship with Ryk, the pressure to stay thin for shoots, and the future of my swimming career. I wasn't even aware of the growing negative emotions inside me.

Those moms who canceled my clinic with their kids had been right. I wasn't a role model to anyone. I was a horrible person, but nobody really knew how horrible. Everyone got to see hot, confident Amanda with a big smile. When I was alone, I felt like I was falling down a huge hill, hitting every bump on the way to the bottom.

Miserable and lonely, I didn't want to leave my house or talk to anyone. To bring myself out of it, make my pain more concrete and manageable, I again turned to cutting. About once a month, I made the little slices in my skin that let me return to my life without pause. I had done it a lot more when I was with Ryk, but now that he was gone, I hadn't stopped looking for the quick fix.

Only once did a makeup artist comment on the scratches on my arm.

"Man, you're banged up," she said.

I gave an excuse from the usual list—a dog, mountain biking, roughhousing.

"No problem. We can fix that," she said, and got to work with concealer and foundation.

Bingeing was no longer a problem, because I had stopped eating. I no longer touched anything fried or with cheese. *Bread* was a dirty word and pasta not on any menu ever. A week or two before a photo shoot, I stopped eating altogether, which had proven successful in the past. Then it was just a lot of plain raw vegetables, coffee, and diet pills. Once during a preshoot fast, I went to the movies to get my mind off my hunger. But someone a few seats away from me was eating popcorn. Rich, buttery, salty, crunchy, delicious popcorn. All I could think about for the entire two hours was her popcorn and how I wasn't going to eat it. *I will not eat popcorn. I will not go to the concession stand. I will not . . .*

I no longer looked like an athlete, although I pretended to be one for the camera. Having lost a lot of muscle tone, I was petite. I didn't look healthy, because I wasn't. I had zero energy. Since I wasn't really training, however, energy wasn't crucial. After the 2004 Olympics, I was at a crossroads. At an age when most swimmers hang up their goggles, I had earned the right to end on a high note. But that wasn't the real reason I stopped focusing on my swimming. The real reason was Carl.

I first met the stock car driver Carl Edwards at a race that Yvette and I attended in Fontana when I was looking to blow off a little steam immediately after the Olympics. The meeting was brief but apparently made an impression on him. Six months later, after being told he was going to do a postrace, on-air interview with an Olympic swimmer, he got himself all dolled up—doing his hair and putting on his best outfit, because he assumed I was the swimmer. The swimmer, however, turned out to be Amy Van Dyken. Although Amy was a six-time Olympic gold medalist, Carl was disappointed.

He wound up confiding in Amy about how he had a crush on me. "You would make such a cute couple!" she said, getting his number and telling him she'd handle it. Amy passed it on to Evan, who in turn called me.

"Carl Edwards is into you and wants you to call him," Evan said.

"I'm not going to call him," I said. "But I'm interested. If you want to give him my number and have him call me, that'd be fine."

Ten minutes later Carl called.

He was incredibly sweet and up-front from the first minute. Like a little boy, he explained exactly what he had been thinking ("After we met in Fontana, I wanted to talk to you.") and what he wanted to happen ("Can we start talking on the phone?"). And that's exactly what we did. For the next three weeks or so, we talked a lot, sometimes a couple of times a day. We were so flirty that the chemistry between us was evident even over the phone. When Carl suggested we meet in person, I wanted to find out how our chemistry would play out in real life just as much as he did.

We decided to meet up in San Francisco one weekend in the spring of 2005, since he was testing cars on the track in nearby Napa Valley, and I could stay with Taryn, who had moved there. Waiting in my sister's apartment for him to come pick me up, I was as nervous as a thirteen-year-old on her first date. Finally the buzzer rang and I bolted outside.

There he was, leaning against his rental car, a blond-haired, blue-eyed all-American boy. He came right up to me, and the first thing he said was, "Don't I get a kiss?" Then he grabbed me and kissed me. A *real* kiss. I didn't have time to think, but if I had, I would have been shocked. We weren't even in his car yet. Then, as if to show the complete opposite side of him, he spit his gum out and tried to kick it before it hit the ground. But when he swung his leg, his shoe flew off his foot and landed on another car. I breathed a sigh of relief; here was an honest-to-goodness dork.

I instantly liked Carl. He was sweet and funny. A well-mannered man, but not so gentlemanly that I didn't get to experience our very, very real chemistry. Everything went so well between us that first weekend, he invited me to join him the following weekend in Phoenix for a race. A huge fan of NASCAR, I love the sound and the smells of the sport, so I said yes. Right after that, he said, he wanted me to fly home with him to meet his family.

This was not a speed I was accustomed to, having just come out of an attention-starved relationship, but I was more than happy to oblige Carl, who showed how into me he was in every possible way. That wasn't the only difference between him and my ex. Unlike Ryk, who had been raised in a perfect family and house tended to by a staff, Carl grew up dirt-poor with a difficult dad. His childhood memories were of his mom crying because she didn't have enough money to fix a broken microwave.

Although he made enough money as a driver to buy his own small plane, he still maintained a mostly frugal attitude toward life. He was a man of very simple tastes. Carl was perfectly content to wear the same shorts and shirt all week. Once I went shopping for him and bought a few really soft, expensive designer T-shirts to class up his look, only to find a few days later that he had cut off all their sleeves, turning them instantly into white-trash wear. He didn't get vanity. "Oh my God, one of the driver's wives spent two hundred dollars on face cream," he said to me. "Isn't that such shit? I could get her fifty bottles of the stuff back home for that." I spent a hundred dollars on my face cream, but I wasn't about to tell him that. "Yeah. That's really stupid," I said.

On my first trip to his hometown of Columbia, Missouri, where the NASCAR scene is a big deal, everyone knew who Carl was. And I had just come off the 2004 Olympics, so a lot of people recognized me too. In the gas station, diner, or grocery store, they got a kick out of seeing the two of us together and wanted our autographs or picture.

Strangers in town weren't the only ones who liked seeing Carl and me together. His brother, mom, and stepdad didn't blink an eye that Carl had brought home a girl he barely knew, and they welcomed me warmly. I got along especially well with his mom, Nancy, an outgoing and beautiful blonde whose makeup, hair, and outfits were always perfectly done.

"Carl told me so much about you," she said in the direct manner her son had inherited. "He said you were beautiful, but my goodness, you're gorgeous."

She was really easy to like, and the two of us spent a lot of time around her kitchen table while Carl visited various local car garages. A couple of times, his mom and I went out to have a glass of wine, which we didn't tell Carl about. He didn't drink alcohol and didn't want anyone around him drinking it either. I quickly discovered why he was so sensitive to it after meeting his dad.

When we visited his dad, who had abused alcohol ever since Carl was a kid, we found him already out of control in the shack where he lived. While showing off his motorcycle to Carl, he pointed to me and said, "Make sure your bitch doesn't fall off if you take her out on it." On the drive back to his mom's house, Carl apologized for his dad. "My dad's always been a jerk," he explained with a tone that said he was used to it.

That was the only dose of reality in my relationship with Carl. From Phoenix onward, he wanted me to fly to different tracks around the country with him to be at his races. We never discussed it outright. Instead, it was just, "Meet me in Kansas City" or Daytona or Richmond or Dover. He kept asking me to whatever track came next until we were inseparable inside Carl's little bubble.

I got caught up in the moment, slipping easily into the typical role of a racer's girlfriend or wife who enjoys riding shotgun as her man pursues his dream. We both had a lot of side projects. I had my responsibilities to my sponsors and was trying to start my own line of skin care products. Carl owned a music label, did TV cameos, and was a spokesman for a series of NASCAR-themed Harlequin romance novels. Freed from my hard-core training sessions, I had a lot of downtime, which I was happy to use following Carl around. It was nice to be tethered to someone else's schedule for a change. For my whole life, I had had so much pressure on me to perform. Supporting someone else came as a relief.

Plus, Carl and I were really attracted to each other. The minute we were reunited after any amount of time, we both got that let's-go-in-the-other-room-for-a-while feeling. He wanted me all the time, and I wanted to be wanted. When we were out to dinner, at a basketball game, or at any kind of event, he treated me like a lady. But there was always that undercurrent of wanting to get back to that other room. Carl made me feel like I was good enough and pretty enough—especially after those separations. During a week when I couldn't get out of my business commitments to be with him, he tortured me on the phone: "Come back, baby, I can't wait to see you." When I finally was able to get back to him, he greeted me at the airport by grabbing and lifting me up *An Officer and a Gentleman*–style. I had gone from an underappreciated and undersexed "wife" to a seductress smack in the middle of a romantic fantasy.

To add the perfect detail to my own NASCAR-themed Harlequin romance story line, Carl owned and piloted his own plane. So whenever we needed or wanted to go somewhere, we hopped in the six-seater and took off (once, he let me do the takeoff). Watching him man the controls as we flew through the clouds, I couldn't believe this was my life. Totally consumed in the thrill of the moment, I didn't have any fear. I was sick of plans and power. I liked the weightlessness of it all with Carl.

On Christmas, Carl and I flew to Aspen, the exclusive ski town with beautiful chalets, snowcapped mountains, and cheerful streets.

The place was like something out of a Christmas movie. We stayed at the home of Lesa Kennedy, a member of NASCAR's board of directors and the chief executive officer of the International Speedway Corporation, which owns and manages racetracks. The house was huge and equipped with every luxury one could wish for. In the morning, we woke to a huge spread of waffles, eggs, bacon, pancakes, fruit salad, muffins, coffee, and freshly squeezed juice. Fortified with our favorite breakfast foods, we hit the slopes, where the powder glistened under the bright Colorado sun. After a fun day of me trying to teach Carl how to snowboard, we returned to Lesa's house, where masseuses waited to massage out any knots or kinks from a day on the mountain.

Being with Carl, I felt like some big-shot fancy pants. Even when we were on the track, I had a front-row seat to the high-octane world of NASCAR. I got to be up close to the action during the races, learning a lot, meeting everyone on Carl's team. Once, Carl even took me out for a spin. The cars they race have only one seat, but he found a two-seater used for special fans like me. Careening around the track, Carl did his professional best to scare the crap out of me, driving super close to the walls as if we were about to crash and turning at the very last possible second. He knew I was an adrenaline junkie who loved stuff like that.

Even Carl's RV was posh. This was no cramped trailer but a million-dollar vehicle with a kitchen, a sizable living area, and a comfortable sleeping section. I had the place to myself most of the time, since Carl was always working while at the racetrack. At first I found the lack of anything to do really refreshing, but soon I was bored to death. As someone used to doing a ton of stuff, I felt like a lazy couch potato watching TV for hours. I don't like to veg out on vacation, so doing it as my regular life, I quickly grew listless.

I looked at all the other women at the track who spent their days hanging out in the RVs, and they seemed perfectly happy. Figuring they had some secret solution or activity that kept them from going stir-crazy, I took one nice blonde's invitation to come over to her RV and join the rest of the gals for a beer. Sitting in her living area, filled with professional portraits of her, her blond husband, and their three blond children in coordinated outfits, I sipped my Corona and listened quietly to the conversation.

"That pileup the other day in Martinsville was pretty bad," said a tiny woman with enormous blonde hair.

"There's too much wreckin' going on," another woman with skin the color of a penny said, before taking a swig of her beer.

"What's NASCAR gonna do," our host said, "hand out penalties? The boys want to take care of it themselves. That's what they do."

For the next hour and a half, all they did was hash out any and every detail regarding racing. There wasn't one single mention of kids, movies, not even beauty tips. Their entire existence revolved around their significant others. Three beers and a thousand predictions later, I wanted to scream, *Don't you guys have lives?*

They were very sweet, but I didn't have anything in common with the rest of the women. So instead of dishing on the ins and outs of NASCAR, I'd spend hours talking on the phone with my family, surfing the Internet, listening to music (absolutely no country), and watching movies. To stay in some sort of shape, I jumped rope in the RV parking lot. If Carl was racing a smaller track, then I ran around the entire outside of the stadium of the track. It was pretty bleak.

Carl, meanwhile, had the opposite existence. He was incredibly busy, racing on average three days a week and spending the rest of his time preparing for his races, doing media, and dealing with his sponsorships. I didn't dare complain about being bored, and on his rare off day, I didn't ask him to take me to a pool to work out or anywhere else I wanted to go. His breaks were infrequent enough that I wanted him to do whatever he wanted.

That suited Carl just fine. He never asked me what I might like to do, because he only wanted to be on Carl time. He couldn't imagine any other kind of time. I thought I was a control and neat freak, but compared with Carl, I was a mellow and laid-back California girl.

Everything with Carl was controlled. Nothing wrong entered his diet. He was healthy to the extreme, eating scrambled eggs every single morning of his life, lean proteins, steamed and raw vegetables for the rest of the day, and that's it. No sauce. Ever.

His RV was as tidy as a military barracks. No one had ever accused me of being a slob—until Carl. Once after I made myself a little snack of crackers and peanut butter, Carl returned from the track and saw the box of crackers, jar of peanut butter, and plate with two crackers left sitting on the counter. "This place is a fucking disaster," he said, putting the box and jar away in the cabinet and throwing the contents of my plate into the garbage.

"I was eating that!" I said.

"Sorry, but I didn't want everything sitting out."

I thought he was nuts, but I couldn't tell him anything. He was adamant that his way was the only right one—even about something as small as the way he worked out. Carl, who was extremely buff, lifted weights every single day, which ultimately isn't good for your body.

"You need to mix things up and give your muscles a break," I said from the treadmill where I was working out next to him. "You shouldn't weight train every single day."

"You have no idea what you are talking about," he said, lifting a heavier barbell and keeping his eyes on his reflection in the mirror. "I know what I'm doing."

Sure, I'm just an Olympic athlete. What the hell do I know about physical conditioning?

When he didn't want to listen to what I had to say, he shut me down in such a rude way that it worked. I didn't argue. I was fine to let Carl do things Carl's way, but then he started trying to control me.

I was on the Las Vegas track hanging out with the whole crew when I experienced Carl's jealousy. A random guy recognized and approached me for a brief chat when, from a hundred feet away, Carl made a beeline directly toward us.

"What's going on?" Carl said with fire in his eyes. "Can I help you with something?"

"I am just a fan of swimming . . . And NASCAR," the poor guy stammered, unsure about what was happening.

"Do you know this guy?" Carl asked me.

"No, we're just talking," I said. "Chill out."

Before I could apologize to the stranger, he had wisely taken off.

"Why would you make a fool of me like that?" Carl asked.

"How did I do that?"

"Don't play dumb. By talking to strange men."

Carl was the most intense person I've ever been around in my life, and as a competitive athlete, I've been around a lot of intense people. If he had something set in his mind, everyone better move out of the way or get bulldozed. Before a race, the intensity would appear in his face like a rigid mask. He was known as a brawler, on occasion grabbing drivers by the neck or taking a swing. I didn't dare talk to him during those times. I also stayed out of his way after a race until the intensity wore off into his boyish grin.

Racing was an obvious source of stress for Carl, but I couldn't always predict what was going to set him off. I never imagined that getting a ride from another driver back to the RV camp was on my list of forbidden activities. I had been walking back from the pit with a girlfriend I had invited to watch the race, when Kasey Kahne pulled up next to us in a golf cart and offered us a ride. Since the walk was more than fifteen minutes back to the camp, we took him up on the offer.

As we pulled up to the RV, Carl was standing outside. He shot daggers at me when he caught sight of the man behind the wheel of the golf cart. After my friend went inside the RV, Carl pulled me aside for a seriously angry talking-to.

"You don't get in golf carts with other drivers," he growled. "You don't associate with them. You don't even look at them."

"I didn't mean anything by it. I said I was getting a ride back to *your* RV."

"Never do it again. Understand?"

"I'm sorry. I won't talk to other drivers anymore."

But Carl didn't want me talking to *any* guys. He didn't want me hanging out with the male friends I'd had for fifteen years—and I had a lot of male friends. He didn't want me to email with them either. Carl's controlling ways were starting to feel as confining as his RV.

Instead of confronting him, which would be pretty daunting with Carl's temper and was also not my style, I decided to tell little white lies. Of course I emailed my guy friends back. And while at home in Tucson, I ended our evening phone call by telling him that I was going to sleep when I was really about to go out with a few friends to have a drink. It wasn't as though I was going out and getting wasted, but he still would have freaked out at the idea of me at a bar. So like a sixteen-year-old with overbearing parents, I lived my life and then I lived another life with him.

Things got a little trickier when Carl started to demand that I stop posing for sexy shoots. Before he met me, Carl had been attracted to the persona I presented to the world. He, like many other men, liked my *FHM* cover. He also liked the attention we received as a "celebrity" couple. He didn't capitalize on our relationship by talking about it to reporters all that much (he wanted to be recognized for his racing, not his girlfriend), but he got a kick out of it when people asked for my autograph at his event appearances. "You're more famous than I am," he said.

"I'm more famous on the pool deck," I responded. "And you're more famous on the racetrack."

Now that we were together, he wanted me to turn down the biggest reason I had any fame at all. "I don't want other guys looking at you," he said.

I couldn't get out of this one with a lie, and I wasn't about to give up my career because he was uncomfortable with it.

"This is what I do," I said. "You can't change everything about me just because we're dating."

About six months into our relationship, everything that had been so much fun at first was wearing very thin. I was so much a part of Carl's life that I had completely abandoned my own. I didn't want to twiddle my thumbs in his RV anymore, and flying to meet him at various racetracks around the country started to feel like more of a chore than a treat.

I continued to work out in a pool once or twice a week—any pool I could find—but it was nothing compared with what I had been doing before the Olympics and for most of my life. Not working with Frank or any other coach, I was on my own, creating little workouts for myself to stay active. It was very obvious to everyone in the swimming world that I was having fun and in no mood to compete. What nobody could tell—including me—was whether I'd ever return to competitive swimming.

It was actually something from Carl's world that got my own competitive juices running again. When Dale Jarrett won at Talladega at the age of forty-eight and Mark Martin in Kansas at forty-six, it made me reconsider the belief, common among the swimming set, that at twenty-four I should be considering retirement. Yes, swimming is a sport where athletes die out early. That fact had been churning around in the back of my mind, but the image of Dale and Mark, two middle-aged, gray-haired men still enjoying the thrill of victory changed my thinking. They were on the same grueling forty-eight-weekend race schedule as the young drivers. Meanwhile, in my sport, I had only one big race a year. All of a sudden competitive swimming no longer felt like a burden but an opportunity. I had toyed with the idea of hanging it up and starting a family or something like that. But after seeing Dale and Mark in action, I said to myself, *Screw that. I am going to keep swimming while I can.*

My relationship with Carl was heading south as I started to resent the fact that everything between us revolved around him. We never had conversations about what I was thinking, feeling, doing, or not doing. While hanging out in his apartment in North Carolina, I tried to drop my mask. I made an insane confession to someone who didn't even want me to have a glass of wine: I told Carl I had experimented with drugs. I started out slow, confessing to trying cocaine once. I'd see how he took that and then I'd tell him more. He didn't take it well.

"Oh my God. Are you kidding me? Please say you're kidding," he said, as a look of disgust spread across his face.

"I just wanted you to know some stuff about me."

"You would never do that again, would you? I don't want to be with anyone who does stuff like that or be with anyone who is associated with anyone who does that."

"No, no, no. I just tried it once. It was awful."

I had shattered his image of me as a good girl and had to quickly backtrack. I knew he'd break up with me in a second if I told him about my drug tour through South Africa. In that moment I decided that I wasn't going to tell him anything more about myself and I never did. It was easy since he never asked.

By the spring of 2006, I was completely disconnected from him. I had no motivation to see him and stopped making an effort, meaning I didn't hop on an airplane to see him the minute he asked. I realized being a jet-setter isn't all that it's cracked up to be. I was in the Tucson airport waiting to fly out to a Speedo photo shoot in L.A. when Carl called me. It had been a month since I'd gone on the racetrack with him.

"Yeah, I've been thinking about it," he said. "It might just be easier if you lived in North Carolina with me."

Huh? We were moving apart and he wanted me to move in? To me that's a huge step in the evolution of a relationship, not something you do to make seeing your girlfriend easier.

"Why do you want me to move in?" I asked.

"I think it would be nice to get to know each other better," he said.

"We've been together almost a year. Can I ask you a question? Do you know what my sisters' names are?"

"No."

"My parents?"

"Um, no."

"Where did I grow up?"

"I don't have a clue. That's what I'm talking about. Do you want to move in with me or what?"

I knew the names of all his aunts, uncles, cousins, and friends. I knew every little detail about him, and he didn't know anything about me. He didn't even know where I grew up. Nothing.

"You know what? I am not moving across the country and changing my entire life so that you can get to know me. If you want to know me so badly, pick up a phone."

There was silence for a brief second, and then Carl delivered the obvious verdict: "Maybe this isn't working out."

chapter 10

I felt guilty on the airplane to L.A. Relaxing in my seat and staring out at the puffball clouds below me, I was slightly bummed about Carl and the end of our yearlong romance. Slightly. Mostly, I was relieved—and energized. Sure, I had just been dumped. But I was too busy thinking about Sacha, the adorable photographer's assistant I had a secret crush on, to care.

I had first met Sacha Brown six months earlier, in September of 2005, on a Speedo shoot. I took note because he was exactly my type: six two, dark skin, pretty eyes, but a scruffy appearance. He also dressed exactly the way I like: a skater T-shirt and beat-up jeans that suited his lean surfer body (I had had enough of big muscles). Almost as if by reflex, I smiled at him and waved. Hauling a ton of gear into the studio, he looked at me as though I was a total weirdo and kept walking.

Later that day, while he was swapping out memory cards in the cameras, I said to Sacha, "Do we know each other?" As soon as it came out of my mouth, I realized it sounded like a really corny pickup line, but I really did think I recognized him from somewhere.

"No," he said, looking uncomfortable.

"What's your name?"

"Sacha."

I could barely hear him.

"Have we worked together?"

Everything about him was familiar to me. Even the tattoos covering his arm seemed like a memory. No color, just thick black lines, already faded with time, they started as a spiderweb on his elbow and snaked around his forearm into blurry stars and an angel figure with wings.

"I don't think so," he said, before ducking back over to the lights to check their placement—again.

Although the guy really didn't want to chat with me—it's an unspoken rule that the crew shouldn't fraternize with the "talent"—I wouldn't let it go. It wasn't like me to be pushy, particularly with a guy, and especially at work, but in that moment I didn't feel like I was crossing any boundaries. During lunch, I broke the rules and sat down with the crew. I had walked by the table with the other swimmers also featured in the shoot, and not being close to any of them, kept walking with my salad to a spot right next to Sacha.

"Well, hi," I said.

He looked like that deer caught in the headlights. It took a little doing, but soon enough I had him caught up in casual conversation. It turned out he had lived in Tucson when he was younger, so we bonded over the Arizona-Sonora Desert Museum, an amazing cross between a zoo and a museum where you can see mountain lions and bears in their natural settings.

"Oh man, I used to love that place," he said, an innocent smile peeking through his four-day stubble.

I was drawn to everything about him—his smile, his voice, even the way he ate his lunch. What was I thinking? I had no idea what I was doing. I had a boyfriend—a famous boyfriend. Still, I couldn't stop flirting with this guy. This never happened to me. I hardly ever click with people, but I felt I had to get to know him. An impossible task, since we only had twenty minutes, which went by in a flash, and then it was back to work.

When we wrapped for the day, I looked around to say good-bye to Sacha, but I couldn't find him. He'd left without letting me know. I guess it would have been awkward or inappropriate for him to seek me out, but I was still disappointed. I was embarrassed by my irrational thoughts. What was going to happen if he had said good-bye? Nothing. I had a boyfriend, I had to remind myself again. So it was better this way.

A couple of months later, my dad forwarded me an email that had come to my website (my dad maintained my site and went through all the fan email) because it seemed like the sender really knew me. It was from Sacha!

"It was really great to meet you at the photo shoot," he wrote. "Maybe if you are ever in L.A., we can hang out."

He was sorry he hadn't said good-bye at the shoot and wanted to get my contact information but couldn't ask the photographer for it. I was surprised and secretly excited; I didn't think I'd ever hear from him again. I wrote back immediately:

"Great meeting you too. Hopefully, we can work with each other again soon."

Appropriate and friendly. In the email, I also included my phone number. If Carl had found out, he would have run me over with one of his race cars, but our relationship was already incredibly shitty and I didn't really care.

Sacha and I started texting each other, which led to phone calls that could last as long as five hours during which we talked about everything and nothing. We enjoyed each other's company and the process of getting to know each other.

I learned that despite his name, Sacha has absolutely no Russian in him. Growing up in Marin County in Northern California, he had hippie parents who just thought the name was cool. Seven years older than me, he moved down to L.A., where for a while he bounced from job to job, not sure what he wanted to do. After playing around with his friend's camera, he was inspired to go to art school. In his late twenties he attended the prestigious Arts Center College of Design in Pasadena, where he graduated with honors.

Ever since then, he had been working in photography, mainly assisting established photographers.

Sacha was also interested in me—my family, friends, likes, dislikes. No detail was too small. Unused to talking about myself, I didn't open up quite as quickly as he did. Since I didn't think he really wanted to know all these things, I assumed he was just trying to be nice. But Sacha kept questioning me, not in an intrusive way, but with sincere curiosity, so that soon enough I was sharing intimate feelings and memories that I would never tell Carl. When we landed on the topic of surfing (one of Sacha's big passions ever since he was a ten-year-old kid), I told him all about afternoons with my dad riding to Balboa Beach before my parents split. He listened to everything about that magical time in my life as if it were magical for him too.

Although we had strong feelings for each other, they remained just that—feelings. We never discussed anything romantic on the phone and never crossed the line of friendship in any way. Sacha knew I had a boyfriend, but I didn't talk about Carl (all he had to do was google me if he wanted any information). And I knew Sacha had a girlfriend of six years, with whom he lived, but I wasn't interested in hearing too much about her, so I didn't ask any questions.

Now on the plane to another Speedo shoot in L.A., I was filled with so much anticipation, I could hardly stay in my seat; Sacha was going to be on set. A free woman, I could finally tell him my true feelings, and maybe, eventually, we could take our relationship to another level.

I'm not usually running to get on location for a photo shoot, but this time I couldn't wait to arrive. I had never felt this way about anybody in my life. When I finally found him hauling equipment into the studio, I was a cliché, my heart beating hard and my stomach aflutter. We exchanged friendly hellos and got to work like two professionals. But at the first free minute available, I took him aside.

In the huge complex of studios, I led him to a smaller room

where we could be alone. As we sat side by side on a couch, the attraction was so strong that I was sure I wasn't the only one feeling it. There was no way I was going to waste this opportunity out of pride. I had resolved to take control of the situation, unwilling to lose out of shyness any chance with this dream man.

"Sacha, I like you a lot," I said, surprised by how comfortably those words came out. "I'd like us to see if there is anything there."

"Shhh," he said, looking around with a panicked expression. "I don't want to get fired."

At this point, I really didn't care about being professional. I was way beyond that point.

"I want to go out with you."

"Look, I like you too and would love to hang out. But it's not that easy. Things haven't been going well with my girlfriend for a couple of years now, but I'm not single. I have to figure out that situation before I do anything."

That was reasonable, but I wasn't in a reasonable mood.

"If you have feelings for me—"

"Amanda! I've been with her for a long time. You don't understand."

It wasn't what I wanted to hear, but I listened. Of course, he was right. If we were meant to be, which I was sure of, then he would sort things out eventually. And for Sacha, I would be patient—a quality I'm not exactly known for.

In the end, I didn't have to wait that long. About a month after I made my confession, Sacha began the complicated process of ending his long-term relationship, moving out, finding an apartment, and, finally, asking me out.

We skipped the typical first date and moved right to soul mates. We already had spent so much time on the phone getting to know each other that sitting across from him at some fancy dinner would have been idiotic. We were way past that. Sometime after he broke up with his girlfriend, Sacha called me to see if I wanted to come out to Laguna Beach, where he was going on location for a photo shoot of the cast of the MTV hit *Laguna Beach*. He didn't have to ask twice. I still wasn't training full-time and I was no longer traveling with Carl, so I had more than enough time on my hands to fit in a quick plane ride to visit Sacha.

I made sure I had a cute outfit when I drove into the parking garage of his hotel. I wore little shorts and low ankle boots with high heels, and my hair and makeup were atypically done. I didn't want him to see me and think, *Oh man, what did I do?*

We didn't even say hello before we had our first kiss, a perfect, perfect kiss. I felt so much chemistry and attraction toward him that he could have been an awful kisser and I would have had no idea. There was no way it wasn't going to be fireworks.

Finally we could be together, in public and alone. Although Sacha had to work during the day, in the evenings we visited the little art galleries in Laguna and took walks on the beach before returning to the hotel. It was so sickeningly romantic that we might as well have sipped champagne from each other's intertwined flutes (we didn't). There was only one awkward moment, but it wasn't between Sacha and me. I was in the hotel lobby picking up a few magazines to take to the beach while Sacha worked when I ran into the photographer who shot all the Speedo stuff. He was also doing the *Laguna Beach* shoot.

"Hey, Amanda. What are you doing here?"

"Just visiting."

"Visiting who?"

Then suddenly I could see in his face that he'd put two and two together before I said it out loud: "Sacha."

It was no big deal. A little uncomfortable, yes, but the big deal was that Sacha and I were now together. The only downside was that our time together was way too short. And that time passed way too fast. I wanted to stay in that hotel room forever and forget about real life in Tucson. Sacha said he felt the same way. "Don't worry," he said. "I'll come to see you soon. We'll figure this out."

He made good on his promise and drove out to Tucson in the

summer, when it's 120 degrees in the shade. The fact that his Honda Civic didn't have air conditioning was proof enough of his adoration, but Sacha insisted on talking to me on the phone the whole way out, which meant he had to keep the windows rolled up to hear anything. I was worried he'd pass out and die of heatstroke in the middle of the desert, but instead we made plans for the future. We listed all the places we wanted to go in the world and planned how we'd go together. I told him how I so badly wanted to travel to Fiji. He described the trip he'd take me on in Paris, one of his favorite places because of its incredible culture and food. "Well," I said, "when you get to Tucson, I'm going to take you to an awesome Mexican restaurant with the best guacamole tableside and a mariachi band."

Sacha was the most communicative person I had ever met. Not only was he completely open and excited to share so much of himself with me, but he also wanted to hear every minor thing going on in *my* life and in my brain. He wanted to know all about my past as well as my present. What was I like as a kid? How did I get along with my parents? How did I feel about swimming?

I was out of my depth. When it came to this one aspect, we couldn't have been more different. Sacha was a talker; I was not. While I had kept everything bottled up from a young age, he was a prodigy at expressing himself. He described when as a small kid his mom, already divorced from his dad, brought home a random guy. Instead of absorbing it and manifesting his pain in a childlike way, he expressed himself directly to his mom. Getting to the heart of the matter and articulating his feelings was an ability he had been born with.

As he made his way along the interminable stretch of Interstate 10, he helped me to open up. We talked about kids and how much both of us couldn't wait to have them. He thought being a father sounded like the ultimate creative experience, and I expressed a desire for a big family—although I had no idea what I was talking about.

When Sacha finally showed up at my house in Tucson, he practi-

cally poured out of his car. He was drenched in sweat from his air-
less car ride, his shirt and shorts sticking to his lean frame. He was
sticky and smelled, but all I wanted to do was rip his clothes off his
body. I led him to the pool in my backyard, and we both stripped
down and jumped into the water to cool off. Sort of.

Sacha's ability to talk made the experience very different from
my past relationships. The other terrific quality he possessed was
his willingness to join me in any adventure and fly by the seat of our
pants.

He proved he was up for absolutely anything later that summer
when I invited him for our annual family vacation at the lake house.
The centerpiece of the trip was a barbecue. But my family couldn't
just have a normal cookout. This was a costume barbecue, and the
theme was "Northwest." It was totally weird, and totally us. I had
been slightly nervous about telling Sacha the plan. I still had the
memory of going to the lake with Ryk, who pouted the whole time.
Trapped in a little cabin with twenty of my family members, you
have to get with the program. I couldn't even get Ryk to water-ski.

Sacha didn't miss a beat. When I told him about the costume
barbecue, he replied, "I have the best idea! Let's be Mariners. We'll
go to the Big Five and buy the whole outfit. It'll be awesome." When
we showed up at the cookout, we were wearing Mariner baseball
uniforms from head to toe complete with cleats, baseball bats, and
black stuff under our eyes. Immediately, Sacha racked up a lot of
points with Taryn, who came as a can of Rainier Beer, and Leah,
dressed like a Starbucks employee. Over that holiday, Sacha became
best friends with all my cousins, uncles, aunts, and sisters. My
grandma, whom I consider to have impeccable taste, confided that
she was in love with him.

I know I was. I was in stupid love with him, head-over-heels,
I-want-to-be-with-him-all-the-time love. At the lake house, we held
hands and kissed so much that even my laissez-faire family let me
know it was getting a little obnoxious.

All of a sudden my life in Tucson didn't make any sense. When I returned to Arizona after our trip to the lake house, I wrestled with the point of staying there and couldn't find a single good reason. I wasn't training full-time even though I'd told myself I wanted to re-enter competitive swimming. If I went to L.A., there were places I could train. So what was keeping me here?

The answer was nothing; nothing was holding me in Tucson, and everything was calling me to L.A. Almost from the beginning of our relationship, I knew I wanted to marry Sacha—and I'm not the type of person who says that. I'm not only a loner but also extremely picky. I dated a guy for five years and never once thought about marrying him. With Sacha, I had a feeling in my gut that I didn't want to be without him.

Still, I knew that if I wanted a future with him, I needed to really know if it was going to work out. For that, we'd have to live in the same place. Long-distance was romantic but not practical. So I decided the only logical thing to do was buy a house in L.A. Then Sacha and I could live happily ever after. I got on it right away, finding a realtor and spending one week looking at properties. By August I had found a little house in Venice Beach, which had a lot of charm—and a big price tag.

I brought my dad, my financial and life consultant, to see the house and give me his opinion. He was hesitant. "Houses in L.A. are not cheap," he said. "Are you sure you want to do something like this? It might be a good idea to rent for a while."

"No, I want to live in L.A.," I said, angry that my consultant wasn't giving me the answer I wanted. "It'll be good for my career. I can do more TV stuff if I'm here. And this is a great house. I can own it for five or ten years, then sell it and make money. I want to live here."

When I get an idea into my head, nobody can talk me out of it, not even the two men who loved me the most in the world. Sacha's reaction was similar to my dad's. He was really excited about my move. But being a practical guy, he also thought I shouldn't rush into the high-stakes world of L.A. real estate but should instead play it safe with a rental. Their little rational talks didn't do any good. Looking for instant roots, I moved into my three-bedroom beach bungalow in Venice in September of 2006.

A half mile off the water, the one-thousand-square-foot house from the 1920s had the charm of an old house with the comfort of a completely new one. The recently renovated interior was simple, modern, and beautiful. Although there was only one bathroom, it included a dry sauna and a huge, sexy two-person shower. The place was perfect, but I still did a little renovating of my own. I converted a detached two-car garage into a clubhouse with a huge TV and couch, where you could be as loud as you wanted for as long as you wanted without disturbing anyone in the house. But perhaps the best thing about my new home was its proximity to an incredible neighborhood. Right off Abbot Kinney, an avenue filled with restaurants and shops, all we had to do was walk out our front door and we could stroll out to dinner, the movies, or the beach.

Despite all the diversions, Sacha and I experienced the growing pains typical of any couple moving in together. My neat freakishness reared its ugly head, since Sacha was not a tidy guy. I could trace his day by the trail of mess he left behind. *Oh, I see. He had lunch on the couch, then walked to the bathroom, leaving his clothes in his wake, took a shower, and dried off in the bedroom, where he left his wet towels on the bed.* Although we had a lot of phones for such a small house, I could never find a single one on the receiver. As someone who likes everything in its place, it drove me nuts to come home and see laundry on the floor, dishes in the sink, and every one of his dresser drawers open and chaotic.

"Those dishes are killing me," I said first thing after walking through the door and spying a pile of dirty ones glaring at me from the kitchen.

"It's not a big deal. I'll clean it up later," Sacha said.

"Why can't you put them in the dishwasher?"

"Why can't you chill out?"

"Because I need everything to be clean and put together at all times of the day and night."

"What you need to do is relax."

"You need to go over there and clean it up, or I'm going to hurt you."

We were alike in our stubbornness. If either of us had an idea of how something was supposed to be, it wasn't easily changed. We butted heads over dirty dishes—and decorating. He might not have been a neat freak, but Sacha had a very specific vision of the way he wanted the house to look. Even though he clearly had a better sense of design than I did, I wasn't used to having a man tell me what kind of furniture to get or where to put it. With Sacha, however, each picture had to be hung at gallery height with the correct lighting, perfectly done down to the last detail. Meanwhile I was, like, bang the nail in the wall and hang the sucker up. Our mini art museum was one thing, but the couch he insisted upon was another. The modern leather couch Sacha picked for our Venice house looked amazing and was totally uncomfortable. This was a couch for sipping martinis in a cocktail dress, not snuggling up and watching a movie.

"I come home from swimming and just want to veg out. You can't lie on that stupid thing," I whined.

"If you want to lie down, there's a bed in the other room," he said.

I didn't know I had moved in with Nate Berkus. It was hard to relinquish control of my habitat so quickly, but eventually I did hand it over. Sacha knew exactly how objects should be placed in a room, and I'll admit that I didn't.

Our fights over décor were child's play compared with my issues with his relationship with his ex-girlfriend. The biggest issues we both faced at that time stemmed from the fact that we both had jumped into our new romance right after ending our previous ones. We could have used a little alone time to heal and have closure, but neither of us had the patience to wait. After we moved in together, Sacha continued to talk to his ex, which drove me crazy. If I saw a text from her or heard them on the phone, I went ballistic.

"You don't see me texting or calling Carl," I shouted.

"We were together a long time," he said. "We shared a bank account, furniture, and cats. It takes a little while to untangle that."

"How long? It seems like you've been breaking up forever."

"Amanda, I don't hate the girl. It crushed her when we ended things, but she's still a friend. I'm not going to be an ass about this."

I didn't understand him at all. I cut ties with Ryk and Carl severely and permanently. Sacha was one of those people who cared about other people's emotions; I didn't.

"Jesus, just drop her."

Being compassionate wasn't the only thing that I began to learn from Sacha. He opened up a lot of worlds for me. Art was a big one—including everything that goes into making a great photo. From my perspective—that of the person who shows up and stands in front of the camera—photography was a lot of hair, makeup, lighting, and someone pressing the shutter. Sacha showed it to me from the other side, giving me a tour through the history of photography through trips to galleries and sessions looking at books. He deconstructed the images I saw every day in magazines, showing the skill behind the image by describing exactly what lights or camera went into making it.

Sacha's lessons helped me understand that more than the model was needed for a beautiful picture. Understanding that the end result is truly a team effort took some of the pressure off me when I was doing shoots or assessing the results after the fact. Sacha was incredibly cool about the shoots I did—including those for magazines like *Maxim* or *FHM*. "My girlfriend is the hot chick on the cover," he joked. He understood that the person on the cover of the mag is a creation of a lot of artists; I didn't need to live up to the perfect image of myself. Still, he appreciated my photos—the good ones at least. He was able to be very honest about my work because when he criticized a picture, it was clear he wasn't criticizing me. "The lighting is crap" or "hair and makeup did not do a good job." It was never me who was flawed.

Sacha had a way of making me feel special. He told me all the time that I was, but his actions spoke the loudest. He often left little Post-it notes around the house, reminding me of our love affair. Having given me the nickname "Fish," for obvious reasons, he stuck a note to the fridge that was a simple "I," a heart, and a picture of a fish. Knowing he was thinking about me made the message more powerful than a Shakespeare sonnet. He never had to spend a ton of money on me because he lavished attention on me. Once I mentioned that I'd love to make a little Halloween town like the one I did for Christmas. (Every year, I put up an entire Christmas town—with choo-choo trains, houses, sleighs, trees, people, and snow—that is so big, the display needs an entire table to itself.) So Sacha went out and got me the perfect miniature haunted house for my birthday.

He listened. Sacha knew what was important to me and how to make me *feel* important. If we were at an event filled with drop-dead gorgeous women, he could have cared less. He didn't check out chicks, openly or secretly, or ever make me doubt that he wanted to be there with me. In that way, I became the most stunning and interesting woman in any room where he was around.

In turn, I gave Sacha the freedom of adventure he'd never experienced before in a relationship. I didn't put any restrictions on the things he wanted to do, like buying a motorcycle. Ever since I had first met him, he had wanted one badly, but his girlfriend had forbidden it. As soon as we started dating, I told him to go get one and "have fun." He was a man and could make his own decisions. I might tell him to be careful (not that I needed to, since Sacha is the most safety-conscious person I've ever met), but I would never say he wasn't allowed. In fact, after he got his motorcycle, I went out and bought my own. I even took racing classes on a track once he started them.

We fed off each other's thrill-seeking natures. If I asked him to jump out of a plane, he would say, "Sweet, let's do that," which is exactly how I am. Still, I have my limits. When Sacha, a really great snowboarder, wanted to take me to a course to go off jumps, I refused. I wasn't nearly good enough for that. But he knew exactly how to encourage me. "You're fine," he said. "Just follow me." I had gotten into misadventures before by listening to men but decided to trust Sacha. And he was right; I was fine. More than fine, the jumps were awesome.

He didn't let me put restrictions on myself. Both certified scuba divers, we took the activity up a notch by diving with sharks in California, the Caribbean, and Hawaii. But my favorite daredevil activity we did together was scuba diving in the dark. At night, all the big stuff comes out, so your chances of running into a really giant sea creature are much greater. But that's not why I loved it so much. The best part is that you can't see anything except for what comes into the path of your flashlight. For a lot of people, this is scary since you don't know what's lurking right behind, below, or beside you. For me, though, I loved the peace of the quiet, watery dark and the focus of that one strobe of light.

The security of our new relationship pushed the adventurous sides in both Sacha and me. Knowing that we had each other's back allowed us to take greater risks of all kinds.

I burst through the front door, slamming it behind me and throwing my keys in the direction of the side table. Then I flopped on the couch, nearly sliding right off the slippery leather. That stupid couch! I was so exhausted and frustrated, and I couldn't even lie on a goddamned comfortable couch.

Just at that moment, Sacha walked into the living room looking as refreshed as if he'd slept twelve hours, which he just might have.

"How was practice?" he asked in the upbeat tone of people who think sports are fun.

"Great. Good. Fine," I said, in the short tone I'd once used with my dad. I only wanted to be left alone. If I could have crawled under a rock, I would have. My sweet boyfriend wanted to talk, and I wanted to kill him for it.

"What did you do?" asked Sacha, who had sat down by my feet.

"If I told you, you wouldn't understand what I'm saying."

"I'm really interested. I want to learn about swimming."

"There's nothing interesting about it."

"Come on. It's what you do."

"Okay," I said, sitting up with the aggression of someone on the attack. "I did ten, one-hundred IM on one twenty. Descend one-three. Four is easy. Five is fast. Happy now?"

I had spewed the jargon for the sets I'd done as fast as I could, as if to add an extra layer of bitch to my reply.

"Take it easy," he said. "Maybe if you explained to me what you're saying . . ."

I was in no mood to give him a lesson in swimming basics. Now that I had started training full-time again, I came home a tired, grumpy, angry mess—every single day. I was so worn out and annoyed when I returned to the house, I didn't want to be alive, let alone talk. What had I done?

Right before I started swimming seriously again, I had had a major change of heart from my previous weariness with the sport. In high school it might have been a hardship to wake up in the mornings and juggle swimming with school and friends. But as I got older, I realized what a great job I had. My office was the pool, where my task was to stay in shape. I looked at other people working their asses off at a nine-to-five job, hardly able to pay their bills or squeeze in a workout. Competitive swimming was a luxury by comparison.

With the goal of medaling at my fourth Olympics, I went back to my old coach Dave Salo, who was in his first season as the men's and women's coach at University of Southern California. The decision to work with Dave again was a no-brainer. Returning to swimming after a two-year hiatus, which was practically forever in swimming terms, was hard enough, but add to that the fact that I was an old lady. Getting in shape was going to be a serious challenge. It was consoling to return to a friendly face. I knew Dave and his training style, so I wasn't going to have to contend with a completely foreign environment while I got back in the game. On top of that, Dave had some of the best athletes training under him. I would be swimming with about another twenty professionals, including the incredible breaststroker Rebecca Soni. Competition like that would definitely get my motor running. I was excited to be back, and Dave was excited to have me: old friends beginning anew.

Then I actually came back.

Every day was virtually the same. It began with me hopping in my car and driving to downtown L.A., where the campus was located. I sat in the car, drinking my coffee and listening to the morning radio shows. Starting off my day with the best of intentions, I felt the motivation draining from me as the minutes ticked by in my daily battle with L.A.'s legendary traffic. Although it wasn't much more than seven miles to the pool from my house, it took me forty-five minutes to an hour and a half to get to practice every single day. Driving three hours a day for a two-hour practice was pretty hard to rationalize. I was wasting my whole life trying to get places.

The commute was only the start. The campus was located in a poor and blighted neighborhood where one of the girls on the swim team was held up at gunpoint for her cell phone less than a block from the pool. From my parked car to the pool, I passed boarded-up buildings, guys hanging out on street corners, and broken glass strewn underfoot. The bleak scenery added to the sense that I was going nowhere good.

Once safely inside the pool complex, I headed straight for the locker room, where I changed as fast as I could to get in the pool as quickly as possible. It wasn't that I was so eager to start practice; I just didn't want to talk to anybody.

At first I had been friendly with some people on the professional team, but that turned out to be a mistake. Most of them were typical backstabbers: sweet to your face, but turn around for a second and they're talking about you. If I confided anything in one of them, I could be sure the other swimmers knew about it before practice had even ended. The drama reminded me of my college days with teammates dating each other, cheating on each other, breaking up with each other, and getting back with each other. It was boring and gross.

Finally, I decided I couldn't associate with the team any longer when one of the boys made a snarky comment about Frank Busch. Just loud enough for me to hear, he said Frank went up to offer his hand to Dave at a swim meet, but Dave wouldn't touch it. I wasn't sure of the point of the story, but when he described my old coach as "a loser," I had it. Their making fun of Frank pissed me off badly, particularly because they knew I loved the man. I shot them a dirty look before I got out of the pool and left practice early.

If Dave noticed, he didn't say anything to me. During his first year of being head coach of a major college team, he was very preoccupied with learning the ropes of his new role. At first, it was hard for him just to find pool time for his professional swimmers. While the college swimmers had scheduled training sessions, we had to work around the pool's many teams, including diving and water polo. Because allowing pros to train with NCAA swimmers is in direct violation of the rules, we could practice only when the pool wasn't filled with college kids—which was hardly ever.

In the beginning, we showed up to practice only to find the water polo team using the entire pool. It pissed Dave off, but he knew he had to establish himself before he could take control of the deck.

Me, not much more than two months old, with my mom.

Check out that hat, crocheted by my mom so that I could be a stylin' four-month-old.

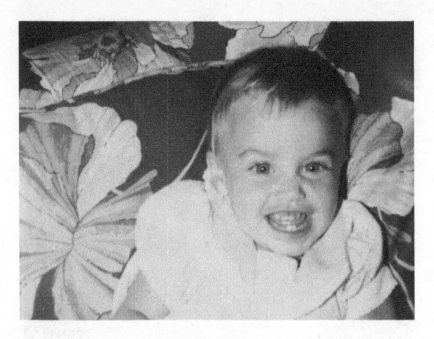

Only a year old and I already have that spunky energy, which would drive my parents crazy.

As a five-year-old member of the Colony Red Hots summer league team, I can't wait to beat all those kids around me.

At the lake house in Washington State.

At eight years old, in my dance outfit hamming it up before a recital.

Me and my sisters, Leah and Taryn, goofing off, as usual.

The Beard Christmas photo circa 1991 (those were some hot outfits) taken three years before my parents split up. Their divorce was very difficult, but my parents remained united in their love and support for me.

Basking in my victories as a Colony Red Hot.

With Coach Dave Salo by my side; I was mortified by the parade of the Irvine Novas held in my honor before I left for the 1996 Olympics.

Me, in the blue suit, at the 1996 Olympics, ready to compete. Look how small I was! At fourteen, I was so young that I didn't even realize I should be nervous.

With my dad as I gave him the fifty-cent tour of the Olympic Village in Atlanta. This was the first time we got to see each other in the three weeks I had been at the Olympics.

My silver medal at the 1996 Olympics!

Me and my famous teddy bear, Harold, made the PR rounds (here on *The Tonight Show with Jay Leno*) after the 1996 Olympics.

Upset with myself after a disappointing race at the Janet Evans Invitational in 1997. I had a growth spurt that year and struggled to swim at the same level in my new body. My self-confidence wasn't helped by the hurtful comments made by the sports media about my new figure. In college, my negative body image only got worse. *Photograph by Todd Warshaw/ Getty Images Sports.*

My friend Ian Thorpe *(left)* and my boyfriend, Ryk Neethling *(right)*, with their medals after the 100-meter freestyle at the 2002 Commonwealth Games. It burned Ryk that Ian always seemed to win gold. *Photograph by Adam Pretty/Getty Images Sports.*

Even though we had broken up, Ryk and I pretended to be a couple for *Vanity Fair*'s 2004 Olympic hopefuls shoot. I began cutting myself during one of the many fights we had over the course of our four-year relationship. The cutting continued long after Ryk was out of my life. *Photograph by Bruce Weber/trunkarchive.com.*

Gold Medal
BEARD AMAN
USA
2:23.37 OR

Accepting my only individual gold medal of my career, during the 2004 Olympics in Athens; I felt that all the hard work over twenty years had finally paid off.

Team Beard: Dad, Mom, and Taryn cheering me on at the 2004 Olympics.

In Fontana, California, September 2005, just hanging out as usual on the racetrack with my boyfriend, NASCAR driver Carl Edwards. I was always flying to a racetrack to be with him, and not the other way around. *Photograph by Getty Images/Getty Images Publicity.*

Don't I look amazing in this modeling shot from January 2008? That's what the wonders of Photoshop can do. *Photograph by Luke Duval/Contour by Getty Images.*

Taryn, my mom, me, and Leah enjoying some girl time in San Francisco.

Five months pregnant, I'm mugging with Sacha, the one man who broke through my tough facade and encouraged me to be myself.

That's our wedding photo, taken on May 1, 2009, in Indonesia! The man standing next to Sacha is the village elder who married us. I have no idea who the guy next to me is.

Our first kiss as husband and wife.

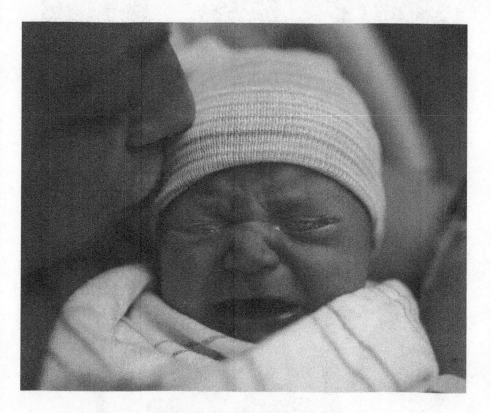

Me kissing our brand-new baby, Blaise, born on September 15, 2009.

Just one of the Wild Things.

My boys in their Angels gear.

My proudest accomplishment.

One of my favorite family pics from our last trip to Oahu in 2011.

While he sent us to the corner to do vertical kicking for an hour, he told us to bear with him, that the situation would get better. For three or four months, our practices were hit or miss, until Dave worked out the kinks and we really got going. But even when our training was more consistent, I didn't enjoy it. Dave ran the sessions very much as he used to back in the days of the Novas—lots of high-intensity sprinting and not a lot of yardage. He always wanted us moving really fast and hard, even if we weren't going that far.

I missed the way I had trained with Frank. Dave's sets lasted about thirty minutes, whereas Frank's easily went over an hour. I couldn't get in the groove without the endurance aspect of the longer sets. As the months wore on into a full year, I was in no better shape than when I had begun. I certainly wasn't swimming any faster. Realizing that Dave's workouts weren't doing anything for me, I went from being annoyed to outright hating them.

Dave shouted orders for a set from the deck: "Ten seven." I wasn't halfway though the first lap when I knew I wasn't going fast enough to make Dave's set. (Because I know how long it takes me to do a lap of any kind of stroke, if I'm off by even a tenth of a second, I know that too.) Easily a second slower than where I should be, I gave up at the first turn. *Forget it. I'm not going to try for the rest of them. There's no point.* Dave screamed at us to go faster and faster. I could have cared less; I just wanted to go home. He didn't care either. Dave never called me out for going slowly. When I was done with the set, I didn't bother to check my time, and he didn't feel it necessary to let me know.

Past the trash, crying babies, and burned cars, I got back into my car in a way worse mood than the grumpy one I'd started with in the morning. Driving home, I couldn't let it go that I had just wasted five hours of my day. Starving and sitting in traffic, I went over and over the same nihilistic thoughts until I had worked myself up to an epic bad mood.

By the time I opened the door of our Venice bungalow, I was on the edge of something very bad. I walked in and threw myself down on the couch—or tried to. God, I hated that couch. Then I saw it: the pile of dirty dishes in the sink.

That was it. I went mental.

"Sacha!"

He came running in from the other room. The way I screamed, he was probably worried I had broken my leg or something.

"I'm so sick of this," I yelled. "This house is a mess. I'm swimming like crap, and now this? What am I doing here? Everything is a mess."

I had worked myself up into such a state that I was now crying while I continued to yell at Sacha, who stood in a shocked daze, completely blindsided by the monster that had returned in the body of his girlfriend.

"Amanda, honey . . ."

Every molecule in my being started to spin. He could have hugged me, told me he loved me, or given me an engagement ring, and I would have flipped out on him. Just like the Hulk, I hated what was happening to me but felt powerless to stop it. I didn't want to kill Sacha, so I had to get away from him. But the house was so small, there was nowhere to escape. I needed somewhere to go to let go of all this. The only option was to lock myself in the bathroom.

Sitting in one of the benches in our "sexy" shower, I heard a soft knocking from the other side of the door. "What's wrong, baby?" he asked. He wanted to console me by talking through things, but in that moment I could have cared less. *I don't want to talk about it. I hate swimming. Don't ask me about it. I'm not talking about it. I'm not talking.*

"I'll be out in a little bit."

He left me alone while I took a couple of hours to come down from being a ball of rage. Once I had returned to my unswimmer self, I was so exhausted that all I wanted to do was jump in bed. Sacha on the other hand was ready to see a movie or have dinner.

His day was just getting started. We had the classic problem of a mixed relationship between an athlete and nonathlete. I woke up at 4:30 a.m., drove three hours, and swam two practices. I wanted to go to bed at 9:00 p.m. Meanwhile, Sacha was a complete night owl, staying up to all hours of the night and sleeping until noon. We were on totally different schedules.

I was so tired, always tired. I was also angry. Pressure was coming down on me from all sides. There were my different sponsors and contracts. I had people constantly breathing down my neck about appearances and photo shoots, while I was trying to battle my issues in the pool. But I couldn't be anything less than a perfect spokesperson, because I had two mortgages (I still owned the house in Tucson) and a crushingly large overhead to pay every month.

Everything was piling up: my issues with swimming, the toxic atmosphere at the pool, my temper at home, my big bills, my troubles keeping up with all my added responsibilities. I felt trapped.

If I wanted to stay in L.A. and continue to train, I couldn't think of any other swim team or facility that would provide me with what I needed to make the 2008 Olympics—which was becoming a bigger fantasy by the minute. In the few competitions I did while training with Dave, I was nowhere near the times needed to win in the trials. It was so hard to race knowing I had zero chance of achieving my goal. I couldn't get on the block, dive in, and give it my all. Too much negativity weighed me down.

Everything became a drag. Things that should have been cool were a pain in the ass. When I got an invitation to the Espy Awards in 2007, instead of thinking it would be a fun night out with Sacha and a chance for exposure, it became a major work hassle with the added hardships of hair and makeup fueling my bad attitude.

Although I was overwhelmed, I didn't do anything to lessen my burden or let anyone know how I felt. I didn't talk to anyone about the major storm clouds brewing around me. I didn't ever discuss my disappointment with swimming with Dave, who was so busy with his own thing, I could have missed practice for two weeks and he wouldn't have known.

Powering through my life like a robot, as my mental state grew darker and darker, seemed like the only viable solution. My routine became an evil Groundhog Day, starting with me getting into my car like a depressed commuter going to a bad job. Sometimes I couldn't handle it, though. When, fifteen minutes into my drive, I was waiting in bumper-to-bumper traffic on Lincoln Avenue and still nowhere near getting on the freeway, I threw in the towel. "I can't do this today," I yelled to myself, before turning the car around and going back home.

But home wasn't much more comforting. I had come to L.A. to be with Sacha. Meanwhile, my swimming and what it was doing to me mentally was killing our relationship.

Deeply, deeply miserable, I had become an awful creature. My temper over the months had escalated from yelling and crying to throwing and breaking. I broke everything around me when I was in one of my states; whatever was in my hand got smashed. I broke dishes, cell phones, frames, vases, and sunglasses—so many sunglasses.

"Thank goodness you have an Oakley sponsor, because you go through so many sunglasses," Sacha joked.

He had taken every tack to deal with my fits of rage. He tried concern, jokes, anger, but nothing worked. When that surge of boiling blood raced through my body, I was helpless to become anything other than a monster.

I went through four pairs of three-hundred-dollar Marc Jacobs sunglasses. I took objects and threw them with all my might so that I made holes in our walls. I broke doors. I had a special and very expensive key made for my Lincoln Navigator with remote navigation so that I could start my car from anywhere. I chucked it at the ground with such force that I smashed it. Hard plastic and metal were no match for my rage.

Sacha understandably grew fed up with my outbursts. At a certain point, no longer wanting to have any part of them, he'd leave the house as soon as I started. "I'm not going to talk to you when you're like this. I'm out of here," he said, going for a walk, to a friend's house, the movies, anywhere I wasn't.

When he got back home after I had cooled off, I felt so pathetic that I pleaded for his affection.

"I just need a hug," I said to him.

"No, I'm not going to hug you," he fumed. "You are acting crazy. Chucking glasses at the wall is not okay. You're going to seriously hurt yourself or someone else. It's like you are a five-year-old who doesn't know how to express herself. You've got to find another way."

chapter II

"Come on. Let me in. Amanda? Hello! Let me in!"

Sacha's pleading from the other side of the bathroom door had turned into yelling, yet I still ignored him; I had work to do.

Anger, that old familiar feeling, shoved me out of my body so that I hovered above. A bad adrenaline surged, making me shake all over and clenching my jaw, hands, and toes in response. I needed to get this tension out before I imploded.

After returning from practice, I had gone straight to the washing machine to clean my workout clothes when I found a pile of Sacha's dirty laundry, which triggered my state of rage. Why did he think it was okay to let dirty laundry sit around? Everything around me was so chaotic and out of control that the only solution seemed to be to destroy it. I couldn't keep up with laundry, dishes, grocery shopping, emails, or phone calls.

I looked around for something to slam or punch or break and found a few things, which brought Sacha running in to make sure I was okay. When he saw the broken glass of the measuring cup scattered across our floor, his look of concern changed into one of anger. That's when I knew I needed to get out of there.

Slipping past him, I ran into the bathroom and locked the door before he could catch up. That's when he began banging on the door and telling me to let him in. My ears, pounding with too much blood, couldn't hear. I had to get a couple of little cuts in quickly. One. Two. Three. And relief.

I was back to reality and now aware of Sacha demanding that I open the door. Eventually, quiet and embarrassed about my secret, I did.

"What's going on in here?" he asked.

"Nothing."

My once- or twice-a-week hysterical trips to the bathroom that left me calm and guilty made Sacha suspicious. With only one bathroom, there was no space for me to hide in our bungalow. I didn't want Sacha to find out about my habit, but I didn't know how not to do it.

It was only a matter of time before I got caught. Still, the day I made a cut that went too deep, when I finally had to come out of the bathroom and admit to Sacha what I had been doing to myself, the humiliation was worse than I could ever have imagined. Sacha examined my wound and determined that I didn't need stitches, but having to explain that I cut myself on purpose made me feel like the lowest of the low. The secret I had kept and that had kept me going for so long was finally out. And all I wanted to do was return it to its hiding place.

Sacha would have none of that. He confronted me head-on. After applying pressure and then tightly bandaging my arm, he said matter-of-factly that I needed help. Just as he had once told his mom how her bringing home strange men had made him feel, so he approached the issue of my cutting—directly, brutally, honestly.

"You need to go see someone," he said.

"I don't know if I can do that," I replied, full of shame and dread.

"Yes, you can, and I'm not talking about in a couple of weeks or months. We are going to look for someone *today*."

"I don't think I'll be able to find someone that I can open up to and tell all my problems."

"This is L.A. There are millions of therapists."

"I don't have time. I have too much going on. And it's too expensive. We spend too much money already."

"No, no, no. This is your future. This is your health. This is your life. You don't get to say no."

Like a cornered animal, I was searching for any way out of this situation. I couldn't talk about the bizarre ways I kept myself running with my understanding, nonjudgmental boyfriend. How was I going to explain it to some weird stranger staring at me from a chair?

"Look, you say you want to have kids," Sacha said in a softer tone. "Do you think this would be a good situation to have a child in? You can't be this kind of a person and raise children."

His words snapped me back to reality like one of my incisions. He was right; I wouldn't be a good mom if I continued with the way I was going. Something needed to change if I ever wanted to have a family, with Sacha or anyone else.

"I don't know how to do this," I said quietly.

"We are going to do this together," he replied. "I will help you find a therapist. I will go with you to therapy. Whatever you need me to do, I will do."

Neither of us had the first clue how to find a therapist, so I did what anyone does in a confusing situation: I googled "therapist" and "Venice Beach." My search offered websites with a bunch of names attached to educational histories, area of specialties, and locations. I found a woman who sounded good enough, mainly because she was really close by in Santa Monica. Now all I had to do was call her. I don't think I've ever been more nervous picking up the phone in my life. I didn't know what to say. How do you explain your problems to someone you've never met? I decided to go with vague.

"My life is very overwhelming and I don't have a lot of friends to talk to," I said. "I need someone to talk to."

Where I got that, I have no idea, maybe some Lifetime movie. It was true but only part of a much bigger truth. Explaining that I should come in to see if we made a good match, the therapist sounded nice enough. So I made an appointment for a session and a week later arrived at her building in Santa Monica. It was after practice and afterhours, so the building was completely quiet as I walked up one flight of stairs and down the hallway to her office before knocking on the door.

Erika—a small, thin woman in her mid- to late forties, wearing fitted slacks and a blousy top in neutral brown and peach linen that looked pretty and comfortable—opened the door.

"Are you Amanda?"

"Yes."

"Come on in and take a seat."

Inside her office there were two big chairs, a couch, and a desk. It was clean and modern but, again, comfortable. Taking a seat on the end of the couch, I noticed a basketful of toys for children in the corner. Out the window to my right, the lights of the passing cars made their way down the road running alongside the beach.

Erika asked me a whole bunch of questions about my background, just what you'd expect: parents, siblings, profession, boyfriends, etc.

"So what are you looking for in therapy?" she asked. "What do you hope to receive?"

"I really don't know. I can't imagine life being any different than it is," I said, searching for what to say although pretty sure I wouldn't find it. "I don't get why, even though I'm successful in my sport, own a beautiful home, can afford nice things, have a great boyfriend, and have lots of other things going for me, I'm still miserable."

Attaching words to my feelings, hearing out loud the thoughts that had been banging around in my head forever, I was surprised by how clear they were.

"I am so sick of being miserable all the time."

I couldn't understand the root of why I was such an unhappy person. Anyone looking from the outside would say I had a lot of great things going on, but I didn't see it that way at all. I couldn't break out of this cycle of being upset and having that state color everything around me in pure negativity. Then I told her about the cutting.

Erika didn't gasp or react with any emotion at all. In her soothing voice, she plugged away with more questions, treating my cutting just as she had my parents' divorce or my life as a competitive swimmer.

When I walked out of her office, I was feeling pleasantly surprised. I hadn't been completely at ease; I still found it awkward to tell a complete stranger my whole life story. At the same time, I had a sense of relief sharing my inner monologue. The volume went down ever so slightly on the negative loop that had been playing in my brain since I was a kid. Erika made it easy to talk to her. She wasn't a friend or a peer, so I didn't have to worry that she would get upset or tell my secrets.

I started seeing Erika once a week, but the thing about therapy is that you don't feel healed right away. In fact, in the beginning, I soon felt worse. Telling Erika all the situations that happened in my life was pretty emotional. It felt like shit to relive painful moments that were horrendous the first time around.

Erika explained that I needed to go through these things with her in the room so that she could understand what was going on in my mind. It was uncomfortable to the extreme. Once I got past the basics of my background and issues, often I found myself unable to find the right words to describe what was going on in my head.

"I just don't know how to get it out," I said many, many times in her office.

"You can't say anything wrong in here," she said.

It was especially hard when it came to cutting. Erika wanted the details of when and why I would cut myself. What was going through my mind in these moments? How did I feel immediately before and after cutting?

I described myself over and over as "a loose cannon" or "a horrible person." Only someone awful could cut herself and not be happy with all that I had been given. Slowly, Erika got me to understand that I was more normal than I thought.

"You know, you're not the only one in the world who does this," she said.

I wasn't sick beyond the point of repair. There were others who had dealt with this and had overcome it. Erika took my problems seriously but didn't punish me for them.

"We need to get it under control, but you are not a crazy person," she continued. "Let's figure out another solution for when you get to that point."

Despite the clarity they brought, I didn't look forward to my sessions. I had to drag myself there as I had to swim practice. Sometimes I felt as if my appointment was a complete nuisance or worse. I'd rather have been doing anything else. The process was a lot more complicated than anything I'd seen on TV. It was weird how much I dreaded sitting in a room where I could say anything I wanted to a really nice lady, who listened attentively.

The sessions I dreaded the most, however, were the ones with Sacha. Erika wanted him to come in once or twice a month to check in. I would have rather poked myself in the eye, but I trusted her enough by this point to know that it was necessary. I worried about it though, because unlike Erika, Sacha was someone in my life outside of therapy. To go from keeping everything inside to suddenly talking about everything was as big a leap as jumping off a cliff.

It was tough telling the man who showed me through affection, communication, and love that he thought the world of me and that I didn't feel good enough for him.

"I'm not pretty enough for you," I said in a session.

"What are you talking about?" he replied. "You are the prettiest person I've ever met."

"I don't know what you see, but this is what I see."

"Why would you think I don't think you're pretty?"

"I don't know."

That was the frustrating part. I didn't have any good answers for anything. In times of pure emotion, there were no coherent arguments to be had. The only reassurance in this confusion of feelings was the fact that Sacha had bothered to come to a therapist with me. No way would my exes have done that or would I have wanted them to. I recognized, through all the pain of these sessions, that it was a good sign that we were willing to work together on our future.

Whether I understood things or not, whenever I left Erika's office, I felt better than when I had arrived. It was just a matter of getting myself there.

A couple of months into the process, Erika began to talk to me about depression. She explained that her training didn't allow her to offer a clinical diagnosis but that I showed many of the signs of the disease.

"I think you should go and see a psychiatrist," she said. "Taking a medication might really help you."

Initially, I bristled at her recommendation. A psychiatrist? Really? Was this going to be another person I'd have to build a relationship with and go through the exhausting routine of explaining the inner workings of my mind? I didn't think I was up to it, but again, I trusted Erika. I really wanted to work on myself, so I didn't offer up any resistance.

"Whom do you think I should see?"

Erika gave me a referral for a psychiatrist, and I showed up at his cluttered office a week later. If I worried about having to divulge my innermost thoughts, I shouldn't have. There were no warm fuzzy feelings or emotional outbursts during the twenty-minute medical consultation.

"What's the problem?" he asked, like any other kind of doctor.

"I am not very happy very often. I am seeing a therapist and she thought it would be a good idea if I saw you. No crazy thing has ever happened to me. I have a good life. I have money. I have love. I don't understand why I am so upset and miserable."

"Maybe we can try some different medications and see what helps."

"Okay."

The psychiatrist wrote me up a prescription for Cymbalta. He wanted me to take thirty milligrams for a few weeks and then return for a follow-up visit.

I didn't run to the pharmacy to fill the prescription. I needed more information before I was going to take anything that would change my brain. I waited until my next session with Erika to discuss the psychiatrist's recommendation with her. She talked me through the whole thing. "Not all medications work on everybody. They can produce side effects that some patients don't think are worth the drug's benefits," she said, listing weight gain, sexual dysfunction, sleep problems, and fogginess as typical. "Sometimes people have to try for years to find what medication works best for them. There are many different drugs out there, so I don't want you to worry that if this doesn't work, that's it. The most important thing is for you to be honest about how you are feeling as you take it. Then we'll assess from there."

Although I started on a very low dosage, I was still really nervous that initial week. My first worry was about swimming. Athletes are very in tune with what's going on with their bodies. We also have a lot of ups and downs that fuel the drive to win. Would taking a med affect that in a bad way? I was scared it might dull my edges and ruin my competitive instinct.

I was also worried about weight gain. Again, as an athlete, any extra weight would totally screw with my swimming, which had enough problems on its own. But more to the point, I didn't want to get fat. Considering all my problems surrounding my self-image, I couldn't imagine feeling better on anything that made me heavier. On top of those two, not-small issues, I still had sponsors to keep happy. I'm pretty sure they weren't looking for a model bloated from antidepressants.

The fears, however, didn't outweigh the hope that the pills could make me feel better. I was excited to see if I had a shot at being an even-keeled person. I was tired of fighting all the time with the guy I loved. I wanted to silence that self-loathing tape loop playing in my head. So I went on Cymbalta.

At first I didn't feel anything—no change, good or bad. So the psychiatrist recommended that I increase the dosage, which I did, winding up on double the amount I started with.

My reaction to the medication was far less dramatic than I could ever have imagined. I didn't notice any weight gain or other side effects, but very gradually I did experience a mood shift. There was no *aha!* moment or huge change in my personality. I continued to have ups and downs, which I liked. I didn't want to become a robot that didn't laugh or cry.

What it did do was take some of the emotion out of the stupid little things that used to send me off the rails. About a month after I started taking Cymbalta, I walked into the house to find a pile of dirty dishes in the sink, and kept right on walking to the bedroom. I was able to let go—in traffic, with Sacha, even at swim practice.

Nobody commented on the shift. Other than Sacha, I was the only person who could really tell the difference. But there was definitely a change. My inner life was getting in order through a subtle, gradual process. The drugs helped a lot, because they gave me a floor to stand on while I did the hard work in therapy.

My response to Evan's call in the spring of 2007 that *Playboy* was interested in putting me on their cover was "Well, for the right amount of money, we can discuss it."

Posing naked would definitely create controversy, but personally I didn't see the big deal. There was no way I was going to let them photograph the downstairs area, so if I agreed to the shoot, the only thing I'd be showing that I hadn't shown previously were my nipples. My relationship with Sacha and being exposed to his artistic view of nudity had opened my thinking. Revealing the human body didn't have to be obscene. Sacha for one thought doing *Playboy*, an iconic magazine that had featured the likes of Marilyn Monroe on its covers, would be an honor.

In the end, for me, it came down to business. Morals, art, whatever: I knew that taking off my clothes was worth a lot of money. Evan went back and forth until the deal turned into a great payday for a few days of work, and I was in.

The shoot started in an L.A. studio, then moved to a Hollywood Hills house and a day in the desert. When I arrived at the studio, everyone was very nice and professional and set about the business of getting ready to take my picture. The hair and makeup girls, who turned out to be friends of Sacha, were outgoing and loosened me up with funny comments on just about everything. They certainly didn't give me a trip about any aspect of my appearance, which I appreciated.

Once I was camera-ready, I went out to the bigger studio, where they had built a little foot-deep pool. In the first shot, the photographer, a woman whom I had handpicked as part of my deal, wanted me to lie topless in the pool. Okay, this was *Playboy*.

I got into the water and tried to lie down. It was awkward in the ad hoc kiddie pool. As soon as I flipped around and the photographer began snapping pictures of my boobs and all, I became aware of lots of sets of eyes on me. There were at least ten guys standing around—from photo assistants to *Playboy* editors to caterers—and when breasts are bared, most guys look.

Suddenly I was annoyed. I didn't care if men looked at a naked photo of me in a magazine when I was nowhere around, but I didn't want them staring at me in the flesh. It takes around two hours for each shot, so I couldn't get uptight now or I'd be miserable for a while. So I tried to tune everything—and everyone—out.

As soon as the photographer said she had the shot, I burst out of the pool and into my robe, grabbed Sacha by the elbow, and pulled him into the bathroom—the one spot where we could have a moment of privacy.

"I don't like everyone out there staring at me," I said, my eyes welling up with tears. "I've worked on a lot of photo shoots, and all these guys don't need to be on set. I have a female photographer, she can be on set, hair and makeup too, you, and no one else. It needs to be a closed set or I'm going to lose it."

Sacha didn't need more convincing than that. He knew all too well what my "losing it" meant. He rubbed my shoulders, told me everything was going to be all right, and then went outside and handled it. When I got ready for the next shot, sure enough, the photographer, hair and makeup girls, and Sacha were the only ones left on set.

It was a long, exhausting shoot of twelve to fourteen hours for four days in a row, so that by the end, I wanted to yell at the photographer, *Just take the picture and let's get it over with already.* I couldn't wait to get home by the last day when, shooting out in the desert, they had me lying naked in the cold on sharp rocks. "How's that rock feel buck naked?" teased Gia, the spunky little makeup artist.

Not great, but it was nothing compared with having a bunch of strange guys circling me like vultures. After the set was closed, I felt confident on the shoot. It was more than a matter of privacy; I had stood up for myself and set some boundaries, which I would never have done in the past. Normally, I would have internalized the problem, pushed it down because I didn't want to make a fuss or offend anyone, only to have the shame and anger resurface in another place and time. Sure, my way of standing up for myself was to tell Sacha to do it for me. Still, it took an ability to figure out what I needed to feel better. That was new for me too. I was proud of myself that I had the guts to tell Sacha and let him help me. It was liberating not to worry about what everyone else was thinking or if I was hurting their feelings. It felt good to feel good.

When the July 2007 issue of *Playboy* with me on the cover hit newsstands, I was beyond proud of the results. It was no small thing for me to open up and reveal so much of myself. Here I was, a very private person with a history of negative feelings about my body, laying it all out for the world to see. I knew people were talking about the spread, and a lot of what they said wasn't nice. Still, I felt secure in and happy with my work. If the *Playboy* offer had come at any other point in my life, I wouldn't have accepted it because I wouldn't have been able to handle the scrutiny. This, however, was exactly the right time.

I went to my local bookstore, where I approached the cashier with five copies of *Playboy*, worried that he was going to recognize me as the person on the cover and wonder what kind of loser goes out and buys copies of her own magazine. But he didn't see the resemblance (ah, Photoshop). Instead, he probably thought I was a weirdo for buying five issues of a men's magazine.

All my friends and family told me they loved the pictures, while many others declared that I had degraded women in general and female swimmers in particular. Doing *Playboy* was cheap and would kill my career, they said. Chuck Wielgus, the USA Swimming executive director at the time, told the *Colorado Springs Gazette*, "As a membership organization that caters primarily to children and teenagers, I don't feel that the appearance . . . is an appropriate portrayal of our sport."

I don't know if he had to criticize me because of his position or if he actually didn't like my pictures, but at this point, I could have cared less what he or anyone else thought about it. I had fun with it. If people couldn't get over the fact that I showed my boobs, they shouldn't buy the magazine. I analyzed the motivations of those making a big fuss over my *Playboy* issue (they were trying to get themselves some media attention too) and put it all in perspective: the magazine was out for only a month, then someone else would be on the cover.

• • •

Unfortunately, my girl-power attitude still didn't extend to my swimming. I hit my lowest point of two very low years in April of 2008 at an event in Palo Alto. It wasn't an important meet in any way, but now that we were nearing the Olympics, everything felt like a big deal. When in the preliminaries I swam the 200-meter breaststroke poorly, as I had been doing all year, I couldn't take it a minute longer.

"I'm not going back for finals," I told Sacha over lunch in between the prelims and finals.

"Fine," he said. What did he care? Sacha wasn't my coach.

"You know what? I don't even know why I am bothering to go to trials. I am just going to make a fool of myself."

"Is there something else you can do?"

"Yeah—quit. It's not worth training anymore. I'm no good."

"Slow down. Slow down," said Sacha, using the phrase he always did when I worked myself up to the point where I had the path to certain doom fully mapped out in my head.

"What about finding another place to swim?" he asked.

"There is no other place."

"What about UCLA and Cyndi?"

Sacha had pointed out an obvious flaw in my previous statement. UCLA was the other big swimming school in L.A. I had thought about Cyndi Gallagher and her Division I team many times while frustrated with my own situation, but moving to UCLA had always seemed impossible. Now, two months before Olympic trials, I knew it was.

"There is no way she is going to let me come and bombard her team and let me train with her. It's too last-minute. It is not even worth calling to ask something like that."

"Being at USC is not going to get you anywhere. You said so yourself. So what's the harm in making a call?"

I would have typically argued with Sacha until we were in a fight about something personal and I could divert from the original topic. What he said, though, made sense, and I was able to hear it. My negativity had lifted, if only a tiny bit. But it gave me enough space to change my mind. I was at the extreme bottom of my swimming career, but that also meant I had nothing to lose.

A couple of minutes later, after getting Cyndi's number through a friend, I left her a message: "My training is not going well. I would love to train with you if you'd allow it. Or at least I'd love to come and talk to you about the possibility."

I met Cyndi a week later at Urth Caffe in Santa Monica, where after a quick friendly exchange she asked me why I wanted to train with her. "Honestly, I want to put myself in the best position possible to make the Olympic team," I said. "And my situation right now is not that. I'd love for you to give me an opportunity."

"Okay," Cyndi said matter-of-factly. "We start practice at six a.m. Monday. I want you to dive in."

It was as easy as that: a phone call, a meeting, and a yes. All I had to do was take the first step. When I was at USC, I was so depressed, my mood distorted my view of everything, including my role. Once it was clear USC wasn't a good fit, there were other options available to me. I just hadn't been healthy enough to see them. Now that I was in a better place, it was almost hard to remember what had kept me from doing this all along.

Even my fear of telling Dave—that he would be so pissed and disappointed—turned out to be false. It wasn't as if any of this was his fault, so there was no reason for him to take my decision badly. When I described my need for a new environment, he was responsive and kind. It didn't affect our friendship at all, as we continued to remain very close long after I left his pool.

Despite the ease of my transition, I was still nervous when I showed up for my first day of practice with the UCLA women's team (the college doesn't have a men's team). I could practice with the women because it was summer and so we were not in violation of the NCAA rules. I didn't know a lot about Cyndi or her training style, so I had no idea what practice was going to be like. I also wondered how the girls would react to my being there. I was starting from scratch all over again—only this time I had two months before Olympic trials.

Any anxiety I had wore off really quickly. Cyndi was a tough cookie who didn't take crap. I was impressed with the sets she gave us; they reminded me of Frank's training. Her exhausting endurance workouts were what I had missed, and they kicked my ass. When it came to the rest of the team members, they couldn't have been more welcoming. The very first week I arrived, a few of them invited me to the senior barbecue for everyone who was graduating. There was no subtext or subterfuge, just an invitation for burgers and hot dogs with the girls.

My relief when I arrived at UCLA was nearly instant. A switch got turned on; I was happier, mellower, and more energized. Even the commute was better. UCLA, only a thirty-minute commute from Venice, is situated right next to Bel Air, one of the fancier neighborhoods in L.A. The difference between this and the USC campus was like night and day.

After a few days of practice with my new team, I was no longer coming home pissed off and arguing with Sacha. Noticing a difference in me, he took a chance of having me bite his head off and asked me how my swimming was going.

"I love it," I said.

"Thank goodness!" he replied, probably more relieved than me.

My training was definitely better, and quickly I felt stronger, but I wasn't sure how much I could do in such a short time before trials. I knew the change had improved my mental state, but had it done enough for me to go to the Olympics? The only way I'd know was by giving it a shot.

The trials held in Omaha turned out to be better than any of my other past experiences—but that had nothing to do with swimming. It had everything to do with my awesome roommate, Kim Vandenberg. Kim was a UCLA swimmer who had become one of my best friends on the team. She and I fed off each other's energy anywhere we were together, from the pool deck to our room at trials. We had so much fun in Omaha that the time almost felt more like a girls' weekend than an incredibly stressful swimming event. In our room, we blew off steam by dancing around to Kim's mixes of obnoxious rap and watching lots of *Nip/Tuck*.

Approaching the trials in a really light, carefree way reminded me of my first Olympics, when I was a fourteen-year-old goofball who didn't take anything too seriously. Twelve long, hard years later, I had reclaimed the good part of my youth. Now that I was older, however, the laughs and silliness weren't an act to mask deeper problems. I had the maturity to realize that I'd done all the work I could by that point, so I might as well just enjoy whatever was going to happen.

And I *really* enjoyed what happened. Despite a bad couple of years swimming and despite changing coaches less than two months earlier, I finished second in the 200-meter breaststroke. I was going to China, becoming one of only three other women in U.S. swimming history to make four Olympic teams!

The thirty family members and friends who had come to watch me went nuts. After the race, they confessed how nervous they'd all been beforehand. "This stupid meet made us sick, it is so stressful," Sacha said. "Your sister had to have a beer before it, she was so worked up. Oh my God, you have no idea what this does to us. It took years off my life."

I was sorry they were having such a hard time, but I felt great. Since I had begun training with Cyndi, I no longer was having the same urges to cut myself. Within the last two months, the bad stuff had faded out while everything good came together. I loved my workouts, had made a good girlfriend in Kim, and was fighting less with Sacha. It seemed like it happened overnight, but I knew it was a progression of my work over the entire year. The messy period of therapy and the medication had paid off.

It was this and not my swimming times that made Beijing seem like the best Olympics ever. After Dara Torres, a freak of nature still competitively swimming in her forties, I was the oldest person on the team at the age of twenty-six. Bringing with me all the best attributes of age, including experience and humor, I was voted team captain. Kim had also made the Olympic team, so I got to have my best bud with me. On top of all that, China had gone all out to make its Olympic Village the most beautiful and best organized I'd ever seen. Unique artistic flourishes popped up everywhere in the form of gardens, sculptures, and even the pool. For the Olympics, the Chinese government had built an amazing building called the Water Cube, which was no ordinary stadium. The walls and ceiling looked like they were constructed from enormous bubbles, which changed colors, from blues to hot pink. Inside, these astonishing bubbles surrounded a state-of-the-art pool and stands.

My positive mind-set couldn't change the fact that I didn't have years of great swims under my belt. I couldn't help but ask myself how I had made it here, but my answer was always the same: *Now I am here, so I will do what I can do.*

When I dove in to swim my 200-meter breaststroke preliminary race, I didn't feel unstoppable but I was good. I didn't push it as hard as I could have, because I always wanted to save something for the finals. I finished in 2:27.70, more than four seconds slower than my Olympic record. It wasn't great for me but still a decent time—one that I assumed would get me to the finals, where I could show everyone what I was really made of.

With another heat to go, I moved to the corner of the pool deck to watch the rest of the races. Within minutes the whole situation shifted. Standing in disbelief, I looked at the times coming up on the scoreboard and the terrible realization dawned on me: I wasn't going to get another swim at this Olympics. My competitors swam really fast and sent me down to eighteenth in the preliminaries, which meant I missed the finals by two places.

As shame and disappointment welled up from old sources of

pain, I knew I had to get out of there. But in order to exit the pool deck, I had to maneuver through the world's longest line of media in the ultimate walk of shame. Wishing I could disappear, I didn't look a single person in the face. I kept my eyes on my feet through the maze of reporters, cameramen, and photographers. I was so angry with myself; I should have gone all out. This was the Olympics. So what that I'd medaled in every Olympics before. Did I think I could just cruise into the finals? How could I have been so stupid?

I didn't need to worry about the media's presence, since not a single one of them wanted to talk to me, which, as it turned out, hurt even more than being confronted on how much I had sucked would have. I had pictured myself walking through the line with a smile on my face and answering hundreds of questions. I wanted to be a winner. Instead, I was embarrassed.

As if on autopilot, I went to the part of the complex where the warm-up pool was located and started to get into it to warm down. Then reality stopped me in my tracks. *I am done with my swimming. It doesn't matter if I warm down now. Nothing matters. I'm finished.*

I sat down near the pool by myself and let doom and anguish wash over me. I had tortured myself with swimming for two years, all those hours in the car commuting, all those mornings jumping into a freezing cold pool, the endless shit I put Sacha through, all our stuff that I broke, for nothing. There was so much buildup to the Games through interviews, commercials, opening ceremonies, and more interviews. The hype grew along with the expectation of bringing home medals for my country and then—*bam!*—two minutes go by and I'm done and all alone. The insane scenario didn't make any sense except to use as a way to torture myself.

Sitting on the stands, suddenly I felt sicker than my eighteenth placement had already made me. A devastating thought made room for itself in my already overwhelmed brain: by failing I had wasted the time and money of all the family and friends who'd made the expensive trip to China for me. Thousands of dollars from people who didn't have tons of money went down the drain in two minutes. *Two minutes.*

I had to find my family right away and tell them how sorry I was that I had let them down. I was ashamed enough without their thinking I didn't care. I needed to let them know I'd make it up to them somehow.

I ran back to the main pool in the Water Cube and called Sacha on his cell to have him meet me at a spot near the stands. But he didn't come alone. Right behind him were my mom, dad, sisters, aunts, uncles, cousins, and friends. As soon as I saw everyone, I began bawling. Sacha enveloped me in a big hug, followed by my dad.

"I'm a failure," I said. "You all wasted your money to see nothing."

All of them looked at me like I was crazy.

"Are you kidding?" my mom said. "We're having a blast running around China. You have no idea."

"Oh man, we went to the Night Market in Beijing, which was a crazy scene," Taryn said. "You can't believe what people eat here. They'll fry anything, including sea horses and starfish. Aunt Sally dared Uncle Joe to eat these fried scorpions on a skewer, and he did!"

"You did too after I dared you," Uncle Joe said.

"Everyone ate them," my dad said. "We've got the video proof to show you later of everyone crunching on scorpion."

I couldn't help but laugh at the thought of my family chowing down on bugs in China.

"That's nothing compared to what happened to us on our way to the Great Wall," my cousin Monica said. "The seats in the minivan we took weren't bolted to the floor, so every time the driver, who was listening to super loud techno, hit the brakes, the whole row of seats went flying forward."

"A chunk of the floor in the car was missing," Leah said. "We could see the road flying by! I totally thought we were about to die."

I had thought their whole trip had centered around me and my Olympic performance, but I understood they clearly didn't feel the same way. I couldn't even get them to shut up for two seconds to tell them anything about my race once they got going on their crazy Chinese adventures.

While the rest of my bizarre family were discussing whether scorpions tasted like the Extra Crispy Strips from KFC, Sacha took me by the shoulders and looked me directly in the eye.

"I understand that it isn't what you wanted. You wanted to be amazing and come home with a gold medal and be a superstar. I get it," he said. "But you are walking away eighteenth in the world. I don't know a lot of people who are eighteenth in the world in anything. You have to realize that with everything you've been brave enough to work through, you cannot call yourself a failure."

The Olympics is a distorted mirror of life. In the world of the Games, you have four years to prepare for a moment—two minutes, five minutes, maybe a little more—where your entire worth is instantly judged. If you don't perform up to a certain standard, no matter the reason—a sudden bout of flu or insecurity—you are a failure and everything you worked for over the last four long years counts for nothing. The artificial construct produces the highest highs and the lowest lows. It's comfortable to divide people into winners and losers (not to mention it makes good television). But in real life the categories aren't so easy. Personal moments of triumph and loss often can't be understood by anyone else. Sometimes success, as Sacha put it, is simply being willing to give it your all.

I wasn't crazy to be upset about losing at the Olympics; anyone in my position would have felt the same way. I couldn't have competed at the level I did if I didn't care *a lot*. If the same thing had happened in 2004, I would have gone off the deep end. I can't even imagine how low I would have sunk. In 2008, however, after an intense year of examining my hardest issues, I allowed myself to feel anger and sadness and then let it go. I cheered on my teammates and celebrated their wins, and I enjoyed my family and did a bunch of sightseeing myself. The difference between being healthy and unhealthy was that I didn't let my failures kill my successes. I had so much to be proud of and happy with—not the least of which was the wonderful man by my side.

chapter 12

By the time Sacha and I had packed up all our stuff and thrown it into the U-Haul, it was around five p.m., kind of late to be starting out for Tucson and leaving our old life behind. We didn't care though. It felt like an adventure, which felt like us.

Right before the Olympics, I had put my Venice house up for sale after a game-changing discussion with Sacha. In a good place and ready to take our lives to the next level, we had been talking seriously about having kids and possibly getting married. We both agreed that we didn't want to raise a family in Venice. It was doable in one thousand square feet—lots of people make do with much less—but it wasn't our dream.

Meanwhile, I owned a gorgeous three-thousand-square-foot house in Tucson that was just sitting empty. There we could live for a quarter of the price in three times the square footage with a pool, acres of land, and a backdrop of the desert and mountains. Or we could stay in our shoe box and battle traffic. The choice for me was obvious, but I didn't know about Sacha. The photography scene in Tucson might not be as happening as in L.A. What about his friends? I didn't want him to sacrifice so much for our family that he turned bitter. I had learned enough about life that I knew we needed at least to talk about it.

A couple of weeks before the Olympics, I asked him directly, "What would you think about moving to Tucson?"

"I love Tucson," he said. "I'd love to."

"Really?"

"Yeah!"

"Awesome, let's sell this house."

Just as in my conversation with Cyndi two months earlier, the plan fell together so easily, it didn't seem real. As Sacha and I talked some more, it quickly became clear he shared my line of thinking: living in Venice as a couple was fine, but Tucson was perfect for a family.

After two weeks on the market, the bungalow sold while we were at the Olympics. So exactly a week after returning from Beijing, we had given away everything we weren't taking to Arizona, packed up the rest ourselves, and started out for our new life with Sacha and one of our four German shepherds in the U-Haul and me and the rest of the dogs in the Navigator. (Yes, we lived with four huge dogs in Venice, which was patently crazy.)

An hour out of Tucson, suddenly a thunderbolt cracked through the enormous sky. Sacha and I, who had been talking to each other on the phone for the entire eight-hour drive, watched in silent amazement. You don't get a lot of weather in Southern California, but in Arizona there are monsoons caused by a shift in the winds that unleash wild electrical storms followed by torrential rain. As our little caravan made its way home, the lightning shot through the night, illuminating our dark surroundings for a brief second and reminding me of the flashlight's strobe cutting the sea during night scuba dives. The storm that turned the sky purple and pink in flashes didn't scare us; it reassured us. *We are doing the right thing.* The electricity ran through us as well as the sky.

When we arrived in Tucson at 2:00 a.m., we dragged a mattress inside, since there wasn't a stick of furniture in the house. Although completely empty, the house felt instantly like home. In the following days (and eventually years), Sacha and I talked all the time about how homey this place was. "Even if I made millions, I wouldn't want to leave," I said. Sacha agreed wholeheartedly: "This is a place where you want to spend the rest of your life."

I love everything about the house starting with its privacy. Trees surround the entire property so that you can't see into our home. Far from claustrophobic, the house boasts an enormous living room with huge sliding glass doors that lead directly onto a backyard that could belong to a five-star resort. Perfectly landscaped by Sacha, who did all the work himself, the yard has flat stones leading to a big pool with a waterfall and Jacuzzi. Comfortable lounge chairs and a fire pit increase the sense of being on vacation.

We have the most wildly beautiful backyard ever. Not too far beyond our land lie mountains covered in the saguaro cacti that only grow in this region. With pitchforked arms reaching to the sky, they grow on average thirty feet into the air. Sacha and I could hop on our bikes or put on our hiking boots and head right from our house into the many trails winding through the savage landscape. One of my favorite things to do became hiking about forty minutes over the other side of the mountain to an outrageously luxurious JW Marriott hotel, where we arrived with a big appetite for the resort's super fancy brunch. After eggs Benedict, we hiked back home.

With both of us taking time off from work and responsibility, we spent our days swimming in the pool, hiking, relaxing, and furniture shopping. Everything was different from life back in Venice—even the décor. We bought a stupidly huge and comfy couch from Crate & Barrel for our enormous living room. Upholstered in soft-brushed suede and covered in tons of pillows, it could fit twenty people easily. It had nothing to do with that torture device Sacha had insisted upon in our bungalow. This beast accommodated all the boys playing video games and my marathon movie watching.

We couldn't have picked a more perfect situation in which to start trying for a baby. So right after we got home from Beijing, I stopped taking my birth control and my antidepressants.

I had wanted to go off Cymbalta before the Olympics, because

I was emotionally ready. It didn't have anything to do with being worried that people would find out I was on the antidepressant. As someone who was drug-tested all the time, I had to write down anything I put into my body—from Advil to Cymbalta. The swimming officials are discreet and would never make a big issue out of any medicine an athlete needed for his or her health. The Olympics didn't change that fact. But I was terrified of going through withdrawal when I needed to be in peak physical condition. If I missed one pill of Cymbalta by mistake, I felt almost drunk. I would get dizzy and sometimes my vision would be blurry. I didn't know how long it took before those side effects went away. It would have been incredibly stupid for me to do anything like that to my body when preparing for the Olympics.

When I left for Beijing, I stopped seeing the psychiatrist and Erika, who left a message on my phone saying that if I ever needed to talk, I could call. Although therapy was a transforming experience, I was ready to be done. Erika had helped me to find my voice for expressing uncomfortable emotions, such as anger and sadness, as well as to develop tools to rely on when I still couldn't find the right words. I didn't need her anymore, because now I could do it on my own.

I was far from perfect. In fact the way I went off my medication showed a secretive side that still masked insecurity. Although on some level I knew it was stupid, I went off the pills without consulting a doctor of any kind. Even though my performance in Beijing had been terrible, I was in a good place when I returned. And I didn't want to be pregnant on Cymbalta. The pace in Tucson was slower and I felt confident I would be okay without the pills, so I came up with my own plan to wean myself off them.

Because the pills were capsules, which meant I couldn't break them in halves or quarters, I decided to take one every two days, and then one every three days, and so on. I don't know what I was thinking; I'm no doctor. I should have consulted a psychiatrist in Tucson and gone off the pills under his or her care. But deep down I was worried the doctor would tell me not to go off the medication, and I didn't want to hear that. So for the next two weeks, I felt like shit. My mood was fine but it was as if I were drunk *and* hungover at the same time. It was not good. After the symptoms disappeared, they never returned. I was just lucky that I didn't experience any devastating mood swings.

I was actually mellower than I can ever remember having been before. I was a really happy person. My temper flare-ups and urges to cut or purge were like an illness when it passes: you remember that you were sick but can no longer recall the suffering. Everything that Sacha and I were doing felt like steps in the right direction. We were simplifying our life, and it was really nice. I wasn't swimming or thinking about swimming at all. We were just having fun and trying to have a family.

If I was happy the minute we arrived in Tucson, by Christmas I was delirious. I'm not one of those people who gets depressed around the holidays. I love everything about that time of year, from peppermint lattes to Christmas commercials on TV. Sacha indulged my Christmas crazies, which included getting a gigantic tree that extended to the top of our thirteen-foot ceiling and covering it with ornaments and lights. Because our house is an adobe structure, it's not the easiest to hang lights from. But I wasn't going to let the desert or its architecture stand in the way of my Christmas spirit. I draped our whole front yard in white lights and covered the trees in huge ornaments. And of course, I had my famous little Christmas town, which wasn't so little anymore. In every corner it looked like Christmas had puked.

Leading up to the holiday, Sacha had been acting kind of funny. He kept leaving the house to go shopping. It was suspicious because Sacha is an Internet guy; he buys everything off the computer. Yet he was ducking out often to go on this continuous shopping trip. When I tried to ask him what he was doing, he told me not to worry. But I did worry; I was both terrified and completely sure that he was out buying me another puppy. We had enough space for five, but I didn't think I could handle it.

On Christmas morning, it was just the two of us under the tree. It's always fun to have a lot of family around during the holidays, but spending this one alone with Sacha was very sweet and somehow fitting. When we were done opening the gifts, I started to get up, but Sacha pointed to a small card on the tree, which read, "Merry Christmas. I love you. You have one more gift. It's hidden and you have to find it."

Thoughtful, romantic Sacha. I began searching around the Christmas tree and the nearby area. I knew he knew how impatient I was and that I wouldn't put up with a housewide Christmas present hunt. It didn't take me long to locate the little blue box that didn't belong in my Santa statue's sack of toys. I could tell right away from the robin's-egg color of the box where it came from: Tiffany's.

After opening the box and finding an engagement ring, I started bawling. We had been through a lot together and I never doubted that he was the man of my life. But we had laid-back attitudes about getting married, since neither of us was very traditional. We had both said we didn't want to do it just to do it. I was thrilled to receive the ring and make things official with Sacha because I now knew it was something he also really wanted to do. An engagement would have been meaningless if we didn't have all the many levels of commitment we did underneath this last one, but it added one more terrific layer.

Sacha grabbed the box out of my hand and put the ring on my finger. "I love you with all my heart. I want to spend the rest of my life with you and have a family with you," he declared. "Will you please marry me?"

Something's weird about you," Sacha said one day in late January.

"Something's weird about you too," I replied.

"No, I'm not kidding. You're different."

"What are you talking about?"

"I think you're pregnant. I know you are."

"Shut up. I'm not pregnant."

That didn't satisfy Sacha, who was so sure, he drove to the pharmacy right away, bought a home pregnancy test, returned, and made me take it. It turned out he was right.

I didn't love being pregnant at all. It wasn't gaining weight that bothered me (although I wound up putting on an extra fifty pounds). It was the morning sickness. I thought I'd lucked out on that awful rite of passage when I didn't have nausea my first trimester. Oh no, unlike what I heard from other women, I started getting morning sickness right around my second trimester and it lasted for the rest of my pregnancy. Almost every single day I was sick, pull-over-on-the-side-of-the-freeway sick. And I have no idea why it's called morning sickness, since I was sick at all hours of the day.

With an energy level at a permanent zero, I could lie on the couch for huge stretches of the day, no problem. I was so tired that I found simple things like taking a shower and putting lotion on afterward exhausting. I hardly had the steam to stand up, let alone put together the nursery. I kept waiting for that nesting phase to kick in and send me into an all-night frenzy of assembling the crib and stenciling the walls with something cute. But it never came. When my dad came to visit, I complained to him from the couch that I just couldn't do it, so my dad did all my nesting for me.

The heat in Tucson didn't help my motivation any. People say when you're pregnant, you run ten degrees hotter than everyone else. I was running about twenty degrees hotter. When folks came over to visit, they had to borrow sweatshirts and blankets to stay warm in my frosty ice palace. At night, I lay on top of the covers in shorts and a tank top while Sacha was buried inside a hoodie, sweats, and three blankets.

If I had no motivation to get up off the couch and make my unborn child's room cute, I had even less to swim. Everyone assumed I'd be doing laps until the bitter end, but the last thing I wanted to do was parade my new body around in a swimsuit. I wasn't one of those people who felt sexy and beautiful with my big old belly. Arriving at a real training pool where everyone was used to seeing me in shape so that they could watch me waddle into the pool and splash around like a sick dolphin: sorry. I have a pool in my backyard that is perfectly suitable for floating in private, which is what I did for the majority of my pregnancy.

While I was gaining weight rapidly, it wasn't as if I was eating like an animal. I did have one bizarre food fixation—well, beverage fixation. My one obsession was Gatorade. I went through the sports drink like it was going out of style. I'm not even sponsored by them, so I actually had to buy cases of the stuff myself, and it's not cheap. But there was nothing I enjoyed more than putting a lemon-lime Gatorade in the freezer for an hour to make a slushy. I literally did that all day long. And when I found myself out of the drink, it wasn't unusual for Sacha to find me crying over it. But that—and crying over life insurance commercials—was the extent of my mood swings.

Even though I could barely pick myself up off the couch to shower, I did rally for a trip to a tiny private island two and a half miles off the coast of Bali when I was a very hefty five months pregnant. We had booked our trip to Wakatobi Dive Resort after we got engaged and before I knew I was pregnant; able to accommodate fewer than sixty people, the five-star resort fills up way in advance. A diver's paradise surrounded by pristine coral reefs, the place is not easy to get to. After flying to Indonesia, you have to take a chartered plane (which only goes in and out of the airport every eleven days) to another nearby island. Then it's a boat ride for the last leg.

From the moment we stepped on the chartered plane, it was nonstop luxury. Flying above, we caught sight of the emerald-green island ringed by white sand beaches and crystalline aqua water. When we arrived, there were people to hold every piece of luggage, plastic bag, or magazine weighing us down. They also greeted us with little bottles of water and moist, lavender-scented washcloths to make sure we arrived at Wakatobi refreshed.

There were two staff members per guest, so it was perfect for a lazy pregnant lady like me. The only thing I was nervous about was the food. According to the website, all the food was top-notch and not going to make guests used to Western hygiene incredibly sick. Still, you never know what you'll find until you arrive. Sacha and I landed on the island just as lunch was being served, and as soon as we saw the spread, we knew we'd be just fine.

In the open, airy dining room with a view of the ocean, there was everything you could ever want: salmon with rice, chicken skewers and salad, hearty steaks, and fresh stir-fries. A pastry chef made fresh cakes, cookies, tarts, and doughnuts to be enjoyed alongside the colorful array of fresh fruit. I chose a freshly blended drink of lime, ginger, and mint to wash it all down.

Because my feet were incredibly swollen from flying for so long, I was directed right to the spa, where I got reflexology—something I treated myself to every single day of our stay. Wakatobi was take-your-breath-away heaven, from my hot chocolate in the morning, where some genius put different designs, such as a fish or palm tree, into the foam on top, to the clear eighty-eight-degree water that was like jumping into a fully stocked aquarium. When I wasn't stuffing myself or checking out sea turtles and brightly colored tropical fish, I was vegging out. We were completely off the grid. Our cell phones didn't work on the island and there was only one computer in the hotel, with dial-up Internet access that didn't work half the time and was too slow to deal with when it did.

Part of the reason we came to Wakatobi was to get married. We knew it wouldn't be official—we weren't going to obtain a marriage license in Jakarta—but we wanted to do something unique and memorable just for us. Before the trip, we had discussed our plans with the staff, who made all the arrangements for our "wedding"—

except one. They had neglected to tell me that the traditional Muslim ceremony (because everyone on the island was Muslim) would require that I be covered up from head to toe. I had brought a couple of sundresses, but nothing appropriate for a conservative culture's traditions. Not even close.

So I went to the resort gift shop (the only place on the island to do any shopping) and bought a long-sleeved black tunic with beading around the neck (fancy!) that hit right below my knees. Under that I wore a maroon and gold-flowered sarong that reached down to my feet. Covering my head I wore a lace scarf as a hijab.

If my garb was out of character, Sacha was in a whole other level of costume. With his sarong, a *taqiyah* (the short, rounded cap worn by observant Muslim men) sitting on top of his head, a black shirt, and a wooden dagger that he had to wear in his waistline for some reason we didn't know, Sacha looked like Aladdin.

I wasn't sure we were going to make it through our beach ceremony without laughing. The village elder—a tiny man with skin the color of a coconut, thick jet-black hair, and a black Pancho Villa mustache to match—came to marry us, because he was the only one with authority to do so. (The village elder doubled as the airport's head of security, so we have a picture of him officiating at our wedding and another one of him in his security guard uniform before we departed.)

On May 1, 2009, I said "I do" to Sacha. Well, actually I'm not sure what I said or what happened, since not a word of English was spoken during the entire ceremony. Still, I'll never forget a moment of it, and I know I could never have done that with anybody other than Sacha.

We may have been husband and wife in the eyes of Muhammad, but when we returned from paradise, we still had to make it legal. Two months after Indonesia, I had a trip to Reno planned for a swim clinic. Sacha and I, being big road trippers, decided to make the two-day drive instead of fly from Tucson. As it turns out, Las Vegas, the city of gambling, stripping, and marriage, was smack in the middle of our journey.

Going to the courthouse and getting hitched by a justice of the peace was way too boring for us. So when we stopped in Vegas, we decided to pick the cheesiest place we could find: the Little White Wedding Chapel. This is the place where the wrestler "Stone Cold" Steve Austin wed WWE diva Debra Marshall and where Britney Spears in a baseball cap was walked down the aisle by a hotel bellman so she could marry a friend from her hometown in Louisiana. This was not exactly the Four Seasons.

We decided to go all the way and opt for the Tunnel of Love ceremony, which is a drive-thru wedding. So Sacha and I, now seven months pregnant, drove into the drive-thru (it had cupids painted on the ceiling in a fresco dedicated to love) and up to the window, where a minister slid open the glass and gave us our vows. It was just like McDonald's, except we ordered commitment until death do us part instead of a Big Mac and fries.

After everything we'd been through already, we wanted to celebrate ourselves and enjoy this blissful time. Too many weddings were for other people, we said. This time was for us.

To please our families, who wanted to be part of the fun, we had a reception at our home in Tucson at the end of June where over a hundred family and friends gathered for an all-day party. Although we pulled out the stops when it came to the food—an amazing local chef created a menu of delicious finger foods that changed every hour—it was strictly a casual affair. Jeans and T-shirts was the attire, the music came from an iPod hooked up to speakers, and absolutely no toasts. The event wasn't about raising a glass to the perfect daughter or friend, it was about drinking, eating, and hanging out with people we loved. And when it was over, it was all about cleaning up. (I don't know why I thought it would be a good idea to host a blowout in my own home when I was seven months pregnant. It took forever to find all the beer bottles in the backyard, and I'm pretty sure I mopped the house ten times to get all the sticky dirt up from the tile grouting.)

By the last week before my September 16 due date, I thought this baby was never going to come. Because I had preeclampsia, a condition that included high blood pressure, I was put on bed rest for the last month of pregnancy, when I watched every Lifetime movie ever made, twice. At my doctor's appointment on the morning of September 14, I was told they were going to induce me on my due date because of my condition.

Sacha suggested we go out that evening and have a last night as non–baby people, having dinner and seeing a movie, the kind of activities we heard we'd never do again. As soon as we left the doctor's, however, I started feeling pain in my back. My back hadn't been great for my whole pregnancy, so I ignored it. But by that afternoon I couldn't ignore it any longer. When I told Sacha that my back was killing me, he turned on the Jacuzzi so I could soak for a while. When he came outside to check on me, I told him, "It's hurting again."

"What do you mean, again?" he asked.

"The pain keeps coming."

"What are you talking about?"

"It's coming every five minutes or so."

"Amanda, I think you're having the baby!"

Getting out of the Jacuzzi, I felt like an ass. What kind of mom was I going to be if I didn't even know I was having a baby?

"I'm going to start timing everything," Sacha said.

He had a whole chart going and going and going until around 8:00 p.m., when the contractions were so bad, my whole body froze during them. That's when we got on the road to the hospital, where I got my epidural and was wheeled into a birthing room. I might be an endurance swimmer known for toughing it out through the hardest set a coach can dream up, but childbirth kicked my ass. It wasn't until 11:00 a.m. on September 15, 2009, that Blaise Ray Brown was finally born.

Blaise was the easiest kid in the world to name. His middle name, Ray, is a family name. It is my paternal grandfather's name, my dad's middle name, and mine too, as well as Sacha's grandfather's name. Our baby's unusual first name was no less obvious though.

The inspiration for his name (which belonged to both the patron saint of sufferers from sore throats and a brilliant seventeenth-century child prodigy, mathematician, scientist, and philosopher) came when I had just starting dating Sacha, who was working on a photo shoot with a lot of little kids, one of whom was named Blaise. As soon as I heard him say it, I loved it.

When we found out that I was pregnant, I told Sacha, "I don't care if it's a boy or a girl, I want to name our baby Blaise."

"Slow down, slow down," he said. "We can put it on the list. I want to research this, look over baby books, and come up with something that's really meaningful."

I was stuck on Blaise, but I returned home the following day with about five different baby name books.

"Here you go," I said, dumping the books on the kitchen table. "Knock yourself out."

Sacha picked up one of the books randomly and said, "I'm going to flip through the book, and whatever name I point to is what we are going to name our kid."

"Terrific. That's super meaningful."

He flipped through the pages with his eyes closed for dramatic purposes and put his finger on a name. After he looked down, I saw his mouth drop. "Holy shit, Amanda," he said. "I just put my finger on Blaise."

"Don't tease me. I love that name."

"I'm not joking. Come here and check it out."

I didn't believe him and almost didn't walk over. I didn't want to see some name like Howard under his finger, but Sacha refused to budge. When I got in front of the book, I saw his finger was pointing straight to the name Blaise.

The magic of the moment was crazy. I felt like Blaise was giving us a message: *I'm coming*.

"Okay," Sacha said, closing the book. "You win. The baby's name is Blaise."

I had never seen so much crap packed into a car in my life. There was a Pack 'n Play, a stroller, a vibrating chair, diapers, bottles, a breast pump, clothes, and God knows what else. The last thing we loaded into the car before we hit the road for a four-thousand-mile, six-week road trip was two-and-a-half-month-old Blaise.

I had never been so excited to hit the road in all my life. Taking care of a newborn when you've never even babysat before—not even an older baby or big kid—is a draining experience. As soon as I laid my eyes on him, I had an instant connection. I was flooded with an overwhelming, nervous kind of love. From the moment we met, I entered into a constant state of worry. Was I giving him the right nutrients? Is he too warm or too cold? Is the car seat really installed the right way?

Although I would have suffered a slow and excruciating death rather than see him harmed in any way, it took awhile for Blaise and me to really bond. For the first month, I couldn't shake the feeling that this was my first babysitting gig and that the real mom was going to show up any minute. The realization that yes, I *am* the mom here, needed some time to solidify. My new identity was a massive and permanent change.

The first pang of my new role came in the form of guilt—over the fact that I was awful at breastfeeding. I found breastfeeding worse than both pregnancy and the actual process of giving birth. Blaise had trouble latching on, and when he did, I found the pain excruciating. I cried as he nursed, it hurt so much, and eventually my poor cracked nipples bled. I dreaded having to feed him, which was terrible because he was my baby and because he wanted to nurse all the time.

You hear so much about the importance of breastfeeding before you have a baby, but few people talk about how emotionally draining and physically painful it can be. For six weeks straight, I felt like the biggest failure as a woman and a mom. This was not the natural, easy, and loving act that I thought it would be from looking at the picture of the mom and baby on the packaging that came with my breast pump. I had already started to screw up and I had just gotten Blaise.

I eventually confided in Leah what a breastfeeding disaster I was, and she said she'd been even worse. With her first child, she got such bad infections that she was only able to breastfeed for two weeks, so with her second she didn't even try. "Don't stress about it," she said. "If you are stressed, you won't enjoy the experience of having the baby and bonding. Just take it one day at a time and do what's right for you. If you can't breastfeed, it's not the biggest deal in the world." Thank God for older sisters. I wound up lasting four months, a record I'm proud of, but I took Leah's advice to figure out my own path to motherhood.

I quickly realized that I was going stir-crazy in the house. It seemed like the only times we went out were to see Blaise's pediatrician. "We can't live like this," I complained to Sacha. "It's not healthy."

Instead of making dinner plans or going on a trip to a resort in Hawaii, we headed out on a crazy trip. From Thanksgiving to Christmas, we meandered through the north and southwest. In San Francisco to visit Sacha's family for Thanksgiving, all of us watched the Christmas tree lighting in Union Square. In Bend, Oregon, we drank cocoa as we marveled at the Cascade Mountains. Then we drove to Astoria on the other side of the state to see the place where they filmed *The Goonies*. We hit Washington, Idaho, and southern Utah before making our way home to Arizona. In Utah, we drove to Bryce Canyon National Park and stopped now and then to take little hikes in the snow. Surrounded by incomparable natural beauty, I stuffed Blaise into the Patagonia snowsuit I'd bought him, covered him with a blanket, and carried him on our walks.

I love the fact that we started Blaise's life with traveling. He was so good in different environments. He was a trooper during the long stretches of driving and as we bounced him from house to house to hotel and more. Some people thought we were nuts, but I thought being stuck in my house all the time was nuts. When we eventually did return to Tucson, going out to dinner no longer seemed like such a big deal: just grab a big bag of junk and go out the door.

I found my groove when it came to the title of "mom," and soon I came to love it more than "Olympian" or anything else I've been called. But I couldn't get used to the body that came with it. Five weeks after Blaise was born, I returned to the pool just to get out of the house and lose some of the weight I'd put on during the pregnancy. Far from doing hard-core training, no more than two or three times a week I would show up at the pool wearing something that invariably had baby puke on it and stay only an hour.

Although I was completely exhausted and nervous about leaving Blaise for even a second, it was nice to swim for an hour. Everyone, even new moms, need a little bit of time for themselves. It didn't matter how slowly I went, the water took pressure off everything. Cleansing and cushioning, I relished my weightlessness.

After a little more than a month, I slowly started to increase my workouts, and by February I was talking to Sacha about returning to swimming. To what extent and for what purpose I couldn't really say. All I knew was that I still loved and missed the sport. Being a mom posed challenges to any kind of participation, but I really didn't worry too much about failing at swimming. Failing my son was my only serious concern now.

The biggest immediate challenge facing me was getting fit again. I'd been out of shape before—particularly when I took two years off between 2006 and 2008—but nothing compared with this. I had not only taken a year off during which I gained fifty pounds, but now I slept for only two hours in a row, max. So much for the days of eating right and getting eight hours of sleep.

I dropped twenty pounds within the first few months of having Blaise, but then the weight loss stopped. Those thirty extra pounds wouldn't come off from my swimming workouts. That had never happened before and it drove me crazy. For the life of me I couldn't lose that weight.

In March when I began training full-time, I hired a personal trainer. Mike LaCoss joked with me later that the first time I walked into the gym, he thought I was a homeless person. Wearing sweats and a baggy T-shirt to hide the belly I still had going on, I was also bleary-eyed and had greasy hair since there hadn't been time to shower. Mike may have thought I looked like a street person, but I was just a new mom.

The first day sucked. He gave me a circuit to do of three different exercises that he wanted me to repeat for a total of four times. But after only two times through the circuit, I keeled over and thought I was going to barf. "Okay, that's enough for today," he said. I had always been able to finish a workout someone's given me, even if I had the flu or was hungover. I had a lot of work to do.

It was brutal but necessary. He dreamed up forms of torture that I could have never imagined, like the time he had me wear a fifty-pound weighted vest to run sprints on a fully inclined treadmill. It was as if I were running up Everest pregnant. Within three months, I had lost twenty-five pounds.

As I got back in shape, I realized that I'd never return to the body I had before. Pregnancy had changed everything. My hips were a little wider, and whereas I used to stay at a weight of 130 pounds, now I was a steady 140 pounds. I regained my six-pack and all the other muscles I had before, but everything was slightly changed.

The amazing thing was that it didn't affect my swimming. Unlike my experience when I went through puberty and my radical new body almost ejected me out of the sport, this time around I was still me, only altered and for the better. My focus was certainly improved. After Blaise's birth, I trained all my attention on having a meaningful practice from the minute my foot touched the pool deck. I couldn't tolerate any other outcome. If I were going to drive thirty minutes to the pool, train for three hours, and drive home for a total of four hours away from Blaise, it had better not be a waste of my time.

Conversely, when I was off the pool deck and at home, the last thing I was thinking about was swimming. Whether changing Blaise's diaper, trying to get him back to sleep, or making dinner for Sacha and me, I didn't have the time or energy to overanalyze my training or anything else. The biggest upside to being fully occupied was that it kept me from straying too far into the past or the future, grounding me firmly in the moment.

I drove into the aquatics complex, already filled with cars. I didn't bother circling around the packed parking lot, but instead headed to a secret spot to the left of the Dumpsters that was completely hidden and legal to park. I knew this place like the back of my hand. This is where I grew up.

The familiarity made my first big competitive meet since having a baby a little easier. I couldn't have asked for a more comfortable situation going into the 2010 USA Swimming Nationals in August. At the biggest meet of the year, held in Irvine, where I trained with Dave and as a Nova, I knew every nook and cranny of the pool. But more important, we were staying at my dad's house, which was a great relief to me since this was my first time spending anything more than a few hours away from Blaise. Now a robust and active ten and a half months, Blaise was in good hands with my dad and Sacha.

Excited and nervous, I wasn't going into this meet to win. I had set a modest but challenging goal for myself: I wanted to be in the top eight swimmers in the whole country in both the 100-meter and the 200-meter breaststroke. I didn't need to win to succeed.

Having Blaise allowed me to ease some of the pressure I was used to burying myself under. I was still competitive, but I also had perspective. Swimming was *not* the most important thing in my life anymore. Sometimes I used Blaise as an excuse, such as when I was so exhausted, I couldn't bring myself to stand up, let alone get down to the pool. "I have to stay home with Blaise today," I said to my coach. Usually, though, this little bundle of energy who stared up at me with his father's eyes simply freed my mind-set.

Blaise got my attention right before my first event, the 100-meter breaststroke, when from the pool deck I found him in the stands with Sacha. I gave my two hipsters in matching skinny jeans and Adidas sneakers a wave and a thumbs-up. The race was like a mini reunion for me. Of course my mom and dad were there, but so were a lot of friends from growing up who never get to see me swim, including Yvette, who showed up with her husband (the high school sweetheart she dated for nine years before getting married) and their adorable two-year-old son.

I came in sixth in the 100-meter, which was decent considering that's not my stronger event. Having made my goal, I wondered what I could do in my signature event, the 200-meter. As Ryk once said, I'm good at surprising people. But this time, I surprised even myself. With a time of 2:26.50, I finished second in the 200-meter breast-stroke. I was thrilled, elated, freaking out. For a minute. Then I was upset.

Right after the race, I grabbed my towel and sweatshirt and ran to the stands, where I waved Sacha down. By the time he got to me, I was crying. "What's wrong with you?" he asked. He and Blaise, in his arms, were staring at me like I was crazy.

"I'm number two in the two-hundred-meter!" I sobbed. "Do you know what that means? I qualified to go to the Pan Pacs to represent the USA at the end of the month."

"Isn't that a good thing?"

"No! I could hardly stand being apart from Blaise at this meet. At Pan Pacs, I'll be totally separated from him for nearly two weeks. I don't think I can handle that."

Now I was full-on bawling, my brain running quickly through all the people I'd disappoint no matter what decision I made.

"Slow down, slow down," Sacha said, putting his arm around me so that Blaise was close enough to yank my hair. "One step at a time."

Sacha had been exactly right. The U.S. swim team coach, Mark Schubert, called Sacha and me into a meeting where he asked what they needed to do to accommodate me. With the competition taking place two weeks later at the Irvine aquatics complex, I didn't have to worry about traveling halfway across the globe or even the country. Team Amanda got into full-force mode. Sacha arranged everything at home so that the dogs would be taken care of, and my mom flew down from Washington State, where she had moved in 2004, to help out with Blaise. Mark offered me terms that were more than generous. He said I could have my own car, not usually allowed for team members, so I could go back home whenever I needed. "I need you at all the team functions and practices," he said. "Otherwise I don't care where you are. Just don't tell me."

I was so grateful to everyone who helped create the best possible situation for my kid and me. I knew as a working mom that I'd never have a meet as convenient as this again, and I took advantage of it by seeing Blaise and Sacha for quick visits during lunch or between practices.

During the Pan Pacific Swimming Championships, I qualified for finals in both the 100-meter and 200-meter breaststroke but ultimately didn't win a medal in either. I landed in fifth place in each event.

Reporters asked me if I was disappointed, and it brought me back to my first Olympics, when they wondered if I was upset with silver. Yes, years earlier I would have been pissed with my results. But with an eleven-month-old son cheering me on, I was extremely satisfied, and not just because I had had to lose fifty pounds and battle the fatigue of being a new mom to get there. I had a different outlook on life; I was excited purely to be part of the race.

My presence showed that starting a family doesn't mean that your life stops—even in an environment that typically demands a completely self-centered existence. I'm always inspired by seeing other moms succeeding and continuing to be relevant in their own way. My number one priority was our family unit and keeping that strong, so I did sometimes feel guilty when I left Blaise for practice. But I truly believed that my working made me a better mom. I not only appreciated my time with him, but I also wanted to be an example of discipline. Already I could see Blaise was learning by watching me, and I wanted to show him what hard work can do.

When earlier in my life people tried to put me in the position of role model, I refused it. How could I hold myself up as someone to follow when secretly I felt like a mess? Maybe it was becoming a mom or maybe it was appreciation for just how far I'd come, but I was ready to be an example to more than just my son.

Before the Nationals in early August, a writer for the *New York Times*, who had started covering my career before my first Olympics, approached me about doing a profile for the paper pegged to my comeback. As we discussed what had happened in my life that would make me worth profiling, I confided in her that my struggles arriving at this swim meet had been about a lot more than losing the baby weight. Listening to my battle with purging and cutting, she said, "That would be a great story."

I told her I had to think about it. I was a lot better at communicating than I used to be, but airing my innermost secrets in the paper of record was a lot of sharing. I worried about opening myself up for criticism on issues about which I'd only received support. I also didn't want people to pity me, treat me differently, or think I was making a pathetic ploy for attention.

"No one is going to look at you like you are weak or lesser," the *Times* writer said. "People will be inspired hearing about what you've gone through. It would really mean something to other women who have the same problems but haven't been strong enough to get help."

Ultimately I went through with it, deciding that this would be a powerful way to resurface. This time I would return to swimming, open to everything and not afraid of anything—even my own past.

Still, I never imagined I'd get the response that I did. When I arrived at Nationals, so many people pulled me aside to divulge their issues. Top-level swim coaches, fellow athletes, men and women—they all had stories, either their own or of someone very close to them, that mirrored mine. "I've experienced a lot of the same stuff that you did," a young swimmer told me. "But I never had a way to talk about it." I realized that many others were hiding negative feelings about their bodies, difficulties dealing with the glare of the limelight, troubles over bad relationships, just as I had. By coming out in the open with my story, I helped to peel away a little bit of the shame.

In fact, I had only one negative moment on the heels of the *Times* piece, which happened during a Pan Pacs team meeting called by Mark, who, as our coach, went over all the rules for the event, such as a prohibition against men in our hotel rooms and a strictly enforced 10:00 p.m. curfew.

"Amanda, I don't mean to single you out, but I read in the *New York Times* that you had your first drink in Atlanta when you were fourteen," he said. "That's unacceptable. If any of you who are underage drink, you'll be thrown off the team. And if any of you are around an underage team member drinking, you'll be thrown off too. We have a no-tolerance policy when it comes to alcohol."

At first I was shocked that someone who had taken extraordinary measures to welcome me back to the sport was calling me to task for something that had happened fourteen years ago. The funny part was that Mark was giving a lecture to a twenty-eight-year-old woman about underage drinking. Less funny was how he completely missed the point of the article. Nobody who makes it to the U.S. swim team is a rule breaker; acts of rebellion aren't always willing but often signs of deeper, hidden motivations.

One silly response was nothing compared with the outpouring

of support and gratitude I received from fans, peers, and mentors. Cyndi Gallagher—a female coach of an all-female team who has seen everything, from depression to eating disorders to catfights— said it best: "By sharing your personal history you've given a voice to those who can't or haven't yet tried to use theirs."

That is the crux of it; despite how I look in a bathing suit or how fast I swim, I'm nothing more than human, with emotions and insecurities that I continue to have but can now deal with. The greatest realization for me is that I have earned more respect *because* of the real-life story behind my image and accomplishments. If being a role model means I don't have to be perfect, then I am all for it.

"Mama!" Blaise shouts from his crib, my daily 6:00 a.m. wakeup call.

I shoot straight out of bed and into his room, where he's bouncing up and down, waiting for me to grab him. I lift him up and the first thing he says is "Watch a movie!"

We begin our morning routine. I put him in his little spot on the enormous couch and prop a special small pillow just for him behind his back. From there he chooses a movie; this morning it's *Mickey's Christmas Carol*. Getting ready for the holidays early, that's my kid. Then he orders breakfast: cereal followed by some avocado. Again, my kid.

When he is done with breakfast and a movie, I slide the glass door open to our backyard, glittering in the late-morning Arizona sun. Blaise and the dogs follow me outside, where we dash around the lawn. The dogs try to stay out of Blaise's way since he has a habit of riding them like horses. After I get in a tickle torture or two, we head back into the house so I can do a few chores.

I've gotten a lot better with mess and learning to tolerate domestic chaos—although laundry and dishes sitting around still don't make me happy. Blaise is, surprisingly, not too messy a kid. He keeps his disasters in his own areas, like his toy table or the fenced-in part of the backyard that we covered in AstroTurf (grass is impossible to grow in Tucson) for his toys. His room may be a disaster of books and stuffed animals, but for some reason that doesn't stress me out.

As Blaise drives his trains around their track, making choo-choo sound effects, he is just over two years old, but there's nothing "terrible" about him. He is a very independent little dude, awesome at playing by himself. At the same time, he's extremely verbal. He makes it very easy for me to meet his needs because he's so good at expressing them. Although he's got his issues (if he sleeps through the night, it's a miracle), Blaise is a great communicator. That's Sacha's kid.

I pour myself a second cup of coffee and start to unload the dishwasher. My thirtieth birthday is coming up in a couple of weeks and I have to collect some of Blaise's artwork for my mom before we go up to the lake house, where my entire family is gathering to celebrate. I'm writing a note to remind myself, when I look up and see Blaise trying to climb the living room bookshelves as if he's Tom Cruise rock climbing in the opening scene of *Mission: Impossible II.*

"Blaise!"

I rush over and pull him down from his perch before explaining why that's a very bad idea. Very adventurous, Blaise thinks he can do anything—which is just like Sacha *and* me. And the two of us encourage that trait in him. I have experienced a lot in my life and want the same for him. School isn't the only place to find an education. There's so much to see in the world, but first you have to put yourself out there.

A couple of weeks earlier, Sacha and I had taken Blaise to an ostrich ranch that had a parrot room where the birds flew all around and landed on the visitors inside. He hated it so much that he was crying. We didn't rush right out but instead stayed for a little bit. "Look at the birds landing on Mommy's head," I said cheerfully, as a couple of parrots nested up there. Nothing doing, I could not get a smile out of him. But as soon as we walked out, he turned to me and said, "Let's do it again!" He's just like his mom and dad: a thrill seeker. While I always make sure he knows safety is important, I also let him know he can't live his life in fear.

After the bookcase incident, I might have to teach a little more about fear. Right now, though, we have to get ready for swim class. *His* swim class. Everyone who doesn't know me assumes I'm some sort of crazy swim parent, but that couldn't be further from the truth. I want my son to know how to swim, because it is a lifesaving skill, not so that he can go to the Olympics. When people (again, who don't know me) ask if he's going to be a swimmer, I say I hope not. I know how much you have to invest for what usually turns out to be little in return.

I'm one of the lucky ones in that I made it to the Olympics. I'm even luckier that I went four times and outrageously lucky that I was able to turn my swimming success into a career that pays the bills. Still, it's staggering when I think about how much time and energy swimming has consumed in my life. An athlete has to sacrifice everything for her sport—something few do for any job or anyone. It's not just the hours working out in the pool or on land. It's waking and going to bed as early as a farmer. It's obsessing about everything you put into your body. It's about tamping down the nerves of any normal person. It's knowing all the right things to say so that your image won't be tarnished. It's about thinking about all these things over and over until you can't think any longer.

I wouldn't want Blaise to go through the ups and downs I went through, especially at the young age they were introduced to me. I want him to worry about prom, not performing in front of millions of people. As I say it, though, I realize that I wouldn't change a thing about my life. It has been an amazing roller coaster of experiences. I guess it's a mom's prerogative to not want her child to suffer—even though it's a condition of any life.

After we return home from swim class and Blaise has eaten his favorite lunch of meatballs, it's time for me to go to the pool.

"Mommy's going swimming," I say, before giving him a kiss and leaving him with the babysitter, which is still hard after all this time. Sacha says we're connected at the hip and could use a little alone time from each other. But there's no such thing as being too connected to my son.

Arriving at the pool at 2:00 p.m., I don't screw around for a second. There's nothing keeping me back from my workouts. I've been swimming so long, I've done it all. Training still kicks my ass and exhausts the crap out of me, but I know there's nothing I can't handle. Still, the first jump is always hard. You would think after twenty-six years of swimming, I would get used to the initial shock of water rushing over my entire body. But you never do.

Once I'm in, though, I feel great. I'm bigger since I had Blaise, but I don't feel bigger; I feel stronger. I push through the water with direction and forceful ease. Becoming a mom changed my body, but it also changed my brain. Moms can handle a lot; we are built to, and now that I am one, I've tapped into this whole new source of strength that I didn't have when I was younger.

In the water, I'm still counting—laps, times, lines at the bottom of the pool, and now months until the 2012 Olympic trials. I want to make the team and represent my country in London. That's why I'm still working at it, because I want to swim until I can't swim anymore.

My sport is a priority because I love it, and because it takes care of my family by paying the bills. And even though I'm trying for another Olympics, my priorities have shifted in my life. The things I used to think were really important—worrying about love handles or ugly cuticles—are now at the bottom of the list. Keeping a roof over our heads, putting good food on our plates, and paying for Blaise's school tuition are foremost on my mind. So is always making sure the bond among the members of our great little family stays strong, which is something at which Sacha works equally hard.

Nobody and nothing is perfect, and like any couple, we've been through those times when you want to sleep in the guest room for a week. When you're together as much as we are, not every day can be rainbows and butterflies. But no matter what, I know that Sacha is my best friend and that I'm good enough to be his.

Though I work to enjoy my mostly wonderful life—whether it's having a date every now and then so Sacha and I can have a meal without Blaise shooting a Nerf gun in our faces, or letting my son cover me in glitter in an arts and crafts explosion—new problems pop up every day. The coffee machine breaks, Blaise pukes on the way to school, I've gained a few pounds, I'm not sure what lies ahead for me after swimming. But it's how I roll with the punches, not how I avoid them, that defines my happiness.

When I'm done training two hours after jumping into the pool, I hop out and get dressed without bothering to dry my hair. I want to get home as fast as I can because I know Blaise is waiting for me. When I arrive home, the first thing I see is him barreling out the back door toward me with his arms wide open as if we were just separated by a war. "Mama back! Mama back!" he shrieks.

I scoop him up in my arms and give him a big kiss.

"Mama went swimming?" he asks, grabbing a piece of my hair to check that it's wet. Consoled that I'm doing exactly what I'm supposed to, he asks, "Play?"

"Yeah," I say. "Let's play."

acknowledgments

This book is a culmination of many years in a sport that I love, but which at times has been a struggle. I wouldn't be a swimmer today if it weren't for my fans, whom I want to thank, first and foremost, for supporting me and keeping me going even during the hardest periods.

I credit my coaches with shaping my career, both in and out of the pool. Dave Salo allowed me to dream big when it seemed impossible. Frank Busch was a second father, helping me navigate through those tough years of my life. Thank you, Cyndi Gallagher, for allowing me to bombard your team only three months before the Olympics and guiding me to my fourth Olympic Games.

Cheers to Evan Morgenstein, my agent and the other driving force in my career. For more than ten years, he has had my back and never once stopped fighting for me.

Thanks to Steve Ross, my literary agent, who had faith in this project from the very first day. I am grateful to Stacy Creamer, my publisher, who gave me the opportunity to tell people my story, and to Lauren Spiegel, my editor, who encouraged and motivated me to give it shape. Thank you to Rebecca Paley for not only capturing my voice but also helping me to sift through years of a hectic life in order to make sense of it all.

Of course I wouldn't have a story to tell if it weren't for my girls, who have always been by my side: Yvette, Erika, Courtney, and April, we'll always have the Spice Girls!

A huge hug to my sisters, who made me the sister that I am. Taryn, you taught me to be tough; and Leah, you nurtured me like a mother. I love you guys.

To my number one fan, my dad: you showed me the world of sports and opened my eyes to my own athletic abilities. Thank you, Dad, for everything.

To my beautiful mom, who allowed me to express myself outside of swimming: you showed me the beauty in everything around me and hugged me through every heartbreak. I love you.

And to my amazing family: Sacha, my husband, who loved me through the dark times, literally saved my life, and put a real smile back on my face; and to our wonderful son, Blaise, who makes me strive to be better every day. When you smile it makes my life worth living. You make me laugh harder than anyone in this world. I love you both with all of my heart.